SOCIAL ACHIEVEMENT MOTIVATION

Motivation and Human Development Series-1
General Editor : **Prayag Mehta**

SOCIAL ACHIEVEMENT MOTIVATION

Needs, Values and Work Organization

PRAYAG MEHTA

CONCEPT PUBLISHING COMPANY, NEW DELHI 110059

ISBN 81-7022-529-9

First Published 1994

Published and Printed by
Ashok Kumar Mittal
Concept Publishing Company
A/15-16, Commercial Block, Mohan Garden
NEW DELHI 110059 (India)

Socially conscious workers, managers and activists who have been trying to evolve a better workplace and a better life-collectively.

General Editor's Introduction

Social and human development has been rather slow in our country. This has been highlighted by the recent UNDP reports. Various government programmes like National Literacy Mission; efforts for activisation of elementary education; health services; employment generation; women and child care; and the recent policy changes for weakening the centralised and bureaucratic controls over industry and the work-place are all supposed to accelerate development in the country. Non-government organisations (NGOs) have been playing an active role in this respect, particularly for empowerment of the urban and rural poor, marginal and small farmers, women and other weaker sections of our society.

Publications under this inter-disciplinary series seek to contribute to theoretical and practical issues in development such as: alienation, motivation, empowerment, participation and collective action, challenge and innovativeness, restructuring of work-place, employee relations, social responsiveness and policy, practice and performance. Thus, the series would deal with important aspects of functioning, management and performance in social and human development policies and programme.

PRAYAG MEHTA

Preface

THE EARLIER research on achievement motivation conducted and published during mid-1960s evoked considerable interest among researchers, educators and trainers. Reviews of studies conducted during this period revealed an important theoretical and practical finding namely, that disadvantaged people showed a higher need for achievement and that they tended to project group/social achievement goals.

A number of studies were initiated in mid-1970s to understand the concern for excellence and for better quality of life involving managers, workers, social activists, government officials, extension personnel, rural development organizers and others. The concept of the need for social achievement, need for influence and other related needs got gradually evolved and tested in such studies. A set of Thematic Apperception Test (TAT) pictures and a scoring system were used and tested in such studies. These concepts and the related behaviour categories and sub-categories were also used as inputs in training programme for worker-resource development, participatory management and rural development which provided further insights in this connection.

The present work, first of a series on 'Motivation and Human Development' is based on various studies and programmes conducted during the past 20 years. It has been divided into four parts. Parts One reports on the formulation of the concept of social achievement motivation and other needs and development of a measuring instrument and scoring system. Part Two contains case studies of two work organizations. Part Three deals with the importance of historical experience and conditions of work in understanding psychological needs, values and organizational behaviour. It also reports some suggested interventions at the work-place for promoting human development. Part Four gives the scoring manual, practice stories and the TAT pictures.

It is hoped that the work would stimulate further interdisciplinary research on social achievement motivation, personal and social efficacy, collective action with practical implications for functioning of the work-place as well as for socio-economic development programmes.

August 18, 1993 **PRAYAG MEHTA**

Acknowledgment

SEVERAL RESEARCHERS have contributed to the present work by their studies on various aspects of the present work particularly towards developing the instrument and the scoring system. Without such studies, the present work could not have been completed. Thanks are due to all of them. Some figures and data have been reproduced in the present work from the earlier publication, *Achievement Motive in High School Boys*, published by the National Council Educational Research and Training (NCERT) in 1969. Two earlier papers, namely, "Employee Motivation and Work Satisfaction in a Public Enterprise" published in *Vikalpa*, 1977 : 2(3), 223-232, and "Efficacy and Alienation in the Imagery of Middle Managers and Worker Representatives" published in *National Labour Instt. Bulletin*, 1976, 302-308, have been used for developing enlarged Chapters 2 and 4 in the present work. Permission of the publishers to use the materials is gratefully acknowledged. Thanks are also due to managers, workers and others who participated in various studies and contributed data and insights.

Thanks are due to several persons for reading the earlier drafts of the present work, particularly to Dr. (Mrs.) Preetam Khandelwal for making valuable suggestions which helped in improving the final draft. Special thanks are due to Shri Jagdish Singh who prepared several drafts of the present work and provided continuous secretarial support to the project.

Last but not least, thanks are due to Shri Ashok Mittal and his team at the Concept Publishing Company for their excellent production job and for marketing the book.

PRAYAG MEHTA

Contents

PART FOUR
Mannual for Scoring Stories

Appendices

PART ONE

Concept and Measurement

In developing countries such as India, the pace of human development has been rather slow. Studies emphasize importance of organization, participation and motivation along with public action in achieving such development goals. People are motivated by the needs for social achievement and for acting on the environment for obtaining a better quality of life and work.

Social achievement and influence motivation play an important role in collective action and team-work. Part One discusses the concept of such motivation and reports on research to understand the imagery of workers, managers and others and on development of a Thematic Apperception Test (TAT) and a system to measure and score such needs.

1

Achievement, Influence and Quality of Life

IT IS now increasingly realized that material wealth is not an accurate measure of development unless human potential is also maximized. The quality of life of the majority of the population of developing countries has worsened in the past few decades because meeting the people's basic needs was pushed to the second place. The U.N. Human Development Report, 1990, once again kindled the hope that it was possible to achieve accessible level of quality of life in a manageable time-frame and at a modest cost. Human Resource Development (HRD) is critical to economic policies and ecological considerations. Not only are technical knowledge and capabilities built up, but new values are created and individuals and nations are enabled to cope with rapidly changing social, environmental and development realities (UNDP, 1992).

I. NEED FOR SOCIAL ACHIEVEMENT : CONCERN FOR BETTER WORK AND LIFE

How do we motivate working people to maximize their potential and enable them to cope with environmental and development realities? How do we stimulate workers to actively involve themselves in work organizations in order to maximize production as well as better their own well-being in developing economies like India? How does social and behavioural research help us to understand and deal with such issues? What do the people themselves think about standards of excellence and quality of life? How strong is their concern for improving their conditions of work and life? Some insights seemed to emerge from studies of need for achievement (Mehta, 1969) among the disadvantaged persons. Results of some early research on achievement motivation suggested that the disadvantaged high school adolescents tended to show a strong need for achievement.

Achievement motive or need for achievement or *n* Achievement has been defined as a concern for doing well in relation to a standard of excellence. Such persons, i.e., those with a high *n* Achievement, when presented with complex tasks, tend to do better and better as they proceed. They are also likely to seek situations in which they could get achievement satisfaction. In TAT stories (Thematic Apperception Test for measuring human motivation in briefly discussed in Chapters 2 and 3), *n* Achievement is scored when there is evidence of a desire for success is relation to some standard of excellence, or when some character is involved in accomplishing other than routine daily task or when someone is involved in attaining a long-term achievement goal—for being a doctor, engineer, etc. (McClelland, *et al.,* 1953:110-115; 1958). Mehta adapted the McClelland's methods to Indian conditions and studied *n* Achievement among high school children (Mehta, 1969). The findings tend to throw some light on questions like the above.

Need for Achievement and Socio-economically disadvantaged Groups

The high school adolescents from socio-economically disadvantaged groups were found to show a comparatively higher need for achievement than their counterparts coming from middle to the lower middle class households. The formers need for achievement was almost of the same level as that shown by the adolescents from high socio-economic status households (Mehta, 1969:51-56).

Social Learning of Need for Achievement

It was found that high school children of fathers with little education as well as of illiterate fathers tended to show a significantly higher need for achievement than their counterparts whose father were secondary school educated. This interesting finding is shown in Fig. 1.1. While college and higher professional education of fathers tended to contribute to greater need for achievement in their children, it was equally interesting to note that children from households of fathers who had some or even no education tended to show greater need for achievement than those from middle category households.

Children's higher need for achievement could not have been due only to the degree of their father's education.

Obviously, there was something in the social learning process, either at home or in school or in the wider social environment or in a combination of these factors, which tended to strengthen the concern for achievement among children from lowly educated households.

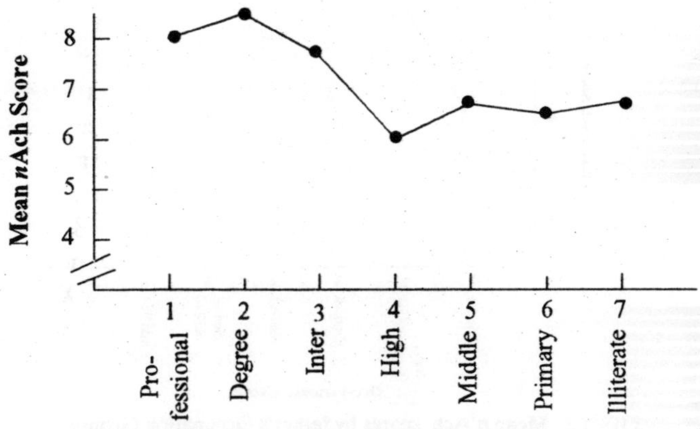

FIG. 1.1: Mean *n* Ach. scores by fathers' Educational Level (Reproduced from Mehta, 1969 : 51)

Some confirmation of the above was available from the results for father's occupational group which also emerged as a very significant factor in children's need for achievement. This interesting finding is seen in Fig. 1.2. It was striking that the need for achievement level of children belonging to households where fathers were engaged in some semi-professional occupation was higher than of all other children. However, another finding, probably more interesting here, was about children coming from households where fathers were engaged in skilled blue-collar occupations. Such children showed a higher need for achievement than their counterparts from households where the fathers were engaged in professional, clerical or petty trading occupations.

Father's occupation, thus, tended to show a very significant influence on their children's need for achievement. This was confirmed when the educational level of fathers was controlled and variations studied for occupation. Children of lowly educated blue-collar workers tended to show a significantly higher need for achievement than their counterparts where the fathers were also equally less educated but were engaged in some clerical/petty trading occupations (Mehta, 1969: 55-57). Results indicated that besides fathers' educations, which was a significant factor in their children's need for achievement, their fathers' occupation also emerged as very important, particularly for children belonging to socio-economically disadvantaged groups like the blue-collar workers.

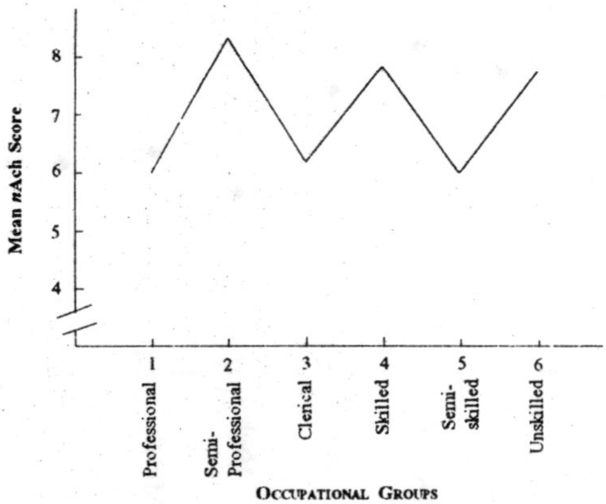

FIG. 1.2 : Mean *n* Ach. scores by father's Occupation Groups.
(Reproduced from Mehta, 1969 : 54)

The higher need for achievement among such high school adolescents as born and brought up in blue-collar workers' households indicated the importance of social environment and socialization obtaining in such homes. The fact that they were all in the high school showed the importance attached to education by their parents. This was, however, a constant factor and the significant difference in their level of need-achievement was probably due to achievement pressures and demands put on them at home. This was particularly true of blue-collar workers, who were not so much educated but were motivated enough to educate their children. The findings implicitly suggested that such parents and homes tended to socialize their children to think in terms of better performance in life, enabling them to internalize some standards of excellence.

An Urge to Improve Conditions of Life

The above findings were unlike those of the Western studies, particularly as reported from the USA, where middle social class subjects were found to have a significantly higher need for achievement than those from the working class (Rosen, 1956; Strodtbeck, 1958; Veroff, 1960). Such Indian research, therefore, underlined the importance of our social conditions in shaping the content of an individual's need for achievement. It was then conceptualized that the need for achievement among the socially disadvantaged secondary school adolescents probably indicated an urge in them to improve their living conditions (Mehta, 1970).

Tribal Children's Need for Achievement

The above findings were confirmed in further research, (Gokulnathan, 1971; Gokulnathan and Mehta, 1972) which found a higher need for achievement among the tribal high school children as compared to their non-tribal counterparts. Another interesting and significant finding of this research was that the urban-based tribal high school boys showed a significantly higher need for achievement than their non-tribal counterparts. Further, there was no difference in the need for achievement among the tribal and non-tribal school girls; within the given tribal groups, there was no gender difference; where as the non-tribal girls showed significantly greater need for achievement than the non-tribal boys. On the whole, school girls showed a significantly greater need for achievement than boys. It was, thus, concluded that the respondents appeared to form two distinct need-for-achievement groups; the tribal boys, tribal girls and non-tribal girls with a greater need for achievement formed one group while the non-tribal boys with a significantly lower need for achievement formed another group. (Gokulnathan and Mehta, 1972:70).

Farmers' Change-proneness

Some research with farmers tended to suggest similar trends, i.e., higher concern for seeking achievement-related information among semi-educated to illiterate small and marginal farmers. Such change-prone and achievement motivated farmers sought much greater production information from electronic media than others including educated and rich farmers. Lack of education did not deter the former from obtaining such information. Such farmers were not only more active in obtaining information but also in diffusing it to others (Sinha and Mehta, 1972). Such a strong achievement tendency was further confirmed by the fact that low-to-middle-size land-holding farmers, although much less educated than the richer farmers, showed a greater need for achievement than the latter, i.e. those with higher land-holdings. The results suggested that comparatively disadvantaged and poorer farmers showed a concern for improving their conditions of life (Sinha and Mehta, 1972a).

Urge to Improve

Reviewing related research on the need for achievement in India, it was concluded that the "disadvantaged groups, whether socially, culturally or economically, such as women irrespective of SES, tribals irrespective of residence and those from relatively poorer homes, tended to show greater urge to improve their conditions of life, resulting in greater need for achievement" (Mehta and Mohta, 1974:326-327).

Sense of Deprivation and Urge to Improve

Socially and economically deprived persons tended to think in terms of group goals rather than/or in addition to personal goals. Do such people perceive the same problems and needs as other members do in their social class? Some answers to such questions are available from research on the sense of fraternal deprivation which predisposes individuals towards group thinking and action (Gurin *et al*, 1969). The person may compare his circumstances with some social standard or a reference group. As a result of this comparison, the individual feels unjustly deprived of power, prestige and material goods resulting in dissatisfaction with the state of affairs (Hyman and Singer, 1968).

Such a sense of unjust deprivation could heighten an individual's concern for a better quality of life. Social situations, therefore promote, thoughts and beliefs about conditions of life and feelings of deprivation. Such thoughts, over time, grow into ideological beliefs and values without intervention of the variables of relative deprivation and relative expectation (Turner, 1957). Emerging beliefs and values and such consciousness, thus, strengthen their concern for a better quality of life, both individually and collectively, as per some perceived standards of excellence. Such a concern for "our quality of life" contribute to motivation for social/group achievement.

Social Conditions, Beliefs and Urge to Improve

Research findings, therefore, suggested that persons from socially disadvantaged and underprivileged groups tend to show a higher need for achievement. Such motivation in them further appeared to contain an urge to improve not only work-related performance, but also, more importantly, the quality and conditions of their life. Such a need for a better quality of life seemed to motivate collective or social achievement goals. Such thoughts were, therefore, different from the usual need for achievement involving competitive personal goals. It has been found, for example, that under conditions of limited resources, as is the case in developing economics like India, as well as in work organizations where resources and rewards are always limited, persons with a high need for achievement tended to aggressively compete with each other (Sinha, 1968). Under such conditions, their personal achievement goals stimulated keen inter-personal competitive and aggressive behaviour.

It has been further observed that such personal achievement goals, by motivating inter-personal competitive behaviour, hindered cooperative behaviour (Pareek and Banerjee, 1976). In some later research with work organizations, it was revealed that under limited resources and restricted reward situations, need for personal achievement motivated competitive and manipulative behaviours, specially among the managers. This in turn tended to promote a work climate of mistrust and mutual negative images (Mehta, 1989a: 45-48).

Social Class and Functional Anxiety

Some results from research on anxiety tended to further suggest the possibility of need for group achievement particularly among the disadvantaged people. Such results (Gokulnathan, 1971; Nijhawan and Chaudhary, 1970) suggested that secondary school children with a high level of anxiety tended to set a realistic level of aspiration and goals for their academic performance. Such findings were contrary to the theory of achievement motivation (Atkinson and Feather, 1966) according to which highly anxious subjects would show either unrealistically high or low aspirations. The results here tended to support the contention (Birney *et al,* 1969) that such fear of failure or anxiety may have a meaning for the individual, implying some sense of responsibility for non-attainment of goals. Gokulnathan's study (1971) further suggested that high anxiety worked as a reinforcing mechanism in expectancy for achievement of realistic goals. In further research (Gokulnathan and Mehta, 1976), school-children with a high need for achievement and a moderate level of anxiety were found to show better school performance. This was particularly true of girls.

Instructional practices, school examinations and admission policies as well as post-school employment and recruitment policies, on the whole, tend to inhibit socially and economically disadvantaged groups in various ways. All such structural and social variables, therefore, tend to promote a sense of moderate anxiety in persons seeking excellence in their academic and other performance situations. Under such conditions, as mentioned above, moderate anxiety, in conjunction with a high need for achievement, probably motivated such children for better school performance.

Discussing the various related concepts of group achievement motivation, Zender (1971) suggested that under group situations, where performance requires inter-dependent efforts, members show a concern for the group outcome as it also helps them to obtain personal satisfaction. He found that, among the group members, those with high fear of failure were more interested in group success than those with high hope of success (Zender, 1971: 86-90). Such research findings, as argued by Forward (1979), suggested the hypothesis that individual and group-oriented achievement tendencies were independent sources of motivation.

Collective Action for Better Quality of Life

The need for social achievement, i.e. an urge to improve and to have a better quality of life for the group/community including oneself, seems to motivate cooperative behaviour and team-work as indicated by increasing documentation of participatory development action. Such projects provide some insights for understanding the importance of social/group achievement goal in motivating people for participation and active involvement in collective action for development. For example, tribals in the Ranchi district of Bihar, motivated by an urge to improve their quality of life, acted collectively and cooperatively in order to obtain literacy, voluntary prohibition, additional water and irrigation facilities, bank credit and government aid for supplementary income generating projects like poultry, piggery, etc. Such significant objective economic and social goals resulted in equally significant subjective gains for the people. These included increased awareness and aspirations, hope of success in collective efforts, sense of vigilance and pro-active action orientation for obtaining various collective achievement goals (Mehta, 1983; Chandra and Mehta, 1984).

Grassroot level collective efforts, motivated by a concern for a better quality of life, help enhance internal capability of the people, for example, in control of drought conditions, in reversing adverse situations for cultivating better crops in obtaining better infrastructural facilities for education, drinking water, health care, etc. A sense of insecurity, induced by uncertain socio-economic conditions, accompanied by a concern for better quality of life, has spurred various social and economic movements like the Chipko (clinging to trees), Movement spearheaded by the Dasholi Gramk Swaraj Mandal (DGSM, 1982), revival of forests and wild-life in Orissa (Behera, 1992) and cooperative efforts of *bidi* workers in Kerala (Mohanan, 1981). Such increasing evidence indicated the strength of collective or social achievement goals in motivating people for a better quality of life.

Such goals arouse people for active participation and involvement in various self-action projects.

Need for Social Achievement

Both, research and experience, therefore, suggested that disadvantaged people, and those involved in self-initiated group activities, tended to show a need for social or group achievement including an urge to improve their quality of life. At personal level, they might think of improving their own standard of living and/or work performance. However, stimulated by an increasing awareness and an increasing sense of deprivation, they learn to think in terms of group or social achievement goals and acquire such a need.

The findings of early studies and field experience therefore, suggested the importance of systematic research on the need for social achievement. The following chapters report the studies thus undertaken. Chapter 2 reports and discusses workers and manager's imagery as contained in their TAT stories. It was found, for example, that they, particularly workers, tended to project a strong concern for collective goals like building small tanks, improved irrigation, school for children and obtaining better facilities and conditions of life for themselves. As discussed further in Chapter 3, such imagery and thoughts revealed needs for social and personal achievement and some other needs.

Such social achievement goals and related behaviour were different from McClelland's concept of need for achievement (McClelland *et al*, 1953) which is conceptually grounded in work and performance related situations. As discussed in Chapter 3, and in later chapters, the categories and sub-categories of the need for social achievement went beyond work situations to a wider context and content of life, containing an urge to improve the conditions and quality of life. It was, therefore, conceptually distinguished from the need for achievement with qualitatively different behavioural and social implications. The concepts, categories and sub-categories for scoring such needs are discussed briefly in Chapter 3 with details provided in the manual in Part Four.

II. EFFICACY, INFLUENCE AND ACTIVISM

Self, as cause of behaviour, is motivationally very important. It has been expressed in several theories of motivation such as effectance motivation (White, 1959), personal causation (de Charms, 1968), self-efficacy (Bandura, 1977), intrinsic motivation (Deci, 1975) and internal locus of control (Rotter, 1966).

In such a conceptualization of motivation, self is conceived as an originating agent. The experience of causing behaviour is fundamental to oneself. As Turner observes, behaviours thought to reveal the true self are also ones whose causes are perceived as residing in the person rather than the situation (1976:991). Historically, symbolic interactionism of Mead (1934/1964; Baldwin,

1986) and Piaget's developmental psychology (1954) have strongly advocated active, creative and agentive view of self.

Generalized View of Self-efficacy Acting of Environment

It is man's primary motivational propensity to be effective in producing changes in his environment. Generalized attitude towards self to view the self as worthy of being taken seriously and capable of producing desired effects seems to lie at the core of motivation that stimulates challenge-taking, coping behaviour, accomplishment and hope as against safe playing and passivity, frustration and pessimism, failure, and fatalism. As Eisenberg (1972) has remarked, "Man is his own chief product. The infant who discovers that he can control the movements of his own fingers transforms himself from observer into actor. The child who masters reading unlocks the treasury of world's heritage..." (1972:127).

Deprivation and Negative Self-concept

Human's natural desire to be effective, to act on and influence his environment is, however, not always satisfied. For example, workers may not be able to exercise any control over their work and work environment. Hence, they feel dissatisfied and alienated. The lower they go in social and/or work hierarchy, the more alienated they may feel. In such cases, the environment works much more on them than they on the environment. Adverse environment, particularly social environment, such as adverse socio-economic and political conditions, have adverse effects on self-concept. For example, as discussed in several studies (Memmi, 1967; Nandy, 1983), the colonized and the oppressed is forced to deny himself even a minimum quality of life and yet, at the same time, he admires the colonizer passionately. Under the impact of unequal social power and interactions, the oppressed take over the definition of their self as held by their adversary. Their thoughts, based on a realistic assessment of the power of adversaries vis-a-vis themselves, as Elias and Scotson have shown (1965), promote in them a negative self-image. They learn to doubt their own worth and capability and develop dependence on powerful others.

The dispossessed and the poor also learn to immitate their dominators' cultural models at the given moment of their oppressed consciousness. There is a tendency to think and behave the way their dominators and masters like them to do (Fanon, 1968). Negative self-image becomes a corner-stone of their cultural strategy. The poor hate and yet reconcile with, and sometimes rationalize, their bad life. They lie low to be able to live (Bailay, 1973).

Sense of Efficacy, Political and Personal

Negative self-concept and self-doubts depress the sense of personal effectiveness which tends to be transferred to social and political situations. The sense of personal effectiveness and the sense of political efficacy are, therefore, closely inter-related. Politically efficacious persons are also generally efficacious (Mehta, 1975a, 1981). A person's sense of control over the outcomes of his endeavours motivates initiative and action in political and other matters. Such generalized attitudes towards self and world are important partly because they tend to be self-confirming. A person who feels ineffective in politics guarantees his ineffectiveness by failing to participate. Conversely a person, who feels effective, is likely to participate in ways that actually make him so. De Charms (1968) came to such a theoretical formulation and suggested distinction between people who regard themselves as the origin of social causation and those who regard themselves as "pawns" of social forces and, because of this attitude, act in ways which perpetuate their being so in fact.

A sense of efficacy in political matters, therefore, indicates rules, general sense of personal efficacy. A citizen who feels that he is competent to follow the functioning of the government and politics, that his vote in elections is important and that there are other means of influencing the government as well, and that he is interested in politics and elections, indicates his sense of perceived effectiveness and interest in the political process. It difines his role vis-a-vis the system either as competent or incompetent, capable of influencing the system for incapable and interested or disinterested in politics and in social and other such matters. Such attitudes show his subjectively perceived sense of competence and not necessarily objective competence. The more the people feel they can influence public matters, the more interested they are in such matters. Such convictions give them energy to care and act and influence socio-political and work-related matters.

Social Learning and Efficacy

Studies suggest that lower social class citizens less educated and illiterate and those engaged in socially low prestige occupations – show a low sense of efficacy. Similarly, unemployed or semi-employed citizens also tend to feel less efficacious than those with full employment. Findings here suggested the key importance of education and work in learning of socio-political attitudes and efficacy. Even a slight movement from illiteracy to literacy and from worklessness to work were found to make a significant difference in the citizens' sense of efficacy (Mehta, 1975 b, 1977a).

Citizens' experience, as derived from socio-economic and working conditions, thus, emerged as an important factor in their sense of efficacy. As mentioned above, unemployment, destitution, illiteracy, rising cost of living and dwindling purchasing power induce bitter and dehumanizing experience resulting in the lowering of efficacy and heightening of a sense of helplessness in them. They develop a sense of being "Pawns" in the hands of the employment market, powerful others including political leaders, work managers and others persons and forces over which, they think, they have no control.

Sense of Isolation, Participation and Involvement

A sense of powerlessness and helplessness is accompanied by feeling of cynicism and meaninglessness which results, as discussed in Chapter 4, in withdrawal behaviour at the work-place. They not only feel helpless but also disinterested in work. This further reinforces their sense of powerlessness. There is a growing body of knowledge to show that attitudes towards work are related to political attitudes. A review of research suggested that, "Persons who feel more effective in their everyday tasks and challenges are more likely to participate in politics" (Milbrath, 1965:59). Following a cross-cultural study of civic culture, it was concluded that "the individual who has consistent opportunity in non-political participation is more likely to generate this to political participation". (Almond and Verba, 1963:366).

Studies show that participation of economically and socially disadvantaged people in mass movements and activities like election campaigns help them weaken their sense of isolation and cynicism.

This in turn, further activates their involvement in such meaningful activities, strengthening their positive attitudes. Such experience helps promote a sense of personal as well as social efficacy in them. For instance, fields functionaries and common people in adult education, self-action for better life and such other developmental efforts were found to have a high sense of political and personal and social efficacy as well as a high level of educational and social activism (Mehta, 1983, 1990).

Sense of Learnt Helplessness : Self-Image of Workers

As mentioned above, the oppressed people are driven to learn a negative self-image and a sense of self-doubts. This was revealed in our study of coal-miners, as reported in Chapter 2, who tended to show a sense of helplessness and powerlessness in their imagery, as contained in TAT stories. Their acquired self-image seemed to reflect their historical experience of severe oppression which was probably reinforced by their contemporary work and life experience. Such coal-miners were recruited from the poorest of the poor who tended to show a chronic sense of inefficiency resulting from their learning that, as Abrahamson *et al* (1978) have argued, one's actions have no effects on one's environment. It has been conceptualized that such a sense of learnt helplessness is likely to occur when an individual attributes his inefficiency to personal failure rather than to universal conditions (Seligman, 1975).

The recent literature on sense of alienation based on Marx's classic formulations (Marx, 1844/1974) is very relevant for our understanding of sense of helplessness and efficacy, at the work-place. The central theme in Marx's view of human nature was of self-creation through efficacious action in the context of work or "praxis". Under condition of alienation, the sense of self-efficacy and self-creation is frustrated or inhibited because of disjuncture between self and work. Studies show that the key feature of such alienation is their sense of powerlessness (Seeman, 1972). There are strong sociological traditions, as discussed in the following chapters, which identify the crucial importance of conditions of life including conditions of work in learning of helplessness or inefficiency.

Personal and Worldly Blocks : Sense of Efficacy

As mentioned in Section I, studies of need for achievement conducted in mid-1960s showed that socially disadvantaged high school adolescents tended to show a relatively stronger need for achievement, indicating an urge in them for improving their conditions of life. The same adolescents also showed much greater articulation of action as well as environmental hardships and difficulties. They tended to think more of blocks from outside than of personal blocks from within (Mehta, 1969:58-59). They, for example, imagined and thought of poverty as an important cause of their not being able to go to college or for not completing their education. The findings suggested that such adolescents, as motivated by an urge to improve their conditions of life, also, probably, showed an element of a sense of personal efficacy by tending to relate their lack of progress to socio-economic causation. In this sense, also they tended to show a sense of efficacy. They seemed to show a desire to influence their socio-economic conditions which, they thought, were likely to come in their way. It seemed, as discussed above, the same process of socialization, which tended to release and strengthen their concern for better performance and better quality of life, probably also facilitated social cosciousness and learning of a sense of efficacy in them.

Influence and Autonomy at Work-place

Studies of work-organization have further identified perceived availability of influence and autonomy at the work-place as the most important factor in employees' overall work satisfaction. This was also the single most significant predictor of the employees' sense of political efficacy, suggesting an intimate interface between the organizational factor of autonomy at the work-place and the psychological factor of a sense of competence and self-determination (Mehta, 1976a). Self-initiated and participatory development action, as reported in Section I, also suggested a desire in such people to act on their environment and influence it to their benefit. Such projects and related research showed the importance of a sense of efficacy in motivating participation and, in turn, the importance of participation in promoting a concern for efficacy and influence.

Influence and Power

Individuals are assumed to have need for power connoting an urge to influence and control other people (McClelland, 1975). In this sense, power is conceived primarily as a relational concept used to describe the perceived power or control that an individual has over others. The relative power of one actor over another is a product of the net dependence of one on the other (Pfeffer, 1981). As discussed above, the individual's disposition to influence life events and cope with them is much wider than inter-personal relations.

Need for Influence

The need for influence as indicated by a desire to act on the ongoing socio-economic and work situations, as reported in Chapters 2 and 3 and discussed in later chapters, is a more inclusive concept than the need for power. Following Mead, the individual is viewed as an actor in the environment shaping his/her world as well as being created by it. The need for influence indicates the need of the individual to play an actor role and to act on the environment. It is related to an active, creative and agentive view of self (Mead, 1934; Baldwin, 1986). Among the studies of self-efficacy motive, White's concept of effectance motivation (1959) and Deci's concept of self-determination (1975) have been the most influential formulations. As discussed in Chapters 2 and 3, the concept of need for influence, as formulated and used in the present research, is the need to experience controlling and being active on one's environment and of influencing the on-going work and other situations. It is, thus, conceptualized as a concern to influence and to act on the wider environment including social and work environment. This is a concern to cause things to happen. Behaviourally, it would mean taking an actor role vs. behaving like a pawn and feeling competent rather than feeling helpless *vis-a-vis* social, political and work environment.

It was decided to study the need more systemically and in the process also study its correlates and implications at the work-place and in development action. Chapters 2 and 3 also report the steps undertaken in this regard. The later chapters discuss the obtained findings and their implications.

III. HUMAN DEVELOPMENT AND QUALITY OF LIFE

As mentioned in Section I, there is now an increasing attention to assessing human development in countries around the world (UNDP, 1990, 1992, 1993). Several decades ago, a UN expert group (1954) had recommended that quantitative measures in the field of health, education, employment and housing be used to assess the standard of living in a country. Calculating the human development index on the basis of longevity, literacy and infant mortality rate in India, Kerala emerged on the top with an index of 651 and Uttar Pradesh at the bottom with an index of 292 (Shiv Kumar, 1991). Studies show that education, awareness, organization, participation and collective action of people along with planned and enlightened public interventions are important for obtaining such social and human development goals (Dreze and Sen, 1989).

Such goals are psychologically social achievement goals which could motivate people for a better quality of life. The need for influence could motivate collective action for such goals.

Work and Human Development

The above formulations need to be understood in the context of work and work-organization. Social and work structures obtaining in work organizations, as discussed in the following chapters, have an important bearing on the individual's well-being. An increasing body of research now points out the importance of the nature and condition of work in the human development of workers as well as managers. Studies (for example, Kohn and Schooler, 1983) show that the greater the freedom experienced on job, and the more complex and challenging the work, the more likely that the worker values freedom and self-direction and also self-efficacy. As reported in Chapters 4 and 5, a historically evolved work-place seemed to have an important bearing on the motivation and attitudes of managers and workers. Such relationships, as shown by Kohn and Schooler, affect workers' self-confidence and their sense of fatalism. These studies underline the importance of reciprocal relationship between nature of work and work-organization, on the one hand, and motivation on the other. However, in all cases, job affects the man more than man affects the job (Kohn and Schoolar, 1973 : 114).

Like development action and participation in such efforts,

conditions of work and history of the work organization were likely to affect the needs of the employees in various ways. Similarly such needs were likely to have implications for functioning of the work-place. Case studies reported in Chapters 4 and 5 throw light on learning and reinforcement of the need for social achievement, need for influence and other needs. These studies also bring out value correlates of such needs and their implications for the well-being of employees. Such correlates throw further light on the concept and functioning of these needs.

2

Sense of Efficacy, Alienation and Achievement

Themes in Workers' and Managers' Imagination

AS MENTIONED in Chapter 1, review of research and experience suggested the need for understanding and conceptualizing the people's urge to improve their quality of life as well as their sense of competence to act and assert on their environment. In pursuance of this objective, it was decided to obtain a sample of thoughts and imagery of working people in response to some TAT (Thematic Apperception Test) pictures. As the main purpose was to locate and study the strength of the respondents' need for social achievement, need for personal achievement, need for influence and other related needs, it was decided to develop a set of pictures, accordingly. Such pictures were required, which could evoke the relevant imagery and thoughts and help in developing a system for scoring the fantasy (stories) for the various needs.

In this chapter, we report the steps taken in order to develop a picture instrument and discuss the dominant themes culled out from the obtained stories. Chapter 3, then reports the steps undertaken to finalise the scoring system for measuring the various needs as contained in the imaginative stories.

I. DEVELOPING THE THEMATIC APPERCEPTION TEST (TAT) PICTURES

Murray (1936; 1938) invented the technique of eliciting imaginative stories (fantasies) from an individual in response to pictures now known as TAT (Thematic Appreciation Test). He conceived personality as a configuration of basic psycho-genic needs or motives. He thought of need as a "force which organizes perception, apperception, intellection, connotation and action in such a way as to transform in a certain direction an existing, unsatisfying situation" (Murray, 1938:123-124). In his view, a need would be overtly manifested in a typical behavioural trend, a typical mode of action, a characteristic emotion or feeling and in manifestation of satisfaction with the achievement of a certain effect or dissatisfaction when there is failure to achieve a certain effect (Murray, 1938:124).

TAT for Need for Achievement

Combining the clinical insight that human motivation is expressed in free associative thoughts with the possibility of manipulating and controlling its strength, McClelland *et al.*, (1953) adapted the TAT to measure human motives.

A series of experiments showed that when the need for achievement, i.e. concern for performing well in relation to a standard of excellence (i.e. pride in skilful performance), was aroused instructionally or in other ways, related imagery was projected to specially designed pictures. Results showed that achievement-related imaginative responses provided a measure of heightened state of motivation produced by achievement-oriented instructions. Results also showed that such pictures as contained obvious achivement-related cues ("two men at work in a machine shop", "a man at the desk in office", etc.) elucidated stories containing significantly more achievement-related imaginative responses than the pictures without such obvious achievement-related cues.

Holding all other factors constant, persons who scored high on the need for achievement in response to a set of pictures also scored high in response to another set of pictures. Such results, therefore, showed that individual differences in the total need for achievement score obtained from a set of pictures referred to something more general than reactions to specific picture cues.

The Thematic Apperception Technique, thus, became an important break-through for measuring human motivation, particularly need for achievement or *n* achievement (*n* Ach. in brief), need for power and other such socially acquired needs. In later research, this technique was utilized for measuring achievement need in Indian high school adolescents. A set of pictures was specifically developed for this purpose, keeping in mind the Indian situation (Mehta, 1969 : 8-19). Some relevant results from this study, and similar other studies using the same technique, have been briefly reviewed in Chapter 1. The same semi-projective technique was used in studies under report here.

The Present Instrument

Available literature and several TAT type pictures were searched in order to identify suitable pictures for the present instrument. This initial research yielded a set of 10 available pictures. These were then adapted, if necessary, to Indian conditions by re-doing for facials, dress, background, etc. The pictures were also re-done for including achievement and efficacy/alienation related vague cues. Such pictorial cues included the following:

(i) A worker-like person standing and another manager-like person sitting across a table;
(ii) A work scene within a factory/mine;
(iii) A group of persons with one person slightly walking away; and
(iv) A group of youth sitting around a table and a standing person looking at them.

Preparation of New Pictures

Besides adapting available pictures, 10 new pictures were also got prepared. Their vague pictorial cues and the suggested themes included the following:

(i) Persons entering a work-place;
(ii) Scene of disturbance, may be a lock-out or strike, and a person looking worried;
(iii) Work scene with persons working on lathes;

(iv) An accident scene;
(v) A destitute woman with a child in her lap;
(vi) A worried person sitting on a cot and a boy sitting on floor;
(vii) A queue of people with a person dropping out; and
(viii) A person facing policeman-like person in uniform.

Initial Try-out of Pictures

The above pictures were tried out on small groups of persons drawn from industry, social work, academic institutions, agricultural workers, rural youth, etc. A set of 3-4 pictures was tried out at a time. The respondents were shown each picture for about 20 seconds and then given four minutes to write an imaginative story in a booklet. On each page of the booklet the following four general questions in Hindi were printed:

(i) What is happening?
(ii) What has led to this situation, i.e. what has happened in the past?
(iii) What have they thought? What is wanted, by whom?
(iv) What will happen, what will be done?

They were told that it was a test of their creative imagination or story-telling and were given usual neutral instructions (Mehta, 1969:10).

The above stories were subjected to initial scrutiny to find out whether the given picture could elicit the desired kind of imagery. On the basis of such preliminary examination, eight pictures were eliminated in the first round. The remaining pictures were arranged in two sets of six each for further try-outs.

Further Try-outs of Pictures

The selected set of pictures were then administered to two comparable groups of 15 persons each, consisting of skilled workers and managers under the usual neutral and standard conditions. The obtained stories were then examined in order to find fantasy-evokability of each picture. One of the criteria was whether the given picture was able to evoke at least one achievement and/or influence-related imagery in about 15 per cent of the stories. The pictures were then arranged in order of their evokability of the desired kind of thoughts/imagery. A set of six pictures was, thus, obtained for a final try-out. The selected set of pictures was then once again administered to a new group of workers and managers. The pictures were administered under the same neutral conditions and instructions without any effort to relax or arouse their motivation. The obtained stories were then subjected to a detailed thematic analysis. This yielded several important behavioural trends which contributed to developing the necessary system for content-analysing the TAT stories for various needs.

II. THEMATIC ANALYSIS OF OBTAINED STORIES

The obtained stories were content-analysed with a view to identifying dominant themes. The related elements, as evoked by each picture, were classified under certain broad themes and processed for a comparative study of the dominant thoughts of workers and managers. The obtained themes or dominant thoughts, thus culled out, are briefly summarized below:

Picture Card I : Group of People

The obtained stories, written on this picture, seemed to contain the following major themes or dominant thoughts:

Leader Asking for Action/Agitation

Such stories talked of a leader explaining to workers, in some cases villagers, as to how some wrong has been done by the management or the landlord and that they should get ready for an agitation – some united action, a strike or a *gherao* – in order to get their demands accepted. The leader also explains that in the past also, assurances were given but not met and that the authorities (management or landlord) do not yield without some kind of action or agitation. Some examples of this theme were:*

(a) Union leader addressing workers; listening to grievances of workers to discuss with management; strike or *gherao* will take place if payment is not made;
(b) Ram approached the workers after being dissatisfied with the

* Translation of original stories written in Hindi, and obtained during 1976.

decisions of the boss; assurances have been given but not implemented; Ram asks his co-workers to be with him to stage an agitation; and

(c) The landlord harassed the people; took forcible possession of Ramu's land; his friends aggrieved not able to do anything; approached Hanuman – their friend in need; he asks them for joint action against the landlord; he emphasizes unity and action.

Action for Production for the Country

Imagery here showed people discussing either among themselves and/or with a leader various problems facing the country or facing the industry and the need for doing something to increase production and to serve the country. The imagery here indicated action orientation and a concern for achievement for the good of a collectivity. Some examples were:

(a) This is a good picture; people are sitting together as friends and talking good things; they are thinking about various things and also thinking in their minds as to what to do for the family and the country; what will be the loss without working.

(b) These persons are trying to establish unity amongst themselves; they are discussing issues of workers of our country who are like our brothers; before this there was no unity in the country. Our education system was not like this; we were fighting with each others. Now people are understanding and thinking how to increase the production of the country; how to establish unity with others so that the family and others also are happy.

(c) In the picture a leader is talking to the assembled village masses and explaining to them as to how the country can be helped; he is telling the employees and the people about their responsibility; there was some accident before it; the leader has now come in their midst and he is telling them not to do things in this way but to cooperate with the management; in this way country will benefit; workers will also be benefited.

Concern for Safety and Dispute Settlement

Imagery of a group of people – workers or villagers – discussing among themselves or with a supervisor or with a village *mukhia* (leader) either some natural calamity or a theft or an accident or some dispute or some of their demands. There was no mention of any agitation in this imagery. Most stories under this category just mentioned that such things were being discussed. Some examples were:

(a) Four brothers quarrelling over landed property represent their case before the *Mukhia* and the Gram Panchayat; the younger brother did not agree with other brothers; he is not satisfied and is abusing the *Mukhia*.

(b) These people are talking about some accident in the mine; they are working in the mine and suddenly there was this accident; people had some quarrel amongst themselves and they also fought each other and, therefore, the accident occurred.

(c) Workers have collected; among them, there is one supervisor; they are exchanging ideas about something; probably they are discussing about some possible accident; people are being explained the correct way and procedure about such an accident so that the work can be completed with safety; people are stunned with the recent accident and are very eager to do things with proper safety; they are eagerly trying to get information from the supervisor.

Agitation Vs Service

Middle managers and skilled workers showed interesting differences in their thoughts/imagery in response to the picture, as seen in Table 2.1. The dominant theme in the thoughts of middle managers was that the workers' demands were seldom met without an agitation and that a strike or a *gherao* would follow. Interestingly, the workers' imagery did not suggest such a concern. They thought more of service to the country and of increasing production. There was a tendency in their imagery to think of problems and grievances and their redressal by mutual discussions.

Picture Card II : A Person Facing an Uniformed Person

Thoughts obtained in responses to this picture showed the following significant themes:

Helper of Exploiter and Oppressor

The respondents recalled the arrest of the union leader during an agitation provoked by the employers' retrenchment of some workers. The dominant thought here was that the police force was used to break the strike, intimidate workers and help managements and other influential elements. Some samples of the dominant thoughts

TABLE 2.1 Percentage distribution of major themes in managers and workers' stories to picture card*

Sl. No.	Themes	Middle Managers	Workers	Combined
1.	Leader asking workers/villagers for action/agitation for their demands	53	10	40
2.	Action for production : People planning for "good" and service			
	(a) with leader	07	20	14
	(b) without leader	00	25	13
3.	Workers/Villagers discussing accidents/ calamities/ demants			
	(a) with supervison/mukhia	27	22	25
	(b) by themselves	10	23	16
	Number of stories	30	30	60

* This card shows a group of people with cues indicating a leader and followers.

indicating this theme were as follows:

(a) Some workers were retrenched by the management. The union went on strike. This was declared illegal. The police was called and they arrested the union leader. The leader is thinking what will happen to the workers.

(b) The police is questioning Shankar. He demanded wages but was thrown out by the musclemen of the management. His friends also deserted him. He has no money.

(c) Landlord and cultivators are discussing something. The landlord wants to take money from the cultivators. The cultivators want their share and disobey the decision. Police has come to help the landlord. Police will arrest the cultivators.

Police as Helper and Enforcer of Law

Another important theme in the stories, almost opposite of theme 1 above, viewed the police as helper and enforcer of law. They were perceived as persons correcting/preventing wrong things like violence, accidents, drug trafficking, violation of traffic rules, etc. Some examples of this theme were as follows:

(a) There is a black market here. The other person taking *ganja* (an intoxicating preparation). Both are in this business. The policeman got suspicious of the business and the black-marketeer is talking to the policeman to explain that he is not involved.

(b) People with their tiffins in hand going to work. There is suspicion on one person. A policeman opens his box and sees that there was a dynamite. The criminal is caught.

(c) A boy committed a theft out of distress. He was hungry. He was caught by a policeman. The boy is sorry. The policeman took pity and released him.

TABLE 2.2 : Percentage distribution of major themes in stories to Card II*

Themes	Middle Managers	Workers	Combined
Police : as Helper of exploiters	40	32	37
Helper and enforcer of law	20	24	22
Police is corrupt	40	44	41
Number of stories	30	30	60

* It shows a person facing another person in uniform looking like a gaurd or a policeman. Two other persons are seen in the background.

The Police is Corrupt

The dominant theme here was that the police let go the offenders and harass innocent citizens. They extort money from the poor and take bribes from the rich. The police was, therefore, perceived as a symbol of corruption. The dominant thoughts here were as follows:

(a) There was a fight in the locality. The police came on the scene and are talking to the people now. Shyam is explaining that he has done nothing and his things have been taken away by other people. Despite protests from Shyam, the police has taken him away. They want money.

(b) There was a theft in the locality. The police have to investigate. People caught Ram while stealing. Ram is in the habit of doing such things. He is known in the locality. Ram offers money to the police and he will get released.

(c) Some persons have been caught with *ganja* (an intoxicating preparation). They do this in the locality and harm workers and their families. There are quarrels. The police comes but they do nothing. The nuisance continues. We have to do something about it.

Widely Shared Image of Police as Corrupt

The managers and workers seemed to share a common image of the police as corrupt. Interestingly, as seen in Table 2.2, workers appeared to be somewhat more sympathetic to the police than the managers. Such images brought out some difference in the consciousness of the two groups vis-a-vis the police.

Picture Card III : An Elderly Person and a Boy with a Book in Hands

The picture evoked a variety of imagery and thoughts. These were coded and broadly classified under the following three themes:

Hope for a Better Future

The stories here perceived the son as a symbol and source of better future. They compared and contrasted the difficult and deprived present life (father's) and a hopefully more satisfying future life (son's) education emerged as means to ensuring better future. There was a resolve to provide education to the boy by saving money, cutting expenditure, borrowing money and to do so at any cost. Some examples of the dominant thoughts here were as follows:

(a) Ram relaxing and his son Kishore studying; he wants him to study intelligently; Kishore will become a good citizen.

(b) The man is thinking about his son's education and expecting that one day his son will enjoy all the comforts of life which he could not enjoy so far.

(c) Worker's own earning low, expenditure more; thinking how to look after his family and give education to children on this small income; boy wants to study but shortage of money; worker thinking to cut expenditure elsewhere and give education to him so that he becomes an able man; he told this to his son who understood it; studied hard and made progress; in this way all his sorrows ended.

Pessimistic Future

Imagery here indicated a fear of dark future – opposite of theme 1 above. Stories talked of the present difficulties and apprehensions that poverty and bad personal habits might jeopardize the future of their children. They appeared pessimistic in this regard. Some examples of this theme were:

(a) Leader sitting in his room while son reading a book; repenting that he has done illegal things, worrying how he will support his family since he has lost his job, he has lost his friends also; he is alone to bear the sorrow.
(b) An employee repenting over what has happened in the past; the boy is his son; thinking seriously as to how to get rid of the situation, visualizing bad days ahead.
(c) Dukhan Ram, the worker, gets poor salary; he cannot look after his family with this amount; he has everything in shortage; his son is reading a book; he has no means to see that he could study and go ahead; poverty blocks people from progress.

Insecurity: Between Hope and Uncertainty

Imagery here neither indicated a clear pessimistic future nor a clear hope. Thoughts here indicated a sense of insecurity with the present and an apprehension of bad time in future. They showed anxiety about children's studies, one's own work, retrenchment and unemployment, support to family, etc. Some examples of this theme were:

(a) Ramu's boy is very mischievous; Ramu wants him to get education and become a big man, but the boy does not read; now Ramu made him sit on the cot; watching him to see whether he is studying or not; Ramu always thinks how to make the boy go ahead and make progress.

(b) A worker wants his son to go to school; not attentive in studies; father worried about the future of his child and wants his life to become prosperous and good; he will bear all expenditure of his education.

(c) The worker deprived of his work due to direlection of duty and indiscipline; worrying about the family and education of his children; thinking about some way out; thinking to persuade co-workers to go to the manager and plead for him so that he could resume work.

Importance of Education

Interestingly, most of the stories written to this picture contained children's education as the main theme. They talked of son's education as a means of improving their life. It was also the source of their worry and uncertainty. It was the fear that fathers might not be able to support their children's education. Education, therefore, emerged as a very important theme in the imagination of the managers as well as the workers.

Hope, Insecurity and Uncertainty

The analysis, as seen in Table 2.3, showed that both, the workers and the managers, were equally hopeful of a better future. The workers

TABLE 2.3: Percentage distribution of themes in Card III*

Themes	Middle Managers	Workers	Combined
Hope for better future (through son's education)	36	36	36
Pessimistic future	24	36	30
Insecurity, between hope and uncertainty	40	28	34
Number of stories	30	30	60

* An elderly person and a boy with a book in hands.

seemed to be more anxious, may be helpless, and pessimistic about their sons' and their own future. They were less sure and assured of their sons' education. Managers showed greater ambivalence–whether they would or would not get a better future. They were hopeful but also uncertain. On the whole, a little more than one-third of the combined sample were clearly hopeful and felt assured of education for their children and of a better future, a little less than one-third of them were pessimistic and the remaining were uncertain.

Picture Card IV : "Queue of People" – One person seen falling out and another looking at him

Disorder, Discipline and Organization for Better Present

The dominant thoughts here contained imagery of disorder, indiscipline, rowdyism, musclemanship, aggressive moneylending and profiteering, physical violence and intimidation and that such things change for the better by organization and discipline. Some examples of this theme were as follows:

(a) All people standing in a queue to take ration according to rules; one wicked person wants to break the line; people are afraid of him; another person reprimands him; he realizes the mistake and runs away and falls down at a distance.
(b) Used to collect things and everybody was in difficulty; somebody advised people to stand in an orderly line; everybody is benefited.
(c) In the past employees did not get their wages properly; now standing in a line for weekly wages they will get this money and look after their family; we should show discipline and develop our country.

Collective and Meaningful Action for Better Life

Imagery here showed concern for a better life and a sense of collective assertion in order to achieve it. Stories contained such thoughts as: collectively building a tank; voting meaningfully; and people checking black-marketing.

Some examples of this theme were as follows:

(a) All people assembled to think that they should collectively build a tank; now coming out of their homes in a line.
(b) All villagers are standing in a line ready to vote; all thinking to vote for some such person so that the future could be good.
(c) Queue in front of a fair price shop; shortage due to hoarding and black-marketing; police now arresting black-marketeers and government opening more shops like this; in this way queues will end.

Sense of Insecurity and Helplessness

The queue of people symbolized hardship, difficulties, harassment, humiliation and evoked anxiety and insecurity. Such thoughts also showed elements of annoyance and resentment mixed with a sense of helplessness in the face of indignities and hardships. Some examples of this theme were as follows:

(a) People standing in a line; one person driven out; weeping, wants to get in; will he get wheat; what happens to his children; consoled by another person.
(b) Employees exhausted by standing in the queue; fatigue writ large.
(c) Every day people rush to ration shops; always crowded; hours of waiting; late for office.

Sense of Competence vs Helplessness

The themes in the stories here suggested concern for order, discipline and organization, a sense of competence for collective action as well as a sense of insecurity and helplessness.

Interestingly, the middle managers and the skilled workers tended to show qualitatively different trends in their imagery, as seen in Table 2.4. The dominant theme in the workers' imagery was of discipline and organization for a better present as compared to managers where the dominant theme was resentment and helplessness. The workers also showed a stronger concern for a meaningful and collective action for better life than the managers. Taking "people in queue" as a symbol of the socio-economic and industrial situation, the workers seemed to feel more at ease with the situation than the managers who seemed to feel alienated. The former appeared more efficacious and hopeful for better life whereas the managers appeared pessimistic. It appeared workers were mentally more equipped to cope with such hardships than managers and, therefore, felt more secured on account of some organized service—may be public distribution. On the other hand, managers felt bad queuing up and, therefore, felt more insecured.

TABLE 2.4 : Percentage distribution of themes in stories in Card IV*

Themes	Middle Managers	Workers	Combined
Discipline and organization for a better present	16	50	33
Collective and meaningful action for a better life	16	26	22
Sense of insecurity and helplessness	68	24	45
Number of stories	30	30	60

* Queue of People—one person seen falling out and another looking at him.

Picture Card V : A "poor looking" woman with a child in her lap, a car and a "better-dressed" person near it

Stories written in response to this picture evoked imagery of poverty and misery. The following themes seemed to emerge:

Poverty and Misery due to Personal Shortcomings

Here the dominant thought was that poverty and misery are caused by personal shortcomings and bad habits. They perceived drunkenness, extravagance and such other personal and social evils as the reasons for the misery of women and destitution of the family. The thoughts were moralistic and self-critical, emphasizing the need for improvement in one's own habits. Some examples of this dominant theme were as follows:

(a) Here is a poor family. They are in a bad and pitiable condition. They have a child. The woman has to feed her family by begging. Before this, it was a good family. But due to the mistake of extravagance and drunkenness of the husband, this thing came. The poor wife and the child have to suffer. They are now beggars. She is thinking how her family will continue? In this country, begging has become common. If these people work day and night, they can earn money for themselves and for their children. In this way, their condition as well as of their country will improve.

(b) In this picture, there is an old woman and a child. The old woman is sitting with the boy in her lap and thinking that her son will grow up and will look after them (father, mother). The old woman hoped but the opposite happened. The boy became a bad boy and the old woman's desire remained in her heart only. After some days, the boy facing all kinds of difficulties came to realize this.

(c) The employee deserted his family. When the employer comes to know that the employee has deserted his family, the former seems to have come to the house of the employee for giving financial help. The woman is the wife of the employee but she appears to have not been satisfied with the aid given to her by the employer.

Personal Tragedies and Uncertain Future

Here the respondents thought of inter-personal conflicts, mutual fights, accidents on roads or in factory, riots resulting in killing of workers, etc. The imagery here was different from the one for personal shortcomings, as here they did not talk of bad personal habits of men resulting in misery for the family and women. The attention here was not on habits but on accidents, uncertainties of life and resultant hardships. Some examples of this theme were as follows:

(a) In this picture, once upon a time there was a road accident near the village. The house of Shivan is beside a road. Shivan's son while playing on the road was knocked by a taxi. The driver shouted, "Whose child is this?" On hearing, Shivan's wife came out running and saw the child wounded and lying on the road. She is praying to God. She has no money.

(b) Without worrying, some person is going to jail after fighting with someone. The policeman is standing at the gate. The wife of this person with a child is weeping, and thinking what would happen to her after this? To whom will she go? In this world, "I have nobody to go to for help."

(c) Radha was staying in Ahmednagar with her husband and her one son Ram happily. Suddenly one night during the month of December 1971, some people came to her house and forcibly opened the door and killed her husband. They were shouting slogans. She was scared and she left the house with her son Ram and ultimately came to Delhi where she has to beg to feed her son and herself and nobody helps her in her need.

Socio-economic Causes of Poverty

Another important theme in the stories written to this picture revealed perception of socio-economic causes of poverty and misery. The dominant theme here was that of inequality, exploitation, money-lending, land-alienation and such other practices. Such a theme revealed social consciousness. Some examples of this theme were as follows:

(a) She is a woman. There is a child in her lap. She is begging. She has neither land nor house. Her land was taken away. Her man has also died. The poor woman begs for her child and also for herself. She feeds her child and thinks that this boy will grow up and work or do some job and look after her.
(b) The mother is begging for maintaining the child. She is the wife of a cultivator. There is low production of foodgrain, the family had a bad crop and many people are in starvation. Nobody supports them. Workers will have to beg from others for maintaining their lives. They will die if they do not get any job.
(c) The picture shows a poor woman sitting with a baby and begging. A rich man has got down from his car and is going for shopping. One is fighting for survival and the other is enjoying life. This is a typical picture of our country.

Response to Poverty and Misery

This picture evoked imagery of poverty and misery which is a living reality in the country. People have been living with misery for a long time. A poor woman with a child in her lap is begging – this is a familiar sight. It was interesting that workers tended to think more of poverty and misery as an outcome of personal weakness and accidents, as seen in Table 2.5, than managers. They also perceived men doing wrong to women by their drunkenness, extravagance and other bad habits. Their consciousness of the socio-economic causes of poverty was rather weak. Their thoughts seemed to show elements of an almost masochistic and/or moralizing tendency to blame one's poverty on himself. Their imagery implied the need for efforts to improve one's habits and to eliminate evils of drunkenness, etc.

TABLE 2.5 : Percentage distribution of themes in stories to Card V*

Themes	Middle Managers	Workers	Combined
Poverty as a result of:			
Personal shortcomings, Wrong habits	33	46	40
Tragedies, accidents	37	40	38
Social reasons, exploitation	30	14	22
Number of stories	30	30	60

* A poor-looking woman with a child in her lap, a car and a better dressed person near it.

Managers, on the other hand, also perceived accidents and bad personal habits as the cause of poverty and misery, but their thoughts indicated a greater social consciousness. They tended to think of poverty as a result of the system marked by failure of crops, money-lenders, dispossession and alienation of land and social inequality. Interestingly, managers also perceived charity as one way of dealing with misery and poverty.

Both, workers and managers, tended to be "moralistic" and "individualistic" in viewing misery and poverty. Both tended to hold the "poor" responsible for their poverty and misery and wanted them to improve their habits and behaviour. There was sympathy for the poor. Thoughts were, however, mixed with pity rather than anger at injustice and misery. Their consciousness did not show much appreciation of universal causes of poverty and the need to act on socio-economic systems for an equitable development. They seemed to be strongly bothered by wrong habits, tragedies and uncertainties of life.

Picture Card VI: Workers working on a lathe and other machines

The categorized themes are seen in Table 2.6.

TABLE 2.6 Percentage distribution of themes in stories to Card VI*

Themes	Managers	Workers	Combined
Good and hard work: personal success	15	20	18
Collective efforts for improving production and prosperity	05	55	30
Fear of injuries, let down by colleagues	45	25	33
Concern for discipline and dispute settlement	35	—	20
Number of stories	30	30	60

* Workers working on a lathe and other machines.

Examples of themes under each category are given below:

Good and Hard Work: Personal Success

Here the main thoughts were concerned with good and hard work, determination and patience for personal success in establishing one's own small factory or business resulting in better prospects in life. Some examples of this theme were:

(a) Blacksmith and barber are friends. Poor people, therefore, doing some work in the town. Gradually, saved money, purchased instruments and now doing their own track. One person became very prosperous in this way. He is explaining to his friends that his hard work, determination, patience, wisdom and savings are reasons for his success.

(b) An engineer in government office thought of increasing his income. Establishes his own firm. Resigned from government service and now working in a village. Now fitting the machines in order to start production as early as possible.

(c) One worker showing his workmanship to others who are appreciating. They also think to do the job with the same good workmanship.

Collective Efforts for Improving Production and Prosperity

The main concern in such imagination was progress and prosperity of the country, collective efforts, good working conditions and increasing production. Some examples of this theme were as follows:

(a) Some talented youth working on a lathe for the progress of the country. They are skilled workers repairing and improving the lathe spoiled by some careless workers. Now all employees working hard with all their enthusiasm and heart for the progress of the country and productivity.
(b) Skilled workers working in cooperation. Before this they used to fight like bulls. Now they have understood that they should work like friends and should organise a united organization. People are enthusiastic and working for the prosperity of the country. This will benefit their families.
(c) People should work with interest and for the progress of the country. In this way, we can save foreign exchange and make our country independent, necessary to help country progress continuously.

Fear of Injuries, Let Down

The dominant themes here suggested a sense of insecurity fear of letting down by others, and fear of accidents at work. Examples of this theme were:

(a) One person injured because of his negligence. Another person disputes it. They are quarrelling.
(b) One person careless, gets injured and leads to an accident. Should not talk while working.
(c) The suspended leader is now back at the job. Has learnt his lesson from past experience. Not interested in others. They deserted him, now not interested in politics.

Concern for Discipline and Dispute Settlement

Here the dominant thoughts centred around settlement of disputes and grievances and the need for discipline. Some examples of this theme were:

(a) Workers need to be disciplined and wages linked with productivity. Should not talk while working.
(b) People in a workshop discussing about their grievances and thinking about the course of action to be taken. Will go to the

authority concerned.

(c) There is some dispute not settled. People are talking about them. Want to now settle it.

Table 2.6 once again brings out interesting differences in the imagery of workers and managers as evoked by a work-related picture. More than half of the workers' stories here showed a concern for collective efforts for improving productivity for better quality of life for all. Their thoughts centred round themes such as hard work, carefulness, united and organized efforts, enthusiasm for production and progress and prosperity of the country including their families. Such thoughts were absent or rare in managers' stories. In their case, the dominant imagery seemed to centre round accidents, negligence, desertion by colleagues in times of distress, dispites and other such contentious matters.

It was interesting that managers tended to imagine such apprehensions in relation to and for workers, whereas the workers themselves thought much less of them. The stories seemed, therefore, to reveal some sense of mistrust and apprehension in managers' imagination as evoked in response to a work theme. Workers, on the other hand, seemed to be more hopeful who mostly imagined of a better performance at work. Such thoughts contained concern for personal as well as collective achievement and for better work production and quality of life.

III VARYING THEMES IN WORKERS' AND MANAGERS' APPERCEPTIONS

As mentioned above, a set of six TAT type pictures were selected from a pool of several pictures, in a series of try-outs, to obtain stories from workers and managers. This was done to identify dominant imagery and thoughts as contained in their stories with a view to understanding elements of efficacy and alienation in their thoughts. The obtained data were also utilized in developing a system to analyse the imaginative content of the stories, as discussed in Chapter 3, to measure the strength of various needs. The present analyses, as discussed above, brought out interesting thematic differences in the imagination and thoughts of workers and managers, as evoked by a same set of pictures, administered under same conditions.

The workers' thoughts tended to centre round individual and collective action; production and prosperity; atrocities on people; corrupt and unhelpful police force; better future through son's education; apprehension about future; discipline and organization for a better present; wrong habits and personal shortcomings causing poverty and misery; tragedies of life; and hard work for personal and collective success.

The managers' dominant thoughts, on the other hand, seemed to centre round agitations; unhelpful police; uncertain future; and helplessness in the face of socio-economic hardships; social causation of poverty and misery; mistrust of colleagues, fear of being let down; and punishment, discipline and disputes.

In the present case, both managers and workers seemed to show an apprehension and sense of helplessness but the former tended to be more surcharged with such feelings than workers. Both were equally disillusioned with the law and order situation. It was understandable in view of the situation and musclemanship obtaining in the coal fields. However, workers thought more of organized efforts for facing problems and for improving both, their work performance and conditions of life, while the managers appeared passive in this respect. At the same time, managers were socially much more conscious about the universal causes of poverty, inequality and exploitation while the workers tended to blame themselves for such miseries which, they thought, were caused by bad habits and personal shortcomings.

Managers' sense of mistrust seemed to surface in their imagination in relation to a work theme, while the workers tended to imagine of individual and collective success. They also thought of collective efforts and hard work, while the managers tended to thing more of injuries, foul play by colleagues, conflicts and disputes.

Managers and Workers : Their Background

As mentioned above, the workers' group included several shop-floor leaders and representatives, while the managers' group consisted of first-line supervisors and junior managers. Both of them were drawn from the collieries which were only then nationalized and integrated in the new undertaking, namely, the Bharat Coking Coal Limited (BCCL), at Dhanbad. One reason for the difference in managers and workers' imagination could have been due to their attitude to the nationalization of private coal-mines and the new public sector undertaking. Amalgamation and integration of the erstwhile private small coal-mines probably released energy and hope among the workers, whereas the same event evoked apprehensions and uncertainties among the supervisors, engineers and middle managers. Another reason could be that the first-line supervisors/ middle managers were responsible for the safety of the mines under the Mines Safety Act. They were, therefore, apprehensive about accidents and injuries, may be, because of unsafe mines and mining. They felt insecured on this count, as they could be held accountable under the law. Similarly, due to their historical experience and the background of private coal-mines, despite their greater social awareness, the middle managers were unable to think of workers as their partners in raising production and in improving the functioning of the organization. This probably, indicated a crisis of identity in them as they showed mistrust of their colleagues and lack of respect for workers.

Managers and workers' imagination and dominant thoughts in their stories could have been, therefore, evoked by an interaction of their personal and historical experience, on the one hand, and the pictorial cues on the other. As the pictorial cues as also instructions were constant for all, the differences in their dominant imagery and thoughts were due mainly to their personal and historical experience and their perception of and attitude toward nationalization of private coal-mines and the new public sector undertaking. Such experiential and attitudinal differences could have contributed to evoking qualitatively different imaginative content and themes in their stories.

Thus, the obtained TAT stories showed rich imaginative content and several dominant themes. These indicated a sense of competence, achievement, assertion and action orientation as well as apprehensions and a sense of alienation of their authors – in this case the managers and workers of a recently nationalized coal undertaking. This varied imagination and its thematic content were then processed for developing the TAT instrument and the scoring system. The results obtained are discussed in Chapter 3.

3

Need for Social Achievement, Need for Influence and Other Needs

Scoring System for Analysing TAT Stories

AN ANALYSIS of the obtained stories indicated several major themes. The variety and the content of the themes, such as those reported for managers and workers in Chapter 2, as well as in stories obtained from others, such as agricultural workers, rural artisans, social workers, organizers of rural poor, officials of public systems, etc. seemed to suggest the following important behavioural trends.

I. DOMINANT TRENDS IN THEMES: EMERGING BEHAVIOURAL TENDENCIES

Emerging Consciousness: Conditions of Work and Life

The imaginative content of the stories revealed work-related issues such as lockouts and strikes; retrenchment and unemployment; accidents and safety; conflicts at workplace, income, etc. The respondents seemed to move between hope and uncertainty with regard to such issues. The stories also indicated a similar concern for atrocities inflicted on the rural poor by landlords, money-lenders, the police and others. Such themes revealed an emerging consciousness and awareness of important issues pertaining to work, employment and conditions of life.

Faith in People and in Themselves

The stories (fantasies) indicated a sense of self-confidence and faith in the people's invidividual and collective strength for coping with pressing problems such as the above. They tended to imagine the need for working together and organized efforts against hardships and for solving such problems. Such themes also indicated an attitude of mutual understanding and respect.

Hope and Apprehension : Sense of Ambivalence

The stories showed mixed feelings of hope and apprehension about the present as well as the future. On the one hand, they showed confidence and a sense of hope for settling their disputes, getting their grievances redressed and for solving such problems. At the same time, their thoughts also contained elements of uncertainty, insecurity and a sense of pessimism. They tended to attach importance to education of their children, hoping that this would improve their future quality of life. There was also a strong apprehension that the sons may not be able to complete their education as desired and that their future would be bleak. They, therefore, tended to move between hope and uncertainty, showing a sense of ambivalence. They hoped for a better future with several "ifs" and "buts" in this regard.

Blaming Self for Misery: Moralistic Approach

The stories were rather strong in articulating the ill-effects of personal habits such as drinking, absenteeism, quarrel-someness, etc., and considered such habits as the cause of poverty and misery particularly for destitution of women and the family. They also talked of negligence at the workplace which caused accidents and injuries. While such thoughts were moralistic, they also contained a concern for positive work and personal habits which could help avoid accidents and miseries, for families and for themselves. In a way, therefore, such thoughts implied a concern for a better quality of life and also a sense of vigilance in this regard.

Concern for Production and Prosperity

The stories were strong on the need for raising productivity and production in order to enhance their own and the country's prosperity. They thought of third word, united action, vigilance, acquisition of skills, proper work habits, etc., in this connection. They also thought of proper functioning of factories and workplace so that such goals of production and prosperity could be achieved. Such thoughts, implicitly as well as explicitly, contained a concern for production, discipline and for a better quality of life for themselves as well as others and the society as a whole.

Sense of Helplessness and Sense of Efficacy

Another important sense of ambivalence, emerging from the fantasies, related to some pressing socio-economic and work problems. On the one hand, they showed determination for solving problems, and, on the other, a sense of helplessness in the face of such problems. They thought of hard work, patience, determination, united action, organization, vigilance, working together, etc., for solving problems facing them at the workplace and in society. At the same time, the stories also contained elements of a sense of helplessness in the face of industrial and social problems. As mentioned above, in some such cases, they tended to blame themselves for poverty and miseries. They thus tended to move between sense of helplessness and sense of competence and efficacy.

Collective Action for Better Future

Another dominant theme in the stories showed a concern for collective action for ensuring a better future. They thought of joint and united action for resisting injustice and atrocities. They also thought of discipline, vigilance and a sense of responsibility in such matters. They tended to think in terms of meaningful individual and collective action such as voting, organizing and acting on the situation in order to ensure a better future and quality of life.

Collective Achievement Goals: Improving Quality of Life

Stories, particularly those written by poor villagers and those working with the rural poor, also showed emergence of common or collective achievement goals such as obtaining wells for drinking water and irrigation, schools for children, health care facilities; employment and proper wages; protection against atrocities of money-lenders and others, elimination of alcoholism and such other evils, acquisition of productive skills for generating income, etc. Projection of such goals indicated their rising concern for a better quality of life. It also indicated emergence of some standards and levels of living for themselves and for their children.

Thus, the TAT stories revealed a whole range of behavioural trends including: awareness of personal as well as social- and work-related problems; faith in people and in their own strengths; hope of success as well as apprehension of failure; moralistic approach to problems; concern for better work performance and better quality of life; collective action orientation; sense of efficacy as well as helplessness and projection of social/collective achievement goals. The dominant themes and the behavioural trends suggested the presence of the expected needs in the obtained TAT stories. The obtained themes and the trends were then utilized to facilitate the scoring of the fantasies for these needs and to develop a system for analysing the content of the stories in this regard.

II. SCORING STORIES (FANTASIES) FOR NEEDS CULLING OUT SUB-CATEGORIES

The obtained stories were first examined for analysing imageries/thoughts showing need for social achievement, need for personal achievement, need for influence and other related needs. As explained in the manual given in Appendix I, stories containing social achievement goals such as concern for improving the quality of life by desiring better water supply, better irrigation facilities, schools for children, education of themselves, increased productivity and production, prosperity of the country and for themselves, better health facilities, etc., were scored for need for social achievement.

Similarly, stories containing personal achievement goals such as desire for competitive success for oneself at the workplace, better quality of life for oneself as compared to others, i.e., thoughts indicating a desire for personal achievement goals, were scored for need for personal achievement.

Stories containing imagery indicating a desire to take an actor role and act on the environment, participation in collective action and assertion for influencing the environment, and influencing others for solving problems, i.e. stories containing a desire to influence the on-going situation whether in wider life or at work were scored for need for influence.

There were some stories where imageries indicated integrated goals showing personal-cum-social achievement goals or influence-oriented personal achievement goals or influence-oriented social achievement goals or influence-oriented personal-cum-social achievement goals. Such stories were excluded from scoring for the purpose of identifying sub-categories associated with the three needs.

Behavioural Sub-categories

The stories were thus identified for the relevant needs, i.e., need for social achievement, need for personal achievement and need for influence. Such stories were retained for further examination for related behavioural tendencies or sub-categories. The remaining stories were eliminated from further scoring for our present task, i.e. toward conceptualizing the related sub-categories.

Further examination of the eligible stories showed presence of the following behavioural sub-categories. Their appearance varied from story to story, thus providing varying strength to the various need-states, as contained in the fantasies (stories).

Personal Action

This was relatively a more frequent tendency found in the relevant stories. For instance, someone would talk of adopting family planning; telling someone what to do in a given situation; planning to do his job with responsibility; leader thinking of action; asking son to read; listening to the problems of others; thinking of raising a loan, etc. A large number of stories were found to show such personal action tendency for obtaining the goal mentioned in the stories.

Social Action

Stories also showed a tendency to plan and engage in social/collective action in pursuance of the goal. For instance, taking a pledge collectively; people talking that they should work together; people thinking and working for the good of the country, trying together to solve mutual disputes; planning a special drive to check some evil practices, etc. Such actions involved working together with other people as a team or collectively in pursuance of the goal.

Anticipatory Action

Some stories showed a tendency to plan or act in advance in pursuance of the stated goal. For instance, family planning to ward off future problems; self-reliance in manufacturing in the country to prevent future dependency on other countries; determination to provide an opportunity to the son to prevent future disappointment; planning agitation to prevent future lock-outs or retrenchment; saving money for higher education, etc.

Articulation of Strength and Internal Resources

Some of the need-oriented stories also showed articulation of strength and internal resources. Either someone talked of some strength or the theme suggested presence of strength or some internal resource which could facilitate the goal set in the story. For instance, presence of a sense of discipline, presence of determination, honesty of purpose, people's or personal strength or intelligence or skills.

Hope of Success

Some stories also tended to show a positive and optimistic approach to the outcome, suggesting hope of success in obtaining the goal. For instance, stories talked of honesty and determination to prevail over smuggling; capability for obtaining a bright future; family planning resulting in happiness; education leading to prosperity, etc. Such statements/words indicated hope of success for the goal contained in the story.

Social Awareness

There was a tendency in some stories to show awareness about socio-economic, work-related and such other issues. For instance, they would talk of a disturbed economic situation prevailing inequality in society, need for controlling population, designs of money-lenders and landlords, etc. Such statements in the context of a dominant theme and goal indicated awareness of the related problems and issues.

Sense of Vigilance

Some stories gave evidence of the presence of sense of vigilance in relation to pressing problems. For instance, walking on the left side of the road to avoid an accident; carefulness about accidents and injuries at the work place; identifying persons planning to create disturbance; thinking about a possible retrenchment; thinking to ward off drought, etc. Such statements indicated a tendency to anticipate future problems and be careful about them.

Thus, the above behavioural tendencies, designated as sub-categories here, seemed to be associated with the need-states as contained in the thought content of the imaginative stories. As could be expected, there were individual differences, both by pictures and for persons. As the stories were imagined in response to different pictures, not all of them, although written by the same person, showed the same imagery. Some fantasies (stories) showed none of the relevant needs. Even among those showing need-related imageries, only a few contained some of the sub-categories. Similarly, different persons writing stories to the same picture differed widely in their imagination, thus yielding varying needs and varying frequency of sub-categories.

III. FURTHER SCORING AND EXPERIMENTAL TRY-OUT

As the above sub-categories were culled out from the same stories as were subjected to a thematic analysis for behavioural trends, it was decided to check them for any presence in another set of stories written to the same pictures under the same standard conditions. A sample of 25 new persons—12 skilled workers and 13 managers—was randomly picked up from the larger pool of respondents and their stories (obtained during 1976) taken up for detailed scoring. The results, thus obtained are seen in Table 3.1

As seen in the table, only 15 per cent of the stories contained need for social achievement (*n*SA) and only a little more showed the need for personal achievement (*n*PA). However, more than one-fourth of them showed the need for influence (*n*Inf)

As the main purpose of the present analysis was to identify the sub-categories, as associated with the imagery of these three needs, only such stories were scored as contained any one of the three needs.

One in every two of the eligible (fantasies) stories showed articulation of personal action (Ap) and about 20 per cent showed presence of the sub-category of strength (S+). About 17 per cent of the stories showed thoughts of social action (As). Articulation of the remaining sub-categories, namely, anticipatory action (Aa), hope (H), vigilance (V) and awareness (Aw) was rather low as seen in Table 3.1

TABLE 3.1 : Percentage distribution of categories and sub-categories

	Under Neutral conditions N-25; Stories-150	Under Arousal conditions N-25; Stories-150
Need for personal achievement (*n*PA)	18.7 (23)*	35.3 (53)
Need for social achievement (*n*SA)	15.3 (23)	32.0 (48)
Need for influence (*n*Inf)	27.3 (41)	36.7 (55)
Number of Eligible Stories	(92)	(156)
Personal Action (Ap)	49.3**	50.8**
Social Action (As)	16.9	26.9
Anticipatory Action (Aa)	7.8	7.7
Strength (S+)	19.4	23.7
Hope (H)	13.0	18.5
Awareness (Aw)	7.8	20.9
Vigilance (V)	13.00	19.9

* Figures in parentheses are frequencies.

** Per cent of number of eligible stories.

The projection of the three needs as well as the related sub-categories thus, appeared to be rather meagre. It was, then decided to see whether arousal of such motives would make a difference in the story-writers' imagination and whether such aroused imagination would be projected to pictures. The same set of six pictures was then administered to a comparable experimental group of 25 persons under arousal conditions. The following short speech was delivered to them before administering the pictures for story-writing. The speech and the instructions were designed to arouse their needs for personal achievement, social achievement and influence as well as the related sub-categories:

> As you know, our country is on the march. Various kinds of problems and difficulties have challenged us from time to time since independence. We have been engaged in efforts to improve our standard of living, achieve a better future for our children, raise production and move toward prosperity for all, particularly the down-trodden. This is possible only when we correctly analyse situations, are watchful of the enemies, foresee the obstacles; each one of us makes an effort, participates in collective action and shows solidarity. Success is possible only when all of us, individually and collectively, actively pursue such goals of improving our work and conditions of life.

Brief remarks like the following were repeated before each story was written:

> "Remember, you are skilled workers, trade union leaders and managers. You are engaged in leading and managing others for production, for better work and for better life."

The Obtained Results

The results obtained under neutral conditions and those under arousal conditions are seen in Table 3.1. The experimental treatment did succeed in arousing the internal strength of the three needs. The relevant thoughts were enhanced in the fantasy of the "experimental" respondents which came out in their stories written to the same pictures as by the earlier group under neutral conditions. As compared to the control group, the experimental group projected a substantially greater imagery of personal achievement, social achievement and influence.

Along with the relevant needs, all the sub-categories, excepting personal action (Ap) and anticipatory action (Aa), were also aroused, as shown by their articulation in the eligible stories. Personal action was already high in the control group – about 49 per cent of the stories showing it. Anticipatory action orientation was not affected by the "arousal" condition. Its articulation remained low – with only 8 per cent of the eligible stories showing it. In view of its conceptual and practical importance, this sub-category was, however, retained. The results thus tended to show that the proposed behavioural tendencies – the sub-categories – were associated with the various need-states and that the same could be used to measure the strength of these needs.

IV. THE SCORING SYSTEM: NEEDS AND SUB-CATEGORIES

A thematic analysis and the obtained behavioural trends suggested the presence of needs for personal achievement, social achievement and influence along with some related sub-categories in the stories written to specifically designed TAT pictures. It was then decided to check these once again by obtaining fresh stories in response to the same TAT pictures from another group. The pictures were then administered to a new group of 204 persons, consisting of 136 skilled workers and 68 first-line supervisors and managers, at the Bharat Coking Coal Limited, Dhanbad. The respondents wrote stories under neutral conditions and instructions.

Scoring of the obtained stories showed, as could be expected, that while most eligible stories showed either the need for personal achievement or need for social achievement or the need for influence, some stories showed integrated imageries containing mixed thoughts for achievement and influence. Thus, some of the stories showed an integrated need for achievement in which both personal and social achievement goals were present. Some other stories contained an integrated need for influence-oriented personal achievement or need for influence-oriented social achievement or need for influence-oriented integrated achievement. A preliminary examination suggested that such integrated needs were different from the three single needs.

Inter-Relationship Among the Needs

The scores thus obtained for three single needs and four integrated needs were inter-correlated to understand their direction in respect to each other. The results, seen in Table 3.2, provided confirmation of the view that there were indeed qualitatively different need-states.

TABLE 3.2 : Seven Needs : Inter-correlation Matrix N = 204

Need	*n*PA	*n*SA	*n*Inf	*n*PA SA	*n*PA-Inf	*n*SA-Inf	*n*PA-SA-Inf
*n*PA							
*n*SA	–.14*						
*n*Inf	–.19**	–.31**					
*n*PA and SA	–.10	.21**	–.21**				
*n*PA and Inf	–.12*	–.10	.06	–.15*			
*n*SA and Inf	–.03	.07	–.19**	.03	.04		
*n*PA, SA and Inf	–.06	–.05	–.14*	–.03	.00	.27**	–

* Significant at .05 level.

** Significant at .01 level.

The results suggested that persons with a strong imagination for personal achievement were weak in thoughts for social achievement. The same was true for the need for influence and *vice versa*. Such persons, i.e. those with a high need for personal achievement, or need for social achievement, or need for influence, seemed to centre rather exclusively around such thoughts. Their thoughts were focused relatively more on only one such goal (need) and much less on the other two goals (needs). All the obtained intercorrelations among these three needs were negative and significant in this respect.

Inter-correlations among the four integrated needs and three single needs yielded some interesting findings. Thus, the integrated need for achievement, containing both personal and social achievement goals, did not correlate with the single need for personal achievement. On the other hand, it was positively correlated with the need for social achievement and negatively with the need for influence. Thus, the integrated need for achievement seemed to be loaded strongly with social achievement thoughts. Such persons seemed to be motivated by achievement thoughts in which social achievement goals such as raising productivity, improving safety and working conditions, digging wells and opening schools in the village formed a strong ingredient.

The integrated need for influence-oriented personal achievement, i.e. where the thoughts contained a desire for personal achievement along with influence, showed no correlations with the need for social achievement and for influence. On the other hand, it showed negative correlations with the need for personal achievement as well as the integrated need for achievement.

The findings here, therefore, suggested that integration of influence-related thoughts with thoughts for personal achievement changed the nature of this need. Such persons thought of their personal achievement goals and of influencing situations and persons, probably for obtaining a better work performance and/or life conditions for themselves as well as for establishing their control and supremacy. Their goal was, thus, not personal achievement alone but a wider achievement with control and influence over the given situation and other persons.

Similar findings emerged for the other two integrated needs, namely, need for influence-oriented social achievement and for influence-oriented integrated achievement. First of all, these two needs were highly inter-correlated, suggesting a considerable overlap of thoughts. Persons high on one were also high on the other. The two needs showed no correlation with the need for influence oriented personal achievement. Both the needs, on the other hand, showed a significant negative correlation with the need for influence. These two integrated, highly inter-correlated needs were not similar to the achievement needs and, more definitely, were dissimilar to the need for influence. The results once again showed that such integrated needs were qualitatively different in nature from the single needs. Persons, high on such needs, were, therefore, likely to behave differently in given situations. It was, therefore, decided to treat all the seven (Table 3.2) as separate needs and process the results accordingly.

Articulation of Sub-categories

A total of 778 stories out of 1224 obtained stories were found to be eligible for further scoring for sub-categories. Of these, one-fourth – about 24 per cent – of the stories showed need for personal achievement, one-fifth – about 20 per cent – need for social achievement; and one-third – about 34 per cent – showed the need for influence. The frequency of fantasies with integrated or mixed thoughts was, on the whole, low. Thus, 7 per cent showed the need for influence-oriented personal achievement, 6 per cent for personal and social achievement; 6 per cent for influence-oriented social achievement; and about 2 per cent fantasies showed the need for influence-oriented personal-cum-social achievement. These stories were also taken up for identifying the presence of the various sub-categories.

The articulation of sub-categories, as was expected, was not evenly distributed over the seven needs. The variation in this respect seemed to be associated with the nature of fantasy evoked and as evidenced in the stories. Such variation was statistically highly significant.

The total output of the sub-categories in terms of the frequency of their articulation was 1,352 as obtained in 778 eligible stories. The need for influence was found to evoke comparatively greater sub-categories followed by the need for personal achievement and then the need for social achievement. Fantasies containing four integrated needs, on the whole, showed a greater articulation of sub-categories, although such stories were only a few.

Personal Action, Social Action and Anticipatory Action Tendencies

Table 3.3 gives the variation in articulation of the sub-categories. The first noteworthy information is that, on the whole, verbalization of the personal action tendency was more than of the social action and much more than of the anticipatory action tendencies. Of the three, the least expressed was the anticipatory action tendency. In fact, it was the weakest among the seven sub-categories with only four per cent of the eligible stories showing it. Personal action tendency was found the most in the stories scored for the need for influence and for influence-oriented integrated achievement. It was equally strong in the fantasies marked by personal achievement as well as the integrated needs. It was found to be the lowest in the stories scored for the need for social achievement.

The reverse was the case in respect to the social action tendency which was found to be the maximum in the stories scored for the need for social achievement-oriented influence followed by those scored for the need for social achievement. This was also expressed substantially in the stories scored for the need for integrated achievement as well as in those with the need for influence. Fantasies marked by the need for personal achievement showed it the least. It

TABLE 3.3 : Percentage distribution of stories (scored for respective needs) showing various sub-categories
N = 204

Sub-categories	Needs							Total Number of sub-categories in eligible stories
	*n*PA	*n*SA	*n*Inf	*n*PA-Inf	*n*P-SA	*n*SA-Inf	*n*Inf-PA-SA	
Ap	68.6 (127)	27.8 (44)	85.8 (229)	70.4 (38)	75.5 (37)	59.2 (29)	87.5 (14)	66.6 (518)*
As	12.4 (23)	53.2 (84)	37.4 (100)	16.7 (9)	46.9 (23)	55.1 (27)	37.5 (6)	35.0 (272)
Aa	2.2 (40	1.9 (3)	4.8 (13)	14.8 (8)	2.0 (1)	4.0 (2)	6.3 (1)	4.1 (32)
S+	14.6 (27)	9.5 (15)	3.7 (10)	25.9 (14)	12.2 (6)	18.4 (9)	43.8 (7)	11.3 (88)
Hs	16.2 (30)*	18.3 (29)	10.1 (27)	40.7 (22)	18.4 (9)	26.5 (13)	56.3 (9)	17.7 (139)
Aw	9.7 (18)	22.2 (35)	14.6 (39)	24.1 (13)	34.7 (17)	34.7 (17)	50.0 (8)	18.9 (147)
V	21.1 (39)	17.7 (28)	16.5 (44)	22.2 (12)	26.5 (13)	22.4 (11)	56.3 (9)	20.1 (156)
Total No. of eligible stories	(185) 23.8	(158) 20.3	(267) 34.3	(54) 6.9	(49) 6.3	(49) 6.3	(16) 2.0	1352
						Total	= (778)	

Note: Figures in parentheses are the number of stories.

* Total number of sub-categories found in eligible stories.

$\chi^2 = 183.413$, $df = 36$, $P < .001$

appeared that the tendency for personal action was associated more with the need for influence and the need for personal achievement while the tendency for social action was associated more with the need for social achievement and also with the need for influence.

The anticipatory action tendency was found the most – about 15 per cent in the stories scored for need for influence-oriented personal achievement. The data suggested that the social action tendency was a behavioural characteristic of persons motivated by the need for influence and/or for social achievement and/or by the integrated need for social achievement-oriented influence. Persons motivated by a desire for personal achievement were least bothered with social action. On the other hand, they tended to act alone. Interestingly, persons motivated by a desire for influence tended to show both, personal and social action tendencies. However, there, dominant characteristic was also personal action orientation. On the other hand, persons motivated by a desire for personal achievement-oriented influence were marked by a tendency for personal action. They also tended to show a relatively greater anticipatory action tendency than others.

Persons motivated by an integrated desire for personal-cum-social achievement as well as those by a desire for influence-oriented social achievement and those by a desire for influence-oriented personal-cum-social achievement tended to show substantial orientation for personal as well as social action. However, except those motivated by the need for influence-oriented social achievement who showed both the action tendencies equal strongly, persons showing integrated needs tended to show a much stronger orientation for personal action. In fact, personal action tendency emerged as the most prominent sub-category with two-thirds of the eligible stories showing it followed by the social action tendency present in 35 per cent of the stories.

Articulation of Low

The articulation of the sub-category of strength was found to be rather low. Its presence was higher than of anticipatory action, but along with it, it was one of the two least expressed tendencies found in only one in every 10 eligible stories. Persons motivated by the integrated needs particularly those by the need for influence-oriented personal-cum-social achievement showed a significantly greater tendency to think of individual and/or social internal resource or strength. As many as 44 per cent of such fantasies contained this characteristic. One-fourth of the stories scored for personal achievement-oriented influence also showed this sub-category followed by those showing social achievement-oriented influence.

On the three single needs, persons motivated by a desire for personal achievement tended to think of their own strength substantially more than those motivated by either the need for influence or the need for social achievement. Interestingly, persons motivated by a desire for influence tended to show it the least.

The data on the whole suggested that persons motivated by the integrated need for personal achievement-oriented influence tended to think much more of internal strength or resource than others. This tendency got a boost when the need for social achievement was integrated with the desire for influence.

Hope of Success

The sub-category of hope was found to be present in about 18 per cent of the eligible stories. Interestingly, it was least found in persons motivated by the need for influence and the most in those motivated by the integrated need for personal-cum-social achievement-oriented influence followed by those by the need for personal achievement-oriented influence and then those by the need for social achievement-oriented influence.

It was interesting to note that this optimistic tendency was associated more with achievement needs and least with the need for influence. It, however, came out substantially when such needs, particularly the need for personal achievement, were integrated with the influence-related thoughts. The results, therefore, suggested that such a sense of one's own success was characteristically associated not with the need for influence alone but when it got integrated with an urge to have a better work performance and/or better life conditions.

Social Awareness

The tendency to show social awareness, i.e. awareness of environment and socio-economic issues and problems, was found in one in every five – about 19 per cent – of the eligible stories. Like other sub-categories, integrated fantasies contained this more than individual needs – with one in every two stories marked by the need for influence-oriented personal-cum-social achievement showing it. Among the individual needs, persons motivated by the need for social achievement showed a much greater social awareness than those motivated by the need for personal achievement. This behavioural characteristic of social achievement motivation was further boosted when it got integrated with influence-related thoughts. Interestingly, personal achievement-motivated persons tended to show the lease social awareness.

Sense of Vigilance

Sense of vigilance – the tendency to anticipate outcomes of events and problems – was substantially present in the obtained stories – with 20 per cent showing this sub-category. As in the case of other sub-categories, here also stories marked by the integrated need for influence oriented personal-cum-social achievement showed it the most. However, this tendency was present almost in equal strength in other stories as well, as seen in Table 3.3. Thus, more than one-fifth – about 22 per cent – of the stories marked by the need for influence-oriented personal achievement and those marked by the need for influence-oriented social achievement contained this tendency. Among the single needs, fantasies with the need for personal achievement, showed its presence the most. The sense of vigilance, thus, seemed to be associated more with those for social achievement. This tendency was, therefore, associated more with achievement needs.

Inter-correlation among Sub-categories

The seven sub-categories were significantly correlated among themselves, as seen in Table 3.4. The obtained correlations showed that the sub-categories were working in unison and in the same direction. When added, these would indicate the strength of a particular need.

One interesting finding, however, was that, the two sub-categories, namely, sense of vigilance and anticipatory action, which should been otherwise inter-related, were found to be unrelated here. It was the only correlation which failed to reach an acceptable level of significance. Thus, these tendencies which were significantly correlated with all other sub-categories, but not with each other, suggested that those showing a greater sense of vigilance were not necessarily high on anticipatory action orientation.

TABLE 3.4 : Sub-categories : Inter-Correlation Matrix
$N = 136$

Sub-category	Ap	As	Aa	S+	Hs	Aw	V
Personal Action	—						
Social Action	.19**						
Anticipated Action	.18*	.14*					
Strength	.23	.19**	.18*				
Hope of Success	.15*	.41**	.21**	.22**			
Social Awareness	.37**	.28**	.17*	.29**	.35**		
Vigilance	.39**	.68**	.08	.50**	.27**	.42*	

* Significant beyond .05 level.

** Significant beyond .01 level.

Further Revisions

A working manual was then prepared containing definitions and criteria with examples of the three needs and seven sub-categories. The ground rules for scoring the content of the stories were similar to those usually used for scoring TAT stories (McClelland et al, 1958).

It was circulated for comments to social researchers and possible users. There was an agreement about the usefulness of the three single needs as well as the four integrated needs and the various sub-categories. Based on the feedback and suggestions, it was decided to add one more sub-category, namely, thema (Th) as is the common practice in scoring TAT stories for motivation. This was to be awarded to stories showing only one and single-minded imagery, i.e. either personal achievement or social achievement or influence. In that case, each story would be scored for the presence of any one of the three needs and eight sub-categories yielding a total score ranging from 0–9. It was decided to enlarge the sub-category of awareness to also included awareness of personal shortcomings, along with awareness of social shortcomings, environment socio-economic issues and such other matters. As a result, this was re-designated as personal and social awareness (PSA).

There was also a positive feedback on the use of integrated needs, as these, as noted above, were found to be qualitatively different needs with important behavioural implications at the workplace, in people's movements and self-action for development and change and elsewhere. It was then decided to simplify the scoring method by treating the need for personal achievement, need for social achievement, need for influence and the four integrated needs, as seven independent needs states and score the data accordingly.

Since its initial preparation in 1976, the scoring system has been used in several research studies with social workers, farmers, public officials, workers, managers, agricultural workers, etc. (Mehta 1976b, 1982; Mishra 1979; Kubde 1979; Ram, 1981; Jha, 1982; Anuradha, 1982; Setty, 1982; Borker, 1987; Mehta, M., 1988). As a result of experience gained in such studies and further in training programmes (Mehta, 1983), the scoring system has undergone some modifications from time to time. The basic categories and sub-categories, however, have remained more or less unchanged. The revised scoring system is shown in Part Four (Appendix I).

PART TWO

Case Studies of Two Work Organizations

All work organizations are not alike. They are separated by their history and conditions of work. They may be comparable, yet different, in the nature of needs and values of their members.

Part Two reports on various needs and values of workers and managers of two work organizations—one from coal and the other from steel industry. The case studies bring out similarities and differences in the objective and subjective conditions obtaining in the organizations.

4

Employee Motivation and Work-Satisfaction:

A Case Study of a Newly Nationalized Coal Undertaking*

AS MENTIONED in Chapter 2, the new public sector undertaking, namely, the Bharat Coking Coal Limited (BCCL) was formed by amalgamating the erstwhile private coal-mines in the Dhanbad area of Bihar. Most of the employees of the new organization thus came from their respective private coal-mines, carrying with them experience of their previous organization. A group of such supervisors, first-line managers and skilled workers, some of whom were also workers' representatives on joint committees, wrote imaginative stories to six TAT pictures (seen in Appendix III in Part Four and as reported in Chapter 3). The stories were written under neutral conditions with standard instructions. The obtained stories were analysed (following the scoring system explained in Part Four (Appendix I) for need for personal achievement (*n*PA), need for social achievement (*n*SA), and need for influence (nInf) and the four integrated needs, i.e. need for personal-cum-social achievement (*n*P-SA), need for personal achievement oriented influence

* The case study is based on data collected in 1976-77.

(*n*PA-Inf), need for social achievement oriented influence (*n*SA-Inf) and need for personal-cum-social achievement oriented influence (*n*P-SA-Inf).

I. NEED-STATES OF WORKERS AND MANAGERS: THE OBTAINED RESULTS

The findings thus obtained for workers and first-line supervisors and managers are seen in Table 4.1. As seen in the table, more than one-

TABLE 4.1 Percentage distribution of stories

Need-States	Managers and Supervisors (N = 68)	Workers (N = 136)	Combined (N = 204)
Need for Personal Achievement (*n*PA)	(60) 24.5* 14.7**	(125) 23.5* 15.3**	(185) 23.8* 15.1**
Need for Social Achievement (*n*SA)	(12) 4.9 2.9	(146) 27.5 17.9	(158) 20.4 12.9
Need for Influence (*n*Inf)	(133) 54.3 32.6	(134) 25.2 16.4	(267) 34.4 21.8
Need for Personal-Social Achievement (*n*P–SA)	(1) 0.4 0.3	(48) 9.0 5.9	(52) 6.7 4.3
Need for Social Achievement Oriented Influence (*n*PA–Inf)	(26) 10.6 6.4	(28) 4.9 3.2	(52) 6.7 4.3
Need for Social Achievement Oriented Influence (*n*SA-Inf)	(9) 3.7 2.2	(40) 7.5 4.9	(49) 6.3 4.0
Need for Personal-Social Achievement Oriented Influence (*n*P-SA-Inf)	(4) 1.6 1.0	(12) 2.3 1.5	(16) 2.1 1.3
Unrelated Imagery (UI)	(163) 40.0	(285) 34.9	(448)
Total number of eligible stories	(245) 60.0	(531) 65.1	(776)
Total number of Stories	408	816	1224

* Percentage of eligible stories.

** Percentage of total stories obtained.

third of the eligible stories showed need for influence, about one-fourth for personal achievement and one-fifth for social achievement. There were only a few stories containing the other four needs with 6 per cent of the stories showing the need for personal-cum-social achievement, 6.7 per cent for personal achievement oriented influence; another 6.3 per cent social achievement oriented influence and only 2.1 per cent for personal-cum-social achievement oriented influence.

It was significant that the same pictures evoked qualitatively different imageries in the workers and managers of this organization. While there was no difference in the level of need for personal achievement, they tended to significantly differ in their other need-states, as seen in Tables 4.1 and 4.2. While the workers showed a much greater need for social achievement, the managers showed much greater need for influence, as compared to each other. The former also showed significantly greater needs for personal-cum-social achievement, social achievement oriented influence and personal-cum-social achievement oriented influence than the managers. On the other hand, the managers showed a significantly greater need for personal achievement oriented influence.

TABLE 4.2 : Need-states in Managers and Workers

Need-States	Managers		Workers		
	Mean Score	S.D.	Mean Score	S.D.	t-value
*n*PA	1.90	1.84	2.26	2.76	1.085
*n*SA	0.46	1.81	2.36	3.37	5.578*
Inf	4.99	3.42	2.65	3.01	4.685*
*n*P-SA	0.09	0.74	1.43	2.87	4.995*
*n*PA-Inf	1.92	3.34	0.58	1.53	3.099*
*n*SA-Inf	0.61	1.39	1.34	2.78	8.508*
*n*PA–SA–Inf	0.27	1.79	0.56	1.76	3.967*

* Significant beyond .01 level.

Need for Personal Achievement, Social Achievement and Integrated Personal-cum-Social Achievement

It was interesting to find that the workers of this recently nationalized public sector coal undertaking tended to think much more in terms of social achievement goals—with as many as 27 per cent of their stories showing such fantasies—whereas only 5 per cent of the managers' stories showed this need. About one-fourth of both—workers and managers' stories—showed need for personal achievement. One in every 10 of the workers' fantasies (stories) also showed the need for personal-cum-social achievement whereas it was almost nil for the managers. It was thus clear that the workers thought much more of achievement goals than managers. They tended to think of personal achievement goals in conjunction with social/collective achievement goals in their work performance as well as in general life. The managers, on the other hand, seemed to think mostly of personal achievement goals only.

Although a different scoring system was used here to derive measures of need for personal and need for social achievement from the McClelland *et al's* (1953) need for achievement, the core, i.e. the desire to compete for some standard of excellence, remained the same. The hypothesis, as stated in Chapter 1, that the disadvantaged lower social class people showed a higher need for achievement, including an urge to improve work and life that their middle class counterparts (Metha, 1969), tended to be confirmed by the present research. Similar trends emerged here—with workers, particularly skilled workers, showing a much greater need for achievement with stress on social achievement goals. Managers, on the other hand, were found to be much more motivated by the need for influence.

The above trends in the workers and managers' motivation were further confirmed by the strength of their need for personal achievement oriented influence and the need for social achievement oriented influence. The managers were much more motivated by the former and the workers by the latter. The trends, therefore, indicated that the managers thought of influence along with personal achievement goals while the workers thought of influence along with social achievement goals. Such a qualitative difference in the thoughts and motivation of the workers and managers indicated some aspects of the social structure, values and functioning of the organization.

The Background : Competitive Private Coal-mines and the New Organization

The present public sector organization came into being after private coal-mines were nationalized in July 1972. Its 85 collieries were formed by amalgamating hundreds of smaller privately owned mines. Prior to nationalization, for about 150 years, private coal-mines competed for generating labour surplus and profits by cutting wages, and keeping workers like bonded labour under a ruthless system of control. Since 1920, a series of committees and commissions had repeatedly drawn attention to the unsafe, slaughter and unscientific mining which threatened the very life of this important national resource. Committees after committee had recommended state take-over of coal-mines in order to conserve the resource and improve the quality of mining by scientific methods (Mehta, 1989 : 43-47).

Soon after the nationalization, several tasks were set for the new organization. It was called upon to promote scientific mining, regularize the work force, implement the awards of wage boards, promote participation of managers and workers at all levels, promote healthy trade union activity, utilize the talents of the workforce, eliminate malpractices, improve working conditions and take steps to conserve coal and improve its quality (Kumaramangalam, 1971/1987, 1973, 1973a).

The management thus took a series of actions, including management and worker-resource development programmes, to streamline the organization. They also organized a productivity and safety fortnight with spectacular results (Mehta, 1989 : 51-66). Such activities and campaigns aimed at releasing a spirit of partnership and a concern for excellence in the organization. Their experiential background—consisting of their earlier longer and deeper experience carried over from the private coal mines and the new experience at the state undertaking—could have affected the imagery of the workers and managers, as revealed in their TAT stories. What was noteworthy, however, is that such factors, if at all, affected their thoughts in qualitatively different ways. While the managers craved for influence and control and for using influence for personal achievement goals, the workers thought much more of social achievement and of using influence for such collective goals.

II. CONDITIONS OF WORK, PERCEPTIONS AND FEELINGS IN THE ORGANIZATION

The managers and workers who wrote TAT stories also participated in a series of small group discussions along with some senior and middle managers. In such problem diagnoses, they provided some insightful data on employee perceptions and feelings and the nature of the workplace. Such small group reports were pooled and content analysed. The results are summarized in Tables 4.3, 4.4, 4.5 and 4.5a.

First-line and Middle Managers' Perceptions

Comparing the situation obtaining now (i.e. soon after the nationalization of coal-mines) and before (i.e. under private ownership), the colliery managers and other first-line supervisors and officers thought that the new management was more effective and that professional management was now in command with greater planning and coordination. However, at the same time, they also felt that the new organization was "bureaucratic" with powers centralized at the higher levels of management. They perceived their work environment as characterized by a high degree of alcoholism among the workers, musclemanship of money-lenders and others, intense trade union rivalries and a general tendency for scapegoating and fault-finding. They felt overburdened with work, with inadequate staff and weak support from the senior and top management as well as from their subordinate staff. They felt excluded from the decision-making process. They felt distressed not only by the lack of support but also the lack of respect of both seniors and subordinates. As far as they—the middle managers—were concerned, the organizational environment was marked by mistrust, rigid rules and regulations, escapism and low job satisfaction. They felt sandwiched between the top and the bottom. They felt alienated and dissatisfied.

The middle managers' perceptions, on the one hand, indicated their sense of alienation and insecurity and on the other a desire for greater respect, participation and powers. They clearly wanted to have a better status and authority in the organization. Interestingly, their perceptions were concerned primarily with their status, power and the role. In fact, they tended to blame the organization for giving them more and more responsibility and less and less power, protection and support. They tended to compare their present status and power with that they enjoyed in the erstwhile private coal-mines. The proprietary management, then, ruled and controlled the workers through them, thereby giving them coercive power over their subordinates.

Their (i.e. the first-line middle managers and other functional officers) sense of dissatisfaction and resentment could not have been only due to their previous experience. This could have been also due to the structure of the present organization, as revealed by their senior managers' (discussed below) perceptions of its functioning. They felt deprived as, probably, their need for influence was not fully satisfied.

TABLE 4.3 : Operational managers' analysis of the organization*

Management	Work Environment	Feelings	Climate
Management more effective now than before	High fault-finding	Lack of mutual respect	Mutal mistrust
More bureaucratized	High alcoholism	People not involved in decision-making	Low morale and job satisfaction
Powers centralized	Musclemanship continues	First-line managers' fear of legal action	Non-participative and dominative behaviour
	Trade union rivalries	All-round sense of insecurity	
	Lack of support from top as well as subordinates	Subordinates and workers make scape-goats	
		Feeling of powerlessness	

* Based on discussions in a series of small groups

Senior Managers' Perceptions

Some senior managers participated in a workshop to discuss problems facing workers' participation in management. Their perception and feelings about the extent of managerial participation in management, particularly of those at lower levels, are summarized in Table 4.4. There was a general agreement that participation in management was not adequate. They thought powers were not adequately delegated. Their own decisions were not supported at higher levels. They were not properly informed about the activities of the Company. With poor inter-communication and sharing, the working conditions were poor and the working hours long. It was interesting, they thought, that their efforts for promoting worker participation in decision-making were not supported by the top management and that such participation if there was rendered ineffective owing to poor working conditions. They tended to explain that, they had to carry a heavy workload including attending all kinds of meetings, statutory and non-statutory, which left hardly any time for convening and participating in shop-floor and joint council meetings.

It is clear from the above that the middle managers, including some senior managers, who were responsible for implementing a government sponsored scheme for workers' participation, then introduced, themselves felt dissatisfied and uninvolved. The dominant concern in the managers' thoughts was for better working conditions for themselves, for greater sense of security and for greater influence and power in the organization.

TABLE 4.4 : Senior/Middle Level Managers' perceptions of the functioning of the organization*

Working conditions	Power and Support	Morale and Participation
Too many meetings, often long and in off-hours	Powers centralized, not properly delegated	Spate of audits leads to demoralization
Township not developed, housing and mines widely scattered	Lack of support from higher levels for decisions taken at lower levels	Inadequate management participation in decision-making process
Overwork and over-responsibility	Flow of information inadequate	
Inadequate supportive staff		Managers not encouraged to consult workers and promote participation

* Based on reports of discussions in a series of small groups.

Workers' Analysis of Organization

Like the managers, workers also analysed the functioning of the organization in a series of small group discussions. They gave their perceptions of its functioning as well as of the people at various levels of the organization. The perceived functioning of the workplace is summarized in Table 4.5. They mainly recalled the quality of organization and work planning of day to-day functioning and decision-making and the quality and nature of welfare and care at the organization.

Functioning of the Organization: Mismanagement

It was interesting that the workers' attention was focused on malfunctioning of the organization. For instance, they recalled the supply of poor quality materials. There was a short supply of low-cost spare parts. However, there was a ready supply of expensive ones. In this respect, they recalled malpractices in the stores and purchase departments. Workers were sore with visible corruption and mismanagement. They were also unhappy with the tendency of taking ad-hoc decisions without proper planning of production targets, etc. This resulted in vague and faulty work plans. Such factors, in their view, were responsible for the lowering of productivity and quality of work in the organization.

Sense of Fear and Insecurity

Workers tended to relate faulty functioning and planning with widespread sense of fear prevailing in the organization. The common workers, therefore, hesitated to speak out and give evidence, when required, of the malpractices. They were afraid of the management's vindictiveness and victimization.

Management's Lack of Interest in Joint Councils

Workers believed that the managers were not interested in the proper functioning of the participatory forums like the joint councils. They supported this by saying that, firstly the minutes were not recorded properly and secondly follow-up action was seldom taken on decisions taken, if any, at the joint councils. Further, they thought, the managers tended to act arbitrarily and did not like the joint councils to have any say.

Accumulation of Grievances

Adhoc functioning and arbitrary decision-making led to accumulation of grievances. The Personnel Department was not able to cope with such problems as it was inactive and inefficient.

TABLE 4.5: Workers' perception of the functioning of the organization*

a. Organization and Planning
   - (i) Supply of poor quality materials; low-cost parts generally in short supply.
   - (ii) Malpractices in stores and purchase departments.
   - (iii) Work not planned in advance: ad hoc decisions.
   - (iv) Production targets not properly fixed.

b. *Day-to-day Functioning*
   - (i) Money-lenders' influence continues.
   - (ii) Workers hesitate to give evidence for want of security.
   - (iii) Minutes not recorded; actions seldom taken on joint councils' decisions.
   - iv. Managers do as they like.
   - v. Personnel department inactive and inefficient.

c. *Welfare Orientation and Practices*
   - (i) Lack of amenities like canteens, hospitals, schools, housing and drinking water.
   - (ii) Misuse of welfare funds.
   - (iii) Absence of cooperative stores.
   - (iv) Indebtedness and money-lenders dominate workers' life.
   - (v) Feudal kind of exploitation continues.

*Based on a series of small group discussions.

Dilution of the Welfare Function

There was a dilution of the welfare function in the organization. The management was not oriented to catering to the workers' welfare. There was lack of canteens, medical facilities, educational facilities, housing and even drinking water. As in stores and purchase departments, here also their was misuse of welfare funds and the workers did not get the intended benefits from such schemes.

Continuing Grip of Money-lenders and Musclemen

In the absence of proper management and worker welfare, the workers' representatives were sore that the workers had been forced to continue in the grip of money-lenders and traders. In the absence of cooperative stores, they were forced to shell out higher prices to such elements. Also due to various socio-economic factors, workers fell into additional indebtedness which further tightened the money-lenders' grip on them. In the workers' view, the management was not really interested in their welfare and as the organization was not properly managed, the usurious and ruthless exploitation of the workers continued unabated.

Workers' Image of Managers and other People

Along with analyses of its functioning, the workers also gave their assessment of the managers and other people in the organization as seen in Table 4.5a. They thought, the managers, by and large, were timid and easily provoked. They tended to victimize workers and treat them shabbily. They did not listen to the workers and prevented them from expressing their viewpoints. They like flattery and wanted workers to act at their bidding.

The shop-floor managers avoided taking decisions. They also did not have adequate powers, but even when powers were there, they were afraid of taking decisions. They also discouraged growth of local labour leadership and tended to divide the workers and rule them.

It was therefore, interesting to find that the workers' image of managers corroborated some of the perceptions and feelings of the managers themselves. For example, managers and workers, both, thought that the operational managers did not have adequate powers and that they were not adequately involved in decision-making. Workers' view that managers were afraid of taking decision supplemented the managers' self-image of insecurity and powerlessness. Both, managers and workers, drew attention to the prevailing influence of money-lenders and muscelmen in the organization. However, the workers went a step further and blamed the management for such a situation. The latter's apathy towards the workers' welfare and their discouragement of the growth of local leadership contributed to and reinforced the hold of outsiders, including money-lenders and musclemen.

Workers' Image of Labour Leaders

The workers were quite critical of various labour leaders also, some of whom, they thought had come to trade unions to get their bread and butter. Some of the leaders used musclemen and coerced the workers in order to keep them under control. Like managers, they were also easily provoked and did not listen to the workers. They, however, perceived some change in the situation and believed that the labour leaders had been forced to pay attention to the interest of workers.

TABLE 4.5a : Workers' image of the other people in the organization

Images of people

a. *Managers*
   - (i) Timid, easily provoked and vindictive.
   - (ii) Inexperienced, tend to victimize.
   - (iii) Treat workers as "slaves"; encourage flattery; do not listen to workers; prevent workers from expressing their point of view.
   - (iv) Not open to new ideas.
   - (v) Shop-floor-level officers avoid taking decisions; do not have adequate powers.
   - (vi) Tend to divide and rule; discourage local leadership.

b. *Labour Leaders*
   - (i) Some selfish people have come to trade unions for their own bread and butter;
   - (ii) Some resort to force, coercion, and use muscle power.
   - (iii) Do not listen to workers, easily provoked.
   - (iv) Some change noticed now; leaders pay more attention to workers.

c. *Workers' Self-image*
   - (i) Timid, fear victimization, easily provoked.
   - (ii) Shy, do not participate.
   - (iii) Lack of education, fear of failure.
   - (iv) Conservative attitudes, easy prey to leaders and officers.

*Based on a series of small group discussions.

Workers' Image of Themselves

In the context of their perception of managers as vindictive and labour leaders as coercive, it was interesting to note that the workers perceived themselves as timid. They were afraid of victimization and shy but were easily provided into conflicts. They lacked education and necessary skills and were afraid of failure and disappointment, were socially conservative and fell an easy prey to leaders and managers.

They, therefore, seemed to perceive no significant change in the managerial behaviours after nationalization and thought that the managers were authoritarian and "bossy". They were also not satisfied with the general level of consciousness among their fellow workers. They wanted better planning and better social and working conditions. Their perceptions indicated a concern for production and general worker welfare and improved working conditions. They also expected better treatment by their supervisors as well as from their own leaders. They also wanted workers in general to be more assertive.

Need-States, Perceived Structure and Organizational Climate

The work climate was, thus, perceived, despite some restructuring and management development programmes, as mistrustful, disrespectful, insecure, anxiety ridden and authoritarian. The managers' persistent grievance for better status, more power and participation was in line with their dominant motivational tendency, i.e. the need for influence. The workers' perception of their managers as ruthlessly dominative; of labour leaders as coercive, easily provoked and selfish; their own (workers) as timid, insecure and submissive explained the need in them for collective assertion. Their concern for timely supply of materials, prevention of malpractices, better planning and production targets showed the need in them for social achievement. Their grievance against the feudal kind of exploitation, and for better quality of working and living conditions revealed their emerging need for influence and influence-oriented social achievement. Such perceptions indicated high expectations among the workforce for a more congenial, more positive and more satisfying workplace. Such expectations were not met by the structural arrangements at the workplace, resulting in disappointment and a sense of deprivation in them.

Profile of the Workplace

Taken together, the managers and workers, perceptions indicated a specific profile of their organization and its functioning. There was a near total agreement about the prevailing work environment which was ridden with mutual mistrust, low morale, low job satisfaction, non-participatory and dominative managerial styles. Managers were afraid of victimization by their seniors and workers were afraid of coercion by their supervisors. The workplace was, therefore, marked by scape-goating, fault-finding and lack of support for each other with power centralized at the top.

On the whole, therefore, senior managers, operational managers and workers perceived lack of influence and autonomy for themselves at the workplace. They were also dissatisfied with the inadequate welfare and care and with the prevailing supervisory practices and behaviour. Such perceptions and feelings indicated a widespread sense of alienation and dissatisfaction not only among the workers but also among some sections of middle-to-senior managers.

III. CONDITIONS OF WORK AND EMPLOYEE NEEDS

The foregoing self-reports indicated widespread dissatisfaction among the employees under report. Their sense of work satisfaction was further checked with the help of a work questionnaire (Mehta, 1976a, 1979). The responses yielded information regarding the managers and workers' view of some aspects of their conditions of work such as degree of influence and autonomy available to them; amenities available at the workplace; trust and support; supervisory practices and behaviors; and the nature of their job. These contributed significantly to their overall work satisfaction (Mehta, 1976a).

Individual need-states, some more than others, and the perceived conditions were significantly inter-related, as seen in Table 4.6. However, the need for social achievement and the combined need for personal-cum-social achievement tended to show negative relationships and the need for influence and to some extent the need for personal achievement oriented influence tended to show positive

TABLE. 4.6 : Needs and work-satisfaction among the managers and workers, (Product Moment Correlations)

Individual Needs	Perceived Conditions of Work						
	Influence and Autonomy	Work Amenities	Trust and Support	Intrinsic Job Satisfaction	Supervisory Behaviour	Relations with Peers	Work Satisfaction*
nPA	−.05	−.01	−.01	.07	−.03	−.05	−.02
nSA	−.23***	−.18***	−.09	−.25***	−.20***	−.16***	−.24***
Inf	.30***	.10	.08	.25***	.24***	.12**	.28***
nPA–SA	−.29***	−.10	−.08	−.25***	−.24***	−.12**	−.25***
nPA–Inf	.14**	.07	−.03	.05	.17***	.11	.12**
nSA-Inf	−.05	−.09	.01	.09	−.05	−.11	−.08
nPA-SA-Inf	−.07	.11	−.05	−.16*	−.11	−.07	−.12**

* Excepting trust and support which showed significant low loading, the other five work-related measures showed high loadings on a common second order principal component factor, designated as work satisfaction. The latter's composite score was derived by multiplying the individual score on each measure by its factor loading, thus obtaining the total score.

** Significant at 5% level.

*** Significant at 1% level.

relationships with the same factors. The results clearly suggested that the influence-motivated managers and the workers motivated by the need for social achievement perceived these organizational factors in qualitatively opposite directions. The former felt satisfied, whereas the latter felt dissatisfied with their conditions of work.

Influence Need and Work Satisfaction

It was thus interesting that the employees' need for influence and the perceived degree of influence and autonomy at the work-place were found to be highly positively correlated. The influence-motived employees (mostly managers) also tended to show significantly greater satisfaction with the availability of work amenities, including rewards and nature of their job and with supervisory behaviour and inter-personal relations obtaining at the work place. The greater the employees' need for influence, the greater was their overall work satisfaction. The findings, undoubtedly, showed that the organizational structure, work processes and interpersonal relations were perceived as much more satisfying by managers with a high need for influence.

Employees (mostly workers) with greater need for social achievement, on the other hand showed uniformly greater dissatisfaction with the same work-related factors. They showed significantly greater dissatisfaction with the degree of influence and autonomy available to them. They were also dissatisfied with the amenities available to them at the workplace, with the nature of their job and with the nature of their supervisory behaviour and inter-personal relations at the workplace. There was no doubt that, unlike those with a high need for influence, social achievement motivated employees as well as those with a high need for personal-cum-social achievement felt highly dissatisfied at the workplace. They wanted greater autonomy, better amenities, more positive and respectful supervisors, more friendly and trustful peer relations as well as more challenging and satisfying jobs. Their was a clear discrepancy between their expectations and the actual situation at the workplace. They, therefore, felt deprived and dissatisfied.

Factors in Workers' Satisfaction at Workplace

In a related study (Mehta, 1976a) involving workers' representatives at the various joint councils in the present organization, who were also represented in the workers' sample for the present study, influence and autonomy at the workplace were perceived as the most important and desirable factor. It accounted for as much as 47 per cent of the total variance in their overall work satisfaction. The working conditions and amenities at the workplace, support and care of the management for their well-being and the nature of job also emerged as important factors accounting for a significant variance in their work satisfaction.

The above study also revealed that 6 out of every 10 workers surveyed were highly dissatisfied on account of lack of drinking water and canteen facilities at the workplace. During group discussion, they expressed their deep dismay over the fact that the workers had to go out in search of drinking water for about a kilometre even during very hot summer nights in the Dhanbad area situated near and around the coal-mines, some of them burning, and where temperatures could shoot up to 50° Celsius or even more. It was interesting to note that their general dissatisfaction was not so much due to the salary scales as due to the lack of primary physical facilities at the workplace.

On the whole, two-thirds of them were not satisfied with the degree of influence and autonomy, more than two-thirds with amenities, and support and care for their well-being and also with the behaviour of the supervisors. Comparatively, they were less dissatisfied with the nature of their job.

It was thus clear that the workers did feel dissatisfied and resentful. They felt neglected by the organization. Their expectations, probably heightened by the nationalization and by the promises made by the political leadership and the management, were not fulfilled. They had neither the desired autonomy, nor the necessary amenities, nor the expected care and support of the organization. They therefore, felt alienated.

Objective Socio-economic Conditions and Individual Need-States

Interrelations between employee need-states and their perceptions and feelings regarding the work-related situation and work satisfaction were further confirmed by findings regarding similar relationships with some objective socio-economic factors. As the inter-correlations in Table 4.7 show, the need for influence showed uniformly significant positive correlations with educational status, salary, housing and occupational level in the organization. The greater the employees' educational level, the higher the salary and better the housing facility enjoyed, and higher the occupational level, the greater was the need for influence. Almost the reverse was the situation for those high on need for social achievement. Barring education which did not show a significant correlation, social achievement motivated employees had a lower salary, lower housing facility and also lower occupational status in the organization.

These objective conditions of work also showed qualitatively different relationships with need for personal achievement oriented influence and for social achievement oriented influence. Employees motivated by the former showed uniformly positive correlations and those motivated by the latter showed uniformly negative correlations. All of them were, however, not significant. The greater the employees' educational level, the higher the salary and better the housing facility enjoyed the greater was their need for personal achievement oriented influence. On the other hand, the lower the housing facility enjoyed and the lower the occupational level, the higher was the employees' need for social achievement oriented influence.

TABLE 4.7 :Socio-economic mobility and need-states
(Product Moment Correlation)
(N = 195)

Need-States	Employees			
	Educational Level	Salary Status	Housing Facility	Occupational Level
*n*PA	.01	.12*	–.10	.01
*n*SA	.08	–.16*	–.12*	–.24**
Inf	.19**	.25**	.22**	.32**
*n*P-SA	–.16*	–.20**	–.12**	.08
*n*PA-Inf	.14*	.18**	.16*	.08
*n*SA-Inf	–.09	–.09	–.17*	–.18**
*n*PA–SA–Inf	.02	.14	.10	–.12*

* Significant at 5% level.

** Significant at 1% level.

Objective and Subjective Conditions of Work and Employee Motivation

The findings, therefore, suggested that both, the objective conditions of work (salary, housing, occupational level, etc.) and the subjective conditions of work (perceived influence and autonomy, nature of job, etc), were significantly interrelated with the employee need-states. Those placed on the high side of the objective conditions scale, as well as those perceiving a satisfying degree of subjective conditions of work tended to show significantly greater need for influence and, to some extent, also for personal achievement oriented influence. On the other hand, those placed on the lower side of both these scales showed a greater need for social achievement and, to some extent, also for social achievement oriented influence.

Another noteworthy finding here was that the employees motivated by personal-cum-social achievement goals were also placed on the low side of both the scales. It was, therefore, somewhat ironical that those who thought in terms of excellence in performance as well as of better productivity, better safety and working conditions, better quality of life for themselves as well as others appeared as highly dissatisfied people. And, such people were also located more on the lower rungs of the organization. As a person went up in the hierarchy of the organization, he thought more and more of influence and control and less and less of achievement and excellence, particularly of social achievement goals. Such a pattern of satisfaction and motivation had important implications for the functioning of the workplace, as well as for the psychological well-being of the people the employees. We discuss these issues further in Chapters 5, 6 and 7.

IV. DEMOCRATIC BELIEFS AND NEED-STATES OF MANAGERS AND WORKERS

The employees' commitment to participation and democratic functioning in the wider society and polity is indicated by their faith in people (v. misanthropy), sense of political efficacy (v. powerlessness, acceptance of regime norms (v. normlessness) and liberal social attitudes (v. conservative attitudes). Data obtained from questionnaire responses revealed the employees' overall democratic v. authoritarian orientation (for the questionnaire, see Rao and Mehta, 1978; Mehta, 1989). Inter-relations between such democratic orientation and employee need-states are shown in Table 4.8.

TABLE 4.8 : Personality and social outlook and need-states in workers and officers (Product Moment Correlation) (N = 195)

Need-States	Mis-anthropy	Political Powerless-ness	Perceived Political Normless-ness	Social Dogmatism	Authori-tarian tendency
nPA	−.10	−.12**	.09	.30	.01
nSA	.10	−.10	.09	−.07	−.13**
Inf	−.02	.15**	.10	.18**	.21***
nP-SA	.09	−.12**	−.03	.00	.05
nPA–Inf	−.08	−.02	.07	.09	−.07
nSA–Inf	−.12**	−.14**	−.01	.06	−.10
nPA–SA–Inf	−.11	−.05	.03	.01	.05

*In a second order principal component factor analysis, powerlessness, normlessness and dogmatic moralism showed high loadings on a composite factor designated as authoritarian tendency. The individual scores on the three separate scales were multiplied by their respective second order factor loadings and a composite score was obtained from the three scales to indicate an authoritarian tendency.

** Significant at 5% level.

*** Significant at 1% level.

Employees with a high need for influence tended to show significantly greater authoritarian beliefs or lower commitment to democratic institutions. Interestingly, they showed not only a high sense of social conservatism but also weak sense of competence and faith in themselves for influencing the functioning of political and social systems. They tended to believe that whatever any one might think and do, he would not be able to influence and change the functioning of the polity and society and that god has created the rich and the poor and such divisions would always remain.

It was, thus, interesting to note that, such employees, mostly managers, placed higher in the hierarchy of the organization, who showed a strong craving for controlling and influencing other at the place, reflected lack of faith and competence in the democratic institutions and processes, revealing a strong authoritarian tendency. On the other hand, employees, mostly workers, who were placed lowly at the workplace and who showed a need for social achievement or an integrated achievement orientation or a need for social achievement oriented influence, were socially liberal and democratic in their beliefs. They showed greater faith in the people and their capability for influencing and changing socio-political situations. They also showed greater faith in social equality and believed that, the rich and the poor have been created not by God but by the society itself, and that such inequality could be removed. In this sense, they seemed to show a greater sense of competence both at the workplace and in the wider social system. More particularly, workers and others who were motivated by the integrated need for social achievement oriented influence (unlike those who were motivated only by need for influence) showed a greater sense of political efficacy.

Thus, the various individual needs appeared to be varyingly inter-related with social and democratic thinking. Managers who were mainly motivated by the need for influence were authoritarian in their beliefs and values with low faith in the democratic institutions. They seemed to be welded to social *status quo* and hierarchy at the workplace and to the belief that workers have to be controlled. On the other hand, workers and their representatives, who showed a high need for social achievement as well as for social achievement oriented influence, showed significantly greater democratic values. They seemed to reject social *status quo* and the rigid and coercive hierarchy and controls at the workplace.

In a related study (Mehta, 1976a), positively perceived supervisory behaviour and inter-personal relationship at the workplace emerged as significant individual correlates of faith in people. Friendly and respectful human relations contributed greatly to promoting faith in people and democratic commitment among the people in the organization. No wonder, powerful persons driven by influence motivated authoritarian tendencies and hierarchical values promoted a fear-ridden and mistrustful work-climate, as was the case with the present workplace.

V. MOTIVATION, PARTICIPATION AND DISSATISFACTION

The findings, as briefly discussed above, suggested several important implication for the functioning of a work organization. There is some evidence (for example, Dingra, 1973) which shows that the older and more experienced managers were more accommodative and participative than the younger ones. However, management practices tended to reward the younger ones more with quick promotions to higher positions. In the present study, employees' age showed a small but significant negative correlation (R = – .13, significant at 1% level) with need for influence. As the employees advanced in the work organizational hierarchy, there was a significant increase in their need for influence. Putting such findings together, i.e., the present one and from some earlier studies, it seemed, work organizations, like the one under study, tended to promote younger as well as less participative managers to higher positions in the organization which in turn, further enhanced their need for influence. In the present case, such a need for influence was associated significantly with the authoritarian and traditional value system of hierarchy, status and domination, revealing the coercive nature of the organization.

It was, therefore, no wonder that, in the present case, the organizational climate was perceived as highly authoritarian and insecure. Several studies (for example, Kohn *et al*, 1969, 1983) have found the conditions of work such as the degree of supervision and routinization and a substantive complexity of the job, to either enable or inhibit self-direction among the workers. On the other hand, a challenging work environment, which allows workers autonomy and self direction, promotes development of a creative and flexible mind, contributing to personal well-being of the workforce. Studies of technological changes and work organization also suggest that degree of autonomy v. Control could serve as an indication of the opportunities available to workers for development and diversification of skills (Spencer, 1988).

Managers' and workers' analyses of the funtionoing of the present workplace showed a widespread and intense feelings about lack of autonomy and participation. Decisions were marked by arbitrariness and ad-hocism. Even some middle-to-senior managers felt excluded from such decision-making process. Such "dogmatic" employees with a high degree of need for influence have been found to resist beilateral discussions and, therefore to inhibit wider participation in the organization (Druckman, 1967). Their authoritarian influence oriented ego was likely to be detrimental to cooperation and team-work where sublimation of self was required (Collins and Guetzhow, 1964).

A sence of power and control over one's own fate and capability for self-direction increase when people are given roles of influence and responsibility (Gottesfeld and Dozier, 1966; Martimer and

Lorence, 1979; Mehta, 1983, 1990). Such opportunities were denied to the workforce in the present organization. It was therefore, no wonder that the workers, in this case, even skilled workers and workers' representatives, showed a low need for influence. A sense of deprivation at the workplace reinforced by coercive management practices and authoritarian beliefs and dominative styles of managers probably contributed to the workers' need for social achievement as well as for influence-oriented social achievement.

One of the important findings of the present research was that the degree of influence and autonomy available at the workplace greatly contributed to the sense of work satisfaction. In view of their democratic aspirations, workers, particularly leading and skilled workers, keenly desired greater autonomy and influence at the workplace. One of the main purposes of participation at the workplace, as several studies have documented (Almond and Verba, 1963; Blauner, 1964; Blumberg, 1968; Pateman, 1970; Mehta, 1976a, 1983) is to promote skills and a sense of assertion and efficacy in the people. Such participation, as Gorupic and Paj (1971) have put it, enables workers to assert their interest against bureaucratic centralism. However, as the analysis of both, managers and workers' perceptions suggested, the present workplace was centrally managed with growing tendencies for bureaucratization. Structurally, it tended to function in a non-participatory centralized way, although at the stated policy level it was supposed to promote workers participation.

The present nationalized undertaking came into being after amalgamating a large number of privately owned coal-mines, which were characterized by arbitrary and personalistic domination over the workforce. As Edward (1979) has discussed, when organization moves from a stage of competitiveness for profit-making and personalistic domination to a higher technology and monopolistic stage, workers tended to be controlled by the technology itself.

When workers resist such developments and management practices, the organization tends to move toward the bureaucratic form of control through rigid rules and regulations. When such bureaucratic controls take over the work, tasks get routinized and fragmented. Such changes further alienate the workforce as they are denied adequate autonomy and influence at the workplace. The findings here suggested that the heightened aspirations of the workforce, for greater autonomy and participation, were largely frustrated and letdown by the coercive and centrally and bureaucratically managed new organization.

Control, Conflicts and Satisfaction

Mutual negative images of workers and managers for each other indicated conflicts in the organization. Such conflicts were expected at the present workplace where the interest of the workers and management openly clashed. As has been found in a large number of studies (for example, Blauner, 1964; Likert, 1961; Argyris, 1964), a sense of satisfaction and conflicts in the organization are linked to its structure control mechanism. Centralized structures drive group members to feel powerless. Consequently, they do not experience the psychological success associated with setting their own goals and objectives. As is now well established, autonomy and influence at the workplace help develop internal competence (White, 1959; Deci, 1975). On the other hand, formalization gives the message that the participants are unable to think for themselves, resulting in low satisfaction and a climate of indignation.

As the findings of the present research showed, workers, and some managers, were dissatisfied with the structure and functioning of their workplace. They talked of centralization, formalization and non-participatory decision-making. As it was a new organization with a specific history and, as the political leadership and top management repeatedly announced, its tasks and challenges were varied and complex. They were not routine kind of tasks. Denied their rightful participation, the employees were not able to contribute to decisions which were sometimes incorrect and sometimes delayed very much, although some of them had greater first-hand information than their superiors. And, as the tasks were complex, it was not possible to lay them down in rules and procedures. As a result, authoritarian controls and rigid enforcement of procedures were not only dissatisfying, but also largely dysfunctional.

Workplace, Personality and Satisfaction

The findings of the present research tended to suggest an interesting theoretical paradigm. Historically, the smaller private coal-mines were marked by ruthless and competitive profit-making and oppressive control of workers. The political leadership as well as the top management posed several complex tasks before the workforce and called for their cooperation and participation, raising their expectations. However, in practice, the organization was centrally managed with a high degree of formalization. Despite the rhetoric of participative management, the leadership styles and work structures continued to be authoritarian.

Such structures and practices contributed to wide spread insecurity and negative mutual images at various levels in the organization. There was also a sharp and qualitative difference in the needs of workers and managers with the former showing a high needs for social achievement and for social achievement oriented influence, and the latter showing a strong need for influence and for personal achievement oriented influence. The need for influence, in the present case, was significantly authoritarian whereas the need for social achievement was accompanied by democratic aspirations. The data tended to suggest an inter-play of psychological factors with objective structural and policy factors resulting in several organizational as well as psychological problems at the workplace.

It was quite expected that the employees placed higher on the occupational and income ladder would show greater need for influence as has been found in similar studies elsewhere (Winter, 1973; Ulleman, 1972). What was interesting here was that the influence-motivated employees tended to be significantly more authoritarian in their behaviours. As research shows (Christie and Gies, 1970), such persons tend to become manipulative and machiavellian in their behaviour towards others in the organization. In the present case also, both managers and labour leaders (mostly from outside the organization) were perceived as manipulative and coercive by the workers. Such managerial and leadership styles reinforced and aggravated the sense of insecurity at the workplace inherited from the erstwhile private coal-mines.

The conditions of work in the present organization and the continuing coercion of money-lenders and musclemen added to their sense of alienation, dissatisfaction and anger. They experienced a wide gap between their aspirations and expectations, on the one hand, and actual functioning of the workplace on the other. This greatly aggravated their sense of deprivation. One interesting and noteworthy finding of the present study was that the leading workers, technicians, engineers and some middle managers tended to resist adverse conditions of work and life collectively, showing a sense of social efficacy as reflected in their need for social achievement and for social-achievement-oriented influence.

5

Need-States and Values of Personnel : The Case of Rourkela Steel Plant

THE STUDY of employee motivation in a nationalized coal undertaking as reported in Chapter 4 suggested the importance of objective social conditions obtaining there. Such conditions seemed to have contributed to individual need-states, managerial organization. The results may be different in another organization with a different social and objective background. With this in view, the study was more or less replicated at a modern steel plant, namely, the Rourkela Steel Plant (RSP).

A group of respondents, working in a series of small groups, provided data on their background, need-states, work-related satisfaction, socio-political outlook, etc.* The respondents included 85 workers—khalasies, operators, chargemen and apprenticeship trainees; 86 supervisory personnel-foremen and technicians; 87 officers including 44 middle managers, mostly engineers; 43 medical doctors; and 101 administrative personnel—clerks, superintendents, etc. The sample thus covered a variety of employees from various departments of the organization, such as general administration, town administration, medical, fertilizer plant and some units of the

* The data were collected in 1979-1980.

manufacturing departments.

Of the respondents 58 per cent were graduates and the rest educated up to matriculation or below. Some 60 per cent of them were in the age group of 36 years and above, and 28 per cent between 25-35 years and some 12 per cent below 25 years. Nearly 29 per cent of them had spent 10 years or more, 27 per cent 5-10 years, 34 per cent up to four years and some 10 per cent up to six months on their current jobs. Some 51 per cent of them had 16-25 years of service to there credit in the same steel plant, another three per cent had been their for 26 years or more, 16 per cent were there from 11-15 years. Only nine per cent of the sample had spent two years and less in the plant. Thus, the respondent were largely educated, fairly experienced, had long service to their credit in the same steel plant and many of them had been working in the same position for quite some time, at the time of their participation in the study.

I. ARTICULATION OF NEED-STATES AND SUB-CATEGORIES : THE DOMINANT THOUGHTS

The respondents were drawn, as mentioned above, from various job positions and departments of the steel plant. Frequency of fantasies containing various need-states, as derived from their TAT stories, is seen in Table 5.1. They wrote a total of 2,154 stories of which 906 were found to contain relevant imagery, i.e. one of the seven need-states.

Nature of Job and Individual Need-States

There was not much variation over the occupational groups in proportion of the eligible stories obtained from them. This ranged from 39 to 44 per cent. There were, however, significant variations among different groups in the strength of some of the specific need-states as shown by the frequency of their articulation, some need-states came out much more prominently, as discussed below, than others, as seen in Table 5.1.

Need for Influence (nInf)

The need for influence was articulated conspicuously more prominently by the personnel of the present organization. On the

TABLE 5.1: Percentage Distribution of Expressed need-states by job position in the organization
N = 359; No. of stories obtained = 2154; No. of eligible stories = 906

Job Position	Needs							Eligible Stories	Total Stories Written
	*n*PA	*n*SA	*n*Inf	*n*P-SA	*n*Inf-PA	*n*Inf-SA	*n*Inf-S-PA		
Workers	9.4**	14.1	56.6	2.8	8.0	6.6	2.3	41.6	
(N=85)	(20)*	(30)	(120)	(6)	(17)	(14)	(5)	(212)	510
Foremen and	10.3	11.2	55.8	0.4	10.4	10.3	1.3	43.0	
technicians	(23)	(25)	(124)	(1)	(23)	(23)	(3)	(222)	516
(N = 86)									
Engineers	11.1	7.4	50.9	0	11.1	16.7	2.8	40.9	
(N = 44)	(12)	(8)	(55)	(0)	(12)	(18)	(3)	(108)	264
Medical Doctors	7.0	17.0	56.0	3.0	8.0	8.0	1.0	38.8	
(N = 43)	(7)	(17)	(56)	(3)	(8)	(8)	(1)	(100)	258
Administrative	8.3	9.8	53.0	2.3	9.5	13.7	3.4	43.6	
Personnel	(22)	(26)	(140)	(6)	(25)	(36)	(9)	(264)	606
(N = 101)									
Total eligible	(84)	(106)	(495)	(16)	(85)	(99)	(21)	(906)	2154
stories	9.3	11.7	54.6	1.8	9.4	10.9	2.4	42.1	

* Figures in parentheses are the number of stories.

** Per cent of eligible stories.

whole, as many as 55 per cent of all eligible stories were found to contain evidence of influence-related imagery. Such projection was uniformly high – 51 to 57 per cent of the eligible stories – in all the groups. The results, therefore, indicated that a large number of employees, at least one in every two, in all occupational groups tended to think in terms of control and influence. Its significance was further enhanced by the fact the articulation of other need-states was very much lower. It was thus clear that influence was the dominant need tendency in the present organization.

Need for Social Achievement (nSA)

The need for social achievement emerged as the second prominent tendency among the employees. Its articulation ranged from 7 to 17 per cent in the eligible stories. It was, however, marked by wide variations over different job positions and occupational groups with engineers showing it in about 7 per cent of their eligible stories while the workers and medical doctors showing respectively 14 and 17 per cent. The results, therefore, suggested that medical doctors and workers needed to be motivated by the need for social achievement relatively more than others in the organization.

Need for Social Achievement Oriented Influence (nInf-SA)

The need for social-achievement-oriented influence emerged as another important need of the employees in the organization. Its articulation also ranged from 7 to 17 per cent in eligible stories. Here also, their were wide variations over the different occupational groups – with engineers showing it in 17 per cent of their eligible stories and the workers 7 per cent. As mentioned above, engineers showed rather low need for social achievement. The tendency seemed to be reversed here, suggesting that in the case of workers, this was more a social-achievement-oriented influence need, whereas in the case of engineers, it was more an influence-oriented-social-achievement need. Viewing the two needs together, i.e. the need for social achievement and need for influence oriented social achievement, the employees on the whole, particularly workers and professional personnel, tended to think substantially in terms of social achievement goals either integrated with thoughts of influence or without such thoughts. Another interesting finding here was that the administrative personnel, i.e. office workers including clerks, typists, etc., also showed this need substantially.

Need for Influence Oriented Personal Achievement (nInf-SA) and Need for Personal Achievement (nPA)

The need for influence-oriented personal achievement and the need for personal achievement were the next two important need-states of the employees in the organization. On the whole, one in every 10 employees tended to articulate each of these two needs. Such articulation did not vary much over various occupational groups/departments. However, technical personnel, such as technicians and engineers, tended to show more substantial personal achievement orientation with or without thoughts of influence.

The Other Needs

The remaining two needs, namely, the need for personal-cum-social achievement (*n*PSA) and the need for influence oriented social-personal achievement (nInf-SPA) were not articulated much. Such thoughts appeared only in few stories.

Thus, going by the frequency of articulation of various fantasies, the employees in the present organization were almost gripped with the idea of an actor role and of influencing others and the environment at the workplace and in society. Some personnel showed concern for excellence in their work and life or for better productivity, quality and safety at the workplace and/or better quality of life for them as a group. This was more so with workers, foremen, technicians and medical doctors than with, particularly, the administrative personnel. On the other hand, engineers including managers and, to some extent, foremen and technicians tended to think of an actor role for influencing either social achievement or personal achievement goals.

Articulation of Sub-categories : Some Important Behavioural Characteristics

There was a marked variation in the articulation of various sub-categories in the eligible stories as seen in Table 5.2. Such articulation seemed to vary significantly from one need-state to

TABLE 5.2: Percentage distribution of sub-categories for needs
N = 359, No. of stories eligible for scoring = 906

Sub-categoreis	Need Pattern							
	*n*PA	*n*SA	*n*Inf	*n*PA-SA	*n*Inf-PA	*n*Inf-SA	*n*Inf-PA-SA	Total no. of sub-categories
Personal Action	(64) 76	(39) 37	(192) 39	(10) 62	(64) 73	(28) 28	(18) 86	(415) 46
Social Action	(13) 15	(37) 35	(202) 41	(05) 31	(05) 06	(44) 44	(03) 14	(309) 34
Anticipated Action	(05) 06	(08) 07	(35) 07	(00) 00	(12) 14	(18) 18	(02) 09	(80) 09
Strength	(13) 14	(17) 16	(34) 07	(06) 37	(21) 25	(07) 07	(03) 13	(101) 11
Hope	(21) 25	(08) 07	(18) 04	(03) 19	(29) 34	(15) 15	(02) 09	(96) 10
Personal-Social Awareness	(24) 29	(43) 41	(120) 24	(08) 50	(24) 28	(54) 54	(15) 71	(288) 32
Vigilance	(30) 36	(41) 39	(131) 26	(06) 37	(34) 40	(49) 49	(09) 42	(300) 33
Total number of eligible stories = 906	(84) 09	(106) 12	(495) 55	(16) 02	(85) 09	(99) 11	(21) 02	

F = 7.792, Significant at .01 level.

* Number of stories in parentheses.

another, suggesting that some of these were, typically, behavioural characteristics of persons with specific need-states.

The Action Orientation

As could be expected, personal action (Ap) was articulated uniformly more prominently in all the stories. However, it tended to be expressed more in fantasies containing the need for personal achievement, integrated need for influence-oriented personal achievement and the integrated need for personal and social achievement. Social action (As) was also found substantially in the stories. It was much more evident in fantasies containing the need for social achievement as well as the need for influence. It was found to be the maximum in fantasies containing influence oriented social achievement thoughts and in thoughts, separately, for influence and for social achievement. Interestingly, stories containing the integrated need of personal and social achievement also contained this sub-category quite substantially with one in every three such stories showing it. On the whole, therefore, social action tendency seemed to be a prominent behavioural characteristic of those motivated by the need for social-achievement-oriented influence.

Anticipatory Action (Aa)

The anticipatory action was the least expressed sub-category in the stories with only nine per cent of them showing this tendency. However, the steel personnel showed it much more than those in the coal undertaking, as reported in Chapter 3. It appeared more in stories containing the integrated need for influence oriented social achievement as well as in those with influence oriented personal achievement as compared to the need for influence. The results, therefore, indicated that anticipatory or pro-active action was more a characteristic of persons motivated by a desire to influence others and the environment and to assert for obtaining goals than those motivated only by personal achievement or social achievement or influence goals. In this sense, the pro-active tendency was associated more with thoughts of an actor role for obtaining some standard of excellence in work and/or life. Such a pre-emptivc/pro-active action orientation, particularly among those motivated by the need for social achievement oriented influence had important implications for functioning of the work-organization as well as other organizations such as trade unions, staff associations, various action groups, etc.

Strength

Fantasies about one's own and/or collective strength were comparatively weaker with about 11 per cent of the stories showing them, as seen in Table 5.2. Persons motivated by integrated thoughts of achievement goal showed this tendency more than others. Persons motivated by personal achievement or social achievement goal also showed it more than those motivated to control and influence others and the environment. The results, on the whole, therefore, suggested that thinking in terms of one's own or group strength was more a behavioural tendency of those who thought of standards of excellence, either personal or social, and more particularly of those who thought of both in an integrated way. It was also present, substantially, in those motivated by the need for personal achievement-oriented influence. The latter thought of their own strength much more than those motivated by the need for social achievement oriented influence.

This was an important finding in view of the fact that the desire to influence, control and assert was the dominant tendency in the present work organization. Did the results mean that the people, here although strongly motivated by thoughts of influencing, did not think so much of their own strength? This could have behavioural implications for the work as well as other organizations.

Hope of Success

Persons motivated by a desire of influencing others for personal achievement goal as well as those who thought of personal achievement goal showed significantly greater fantasy of hope in their stories. Interestingly, persons motivated by the influence need showed it the least. The results showed that the hope of success was associated more with the thought of personal excellence more so when such thoughts were integrated with a desire for an actor role for asserting for such goals. It also got articulated more in those thinking of asserting for collective achievement. The finding was particularly important for the present study where the employees' need for influence was the dominant one. It was significant that such influence motivated personnel did not appear to be optimistic and/or hopeful of success. Such a hope seemed to emerge more explicitly only when influence thoughts got integrated with achievement goals.

Personal and Social Awareness

It was interesting to find that there was substantial personal and social awareness among the personnel—with one-third of the eligible stories showing it. It was found much more in the present organization as compared to the coal organization (as reported in Chapter 4). This was also expreseed substantially more than the sub-categories of anticipated action, hope and strength. Such awareness was evident more in persons motivated by the need for social achievement than those motivated either by the the need for personal achievement or by the need for influence. However, the greatest articulation occurred in stories marked by integrated imagery of influence-oriented personal-cum-social achievement followed by those scored for the integrated needs of influence oriented social achievement and personal-cum-social achievement.

Such awareness of personal problems and social issues appeared, therefore, to be a behavioural characteristic of the need for social achievement which got further boosted when such thoughts got integrated with thoughts of an actor and assertive role. The finding was noteworthy, suggesting that the concern for social and collective achievement was significantly accompanied by greater social consciousness. Such socially conscious persons would have an important role to play both at and outside the workplace.

Sense of Vigilance

Like the articulation of personal and social consciousness, the employees of the present organization also tended to show a substantial sense of vigilance, with one-third of stories showing this sub-category. Persons motivated by the need for social achievement, and, still more, those motivated by the need for social achievement oriented influence tended to be more vigilant than others particularly those motivated only by the need for influence. The results seemed to show that the sense of vigilance was behaviourally associated more substantially with the need for social achievement particularly when it got integrated with thoughts of influence. Social consciousness and sense of vigilance emerged as prominent characteristics of social achievement influence motivated persons.

The Dominant Motivational Trends

Thus, the personnel of the present work organization tended to show a conspicuously strong need for influence followed by the need for influence oriented social achievement and the need for social achievement. The strength of the latter two needs, although substantial, was much less than that of the need for influence.

It was thus clear that the personnel here differed widely from those of the coal undertaking in their need-states. There also, the need for influence appeared to be dominant but not in such strength as found at the steel plant. At the former, the two achievement needs, namely, the need for personal achievement and the need for social achievement, appeared much more substantially than found here. On the whole, therefore, the steel personnel tended to imagine and think much more of influencing others and the environment than of achievement–personal or social–as compared to the coal personnel. This was true for workers as well. However, more than one in every 10 persons also tended to imagine of social achievement and social achievement oriented influence goals. Similarly, little less than one-tenth also thought of personal achievement and personal achievement-oriented influence goals.

The steel personnel also tended to show substantial action orientation-both personal and social action. The personal achievement motivated persons tended to think more of personal action, while those moved by thoughts of influence as well as those moved by social achievement verbalized social action more frequently. They also tended to show substantial personal and social awareness as well as sense of vigilance. These tendencies seemed to characterize their fantasies much more than the remaining three, namely, thinking about anticipatory action, strength and hope of success which appeared in one in every 10 stories whereas the former were present in one in every three stories.

As mentioned in Chapter 4, persons motivated by the need for social achievement and, more importantly, by the need for social achievement oriented influence showed a scense of social efficacy. Such persons tended to think in terms of better quality of life and work for the society. More active among them thought of an actor and assertive role for obtaining a better quality of work and life. They tended to define productivity in terms of better life for the society. Such persons also tended to be socially more conscious, linking poverty and poor quality of life with socio-economic reasons, thus showing efficacy as against sense of helplessness. They were highly collective-action-oriented with a sense of vigilance and pro-active action orientation.

In the present case, the steel personnel appeared to be strongly motivated by the need for influence. However, there was a substantial degree of social efficacy in the origination, as discussed below.

II. CORRELATES OF NEED-STATES : FACILITATING AND INHIBITING FACTORS

As mentioned above, a cross-section of personnel representing various occupational groups, and departmental and personal background participated in the present study. They differed in their age, education, origin, i.e. rural/urban background, departmental location, length of service, access to promotion of the organization, exposure to training, income status, etc. Did such back-ground variables make a significant difference in need-states of the personnel? The answers were sought first by an analysis of variance and then by a multiple regression analysis.

Need for personal Achievement (nPA)

The analysis of variance revealed significance of occupational position, age, length of service and degree of exposure to urbanization (urban-rural background) for explaining variance in the need for personal achievement. The apprentice trainees, followed by foremen and engineers, needed to show this need significantly greater than others such as administrative and medical personnel. On the whole, younger employees, as well as those with a shorter period of service in the present organization, tended to show this need greater than the older ones and those with 10 and more years' service to their credit in the organization. Personnel with a greater exposure to urbanization having been brought up in metropolitan cities and such other urban areas also showed this need much more than those who originated from rural areas.

Thus, the younger employees, comparatively fresher in the organization, technical personnel particularly trainees and workers, and the urbanized showed a much greater need for personal achievement than the older ones, those with longer service, those less urbanized with greater rural back-ground and those serving in administrative and medical jobs. The association of personal achievement need with degree of urbanization suggested the role of urban socialization in promoting and reinforcing the desire for individual excellence in one's own work and life. The fact that such persons (i.e. those motivated by this need) tended to show a greater tendency for personal action, perhaps, indicated an emerging sense of individualism in them.

Need for Influence and Other Need-States

None of the background variables was significant in explaining variance in the need for social achievement. Several of these variables such as employees' departmental location, educational level and income, status in the organization, however, emerged as significant factors in explaining variance in the needed for influence. Education and income indicated the employee's occupational status in the organization. Its significant association with the need for influence was, therefore, understandable. More important here was the emergence of departmental location as a significant factor. Interestingly, personnel engaged in administrative jobs and located in administrative and works departments showed a significantly greater need for influence than those located in other departments particularly in training and town planning departments.

Employees' education also emerged as a significant factor in their need for personal and social achievement. Higher the education, the greater was this need. Similarly, education was a significant factor in their need for influence oriented personal achievement along with the length of service in the organization. The higher their education and the longer the length of service the greater was this need. Interestingly, access to promotion and growth in the organization tended to enhance the employees' need for personal achievement oriented influence.

The departmental location was also significant in explaining variance in the need for influence-oriented social achievement. Those located in the department of town administration showed it much more than others. However, more important in this respect was the emergence of the place of birth and upbringing of the employees. Those born and brought up in rural areas indicating a lower exposure to urban socialization showed a significantly greater need for influence oriented social achievement than those born and brought up in urban areas. Education also emerged as an important factor in explaining variance in the need for influence oriented personal and social achievement.

The results tended to suggest that the steel plant employees with a greater exposure to rural socialization tended to imagine and think more in terms of influencing others and the environment for collective (social) achievement goals. Interaction of rural socialization and workplace (factory) socialization, therefore, seemed to promote and reinforce a *sense of collectivism* in the employees.

The analysis of variance did identify, as mentioned above, certain important personal and organizational background variable in explaining variance in employees' need-states. However, these variables, such as education, income, age, length of service, were themselves inter-correlated, making it difficult to draw clear conclusions. The data were, therefore, further submitted to a multiple regression analysis, so as to analyse such overlapping variance, using a set of 28 independent variables. Such analyses helped in identifying significant factors and predictors of various need-states.

Independent Variables

The independent variables included, four variables of perceived work situation; four variables of socio-political outlook; three variables of life-satisfaction and the remaining six need variables (i.e. excepting the one in the seven need-states which was to be predicted as dependent variable). These variables are briefly described below:

Variables of Perceived Work Situation

The four variables here were: employees' perceived influence and autonomy at workplace, perceived amenities at work, perceived nature of job and perceived supervisory behaviour. The datas were collected with the help of a work Questionnaire (WQ) (Mehta,

1976a; Mehta, 1977; 1989). The obtained results indicated a degree of satisfaction (or dissatisfaction) with each of the four workplace dimension as well as overall work satisfaction.

Socio-Political Outlook - Personality Variables

Four variables here were: conservative *vs.* liberal social outlook, misanthropy vs. faith in people, sense of political powerlessness *vs.* efficacy and sense of political normlessness *vs.* acceptance of regime norms. This questionnaire, namely, the General Opinion Questionnaire (GOQ) has been used in earlier studies of some aspects of authoritarian-democratic outlook (Rao and Mehta, 1978; Rao and Mehta, 1979; Mehta, 1981; Borker, 1987; Mehta, 1989).

Life Satisfaction

The respondents provided data on a ten-point self-anchoring instrument regarding the level of satisfaction with their life conditions as obtained five years ago, as obtained presently and as might obtain five years later.

The independent variables are further explained below while discussing the results of the analysis to predict variance in the seven individual need-states.

Dependent Variables

Need for Personal Achievement (nPA)

The independent variables, taken together, explained 10 per cent variance in the employees' need for personal achievement which was statistically significant at 01. level, as seen in Table 5.3. Individual factors like length of service in the organization, place of birth and upbringing sense of political normlessness sense of satisfaction with the present life conditions, and the need for influence and for personal achievement oriented-influence emerged as significant correlates of this need-each factor on its own, when the effect of other simultaneous factors was controlled and held constant.

It was, therefore, definite that the employees' length of service in the organization tended to significantly depress the need for personal achievement. As seen in Fig. 5.1, this need went down as their length of service increased in the organization. The importance of urban socialization was also confirmed here. As seen in Fig. 5.2., the

TABLE 5.3 : Significant contributors to variance in need for personal achievement

N = 359

Positive Contributors			F Value	Negative Contributors			F Value
Variable	Change in variance	BETA		Variables	Change in variance	BETA	
Urban origin and upbringing	.01	0.07	1.81	Length of service in present organization	.03	0.24	9.35
Satisfied present	.01	0.16	4.13	Need for Influence	.01	0.13	5.97
Political normlessness	.01	0.12	3.81	Need for Influence oriented personal achievement	.02	0.14	7.87

$R^2 = 0.1519$; $F = 2.1$; $P < .01$

greater the exposure and degree of urbanization (i.e. those born and brought up in metropolitan cities), the greater was their need for personal achievement. The employees' view of the functioning of the political system and regime also emerged as an important predictor here. The greater the sense of such normlessness, the greater was their need for personal achievement. This probably indicated that persons motivated by a desire of some standard of excellence in their personal life and work were not happy with the functioning of the political regime which they perceived as not in accordance with the established civic norms.

Interestingly, persons satisfied with their present conditions of life showed this need more than those not satisfied. The satisfying quality of life, therefore, tended to enhance the desire to compete for success in work and life, in relation to some standards of excellence. Such persons were not swayed by thoughts of controlling and influencing others and the environment, not even by thoughts of influencing the personal achievement goal itself. It was interesting to note that the thoughts of influencing and controlling others and the

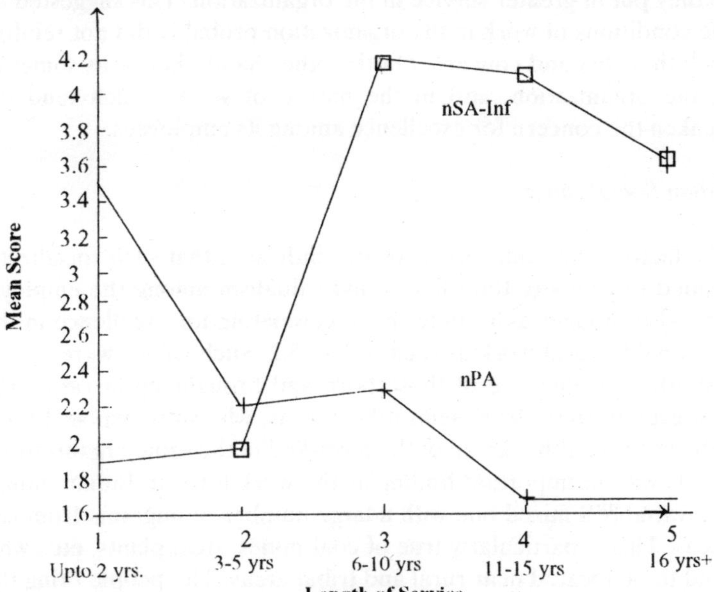

FIG. 5.1: Length of Service in organization and employees' need for personal achievement and need for social achievement oriented influence.

environment tended to weaken the desire for excellence. It was an important negative factor in this respect.

Length of Service

Among the significant factors, length of service in the organization emerged as the most important factor explaining three per cent variance in the employees' need for personal achievement. The result clearly suggested that fresh appointees, or those inducted laterally in the organization, were motivated much more by the thoughts of excellence and concern for a better quality of work and life than those who had put in longer service in the organization. Its importance was further supported by the finding from the coal undertaking (as discussed in Chapter 4) that younger persons showed a greater need for personal achievement than the older ones.

The finding, therefore, suggested that the youthful and those newly inducted in the organization, who seemed to start with enthusiasm for excellence in work and in life tended to lose this zeal as they put in greater service in the organization. This suggested that the conditions of work in the organization probably did not reinforce such thoughts and concern. On the other hand, there was something in the organization, and in the nature of work, which tended to weaken the concern for excellence among its employees.

Urban Socialization

The factor of urbanization probably indicated that such socialization tended to promote the value of individualism among the employees who also thought more in terms of competing for excellence in their personal life and work as seen in Fig. 5.2. Such values were not that important in the case of those born and brought up in rural areas, and even in those from semi-urban areas, who were exposed less to urbanization, although all of them worked in the same organization.

It was an important finding as the work force in Indian industry is invariably a mixed one with a large number of migrants from rural areas. This is particularly true of coal-mines, steel plants, etc., which tend to be located near rural and tribal areas. The people bring their own values and needs to the work organization with important implications for its functioning as well as for the people who work there.

Conditions of Life

The significance of the conditions of life suggested the importance of interface between such conditions and the employees' need-states. This showed the value of the employees' quality of life for functioning of the organization itself. Such satisfied personnel were likely to show a greater concern for quality and excellence to the great advantage of the work-organization.

Thus, the younger employees, the fresher ones; those with greater exposure to urbanization; those dissatisfied with the functioning of the political regime, those who were not interested in influencing others and asserting, and those who felt contented with their life tended to show a greater concern for personal excellence. Longer length of service in the organization and employees' rural background tended to weaken such a concern and values for personal excellence. The results suggested the importance of both, organizational experience and life experience, and socialization processes involved in such experience, for promotion and sustenance

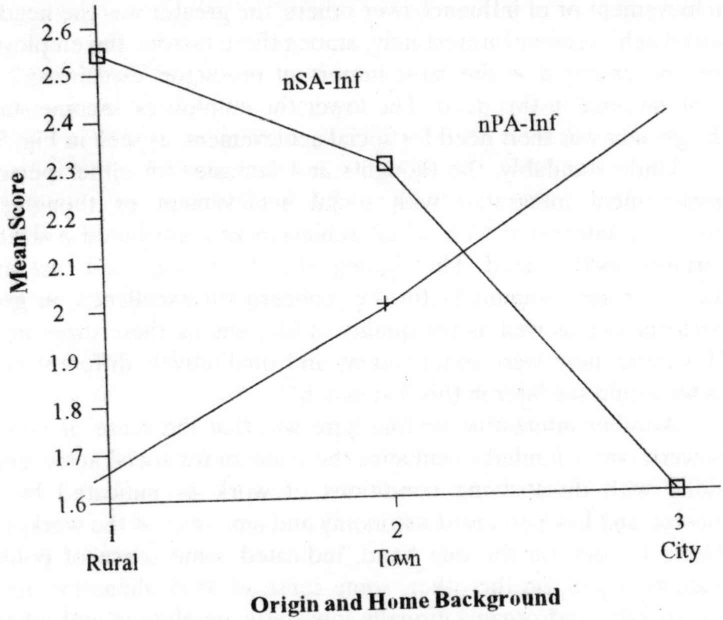

FIG. 5.2: Home background and employees need for social achivement oriented influence and need for personal achievement oriented influence.

of the employees' need for personal excellence in their work and life.

Need for Social Achievement (nSA)

The independent variables explained only 10 per cent variance in the need for social achievement which was statistically not significant, as seen in Table 5.4. Obviously, there were other factors which were probably more important as predictors of this need. However, the individual factors of income, perceived influence at the workplace, amenities at the workplace and a sense of political powerlessness and thoughts for influence oriented social achievement and personal-cum-social achievement emerged as significant predictors and correlates of this need.

The lower the income, the perceived influence and autonomy and the perceived amenities at workplace, the greater was the employees' need for social achievement. Similarly, the greater the sense of their political powerlessness and the more their thoughts of social achievement got integrated either with thoughts of personal achievement or of influence over others, the greater was the need for social achievement Interestingly, among these factors, the employees' income emerged as the most important predictor, explaining 2 per cent variance in this need. The lower the employees' income status, the greater was their need for social achievement, as seen in Fig. 5.3.

Understandably, the thoughts and fantasies for either personal achievement integrated with social achievement or thoughts of influence integrated with social achievement contributed a sizeable variance in this need. The finding, therefore, suggested that there was a strong common factor, i.e. concern for excellence, in group performance as well as for quality of life, among these three needs. However, these were independent and qualitatively different needs as we would see later in this discussion.

Another interesting finding here was that the sense of political powerlessness tended to enhance the concern for social achievement along with dissatisfying conditions of work as indicated by low income and low perceived autonomy and amenities at the workplace. These factors, on the one hand, indicated some sence of political alienation and, on the other, some sense of work-alienation among the socially and organizationally low-status employees and citizens. Such a sense of alienation was therefore, a very significant factor in the need for social achievement. Did such alienated people tend to

TABLE 5.4 : Significant Contributors to Variance in Need for Social Achievement
N = 359

Positive Contributors			F Value	Negative Contributors			F Value
Variable	Change in variance	BETA		Variables	Change in variance	BETA	
Need for personal achievement and social achievement	.04	0.20	14.52	Income	.02	0.12	3.43
Need for influence oriented social achievement	.01	0.12	4.76	Influence at workplace	.00	0.10	1.78
Sense of political powerlessness	.01	0.12	3.89	Amenities at workplace	.01	0.12	3.89

R^2 = .105; F = 1.3; not significant

weaken their personal sense of powerlessness by imagining collective achievement goals and by projecting a sense of collectivism as a value?

Need for Influence (*n*Inf)

The independent variables explained 15 per cent variance in the need for influence which was statistically significant at 01 level. Nine factors emerged as individually significant in this respect, as seen in Table 5.5. These factors included employees' education, income, departmental location as positive predictors, and exposure to training, length of service in the organization, future life aspiration, misanthropy, conservative social outlook, need for personal achievement and need for social achievement as negative predictors.

Interestingly, the organizational status, as indicated by eduction and income, seemed to work in the opposite direction for the need for influence as compared to the need for social achievement as seen in Fig. 5.3. The greater the occupational status and mobility in the

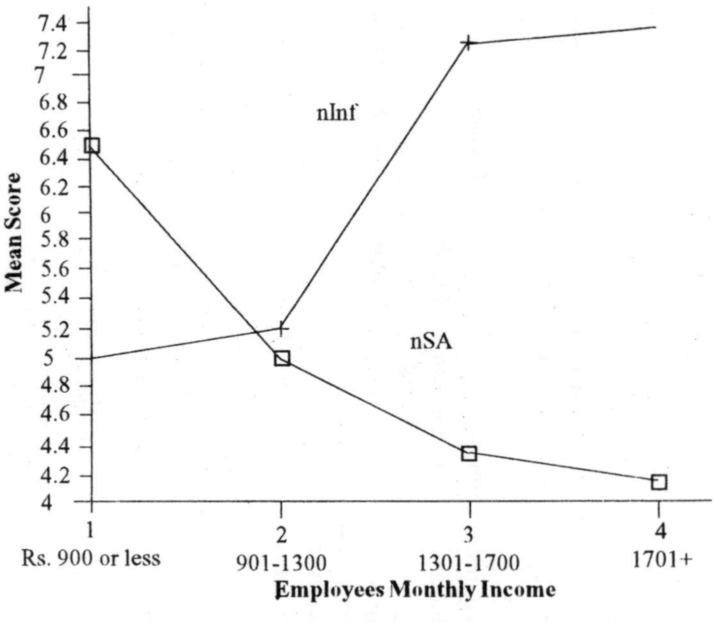

FIG. 5.3 : Employees income and need for influence and need for social achievement

TABLE 5.5 : Significant contributors to variance in need for Influence

N = 359

Positive Contributors				Negative Contributors			
Variable	Change in variance	BETA	F Value	Variables	Change in variance	BETA	F Value
Education	0.05	0.13	4.26	Training	0.01	0.06	1.58
Income	0.02	0.17	7.42	Length of service in same orgn.	0.00	0.17	4.56
Department	0.01	0.12	3.21	Hopeful/satisfying future	0.01	0.09	1.42
				Misanthropy	0.01	0.11	3.46
				Conservative social outlook	0.00	0.09	2.45
				Need for personal achievement	0.02	0.13	5.97
				Need for social achievement	0.01	0.11	4.44

$R^2 = 0.152$; $F = 2.1$; $P < 10$

organization the greater was the employees' need for influence. However, the length of service emerged here also as a negative factor. As the employees acquired longer service (and length of experience) in the organization, the weaker became their need for influence. Interestingly the greater was their training exposure the lower was their need for influence.

Results, therefore, indicated that occupational status, short period of service, liberal social outlook, faith in people, apprehension about future and lack of interest in excellence, either personal or social, were significant correlates of the need for influence. Going by the results of the coal study, as discussed in Chapter 4, influence motivated persons also enjoyed greater satisfaction at the workplace although these work variables did not emerge as significant at the RSP. One striking difference in the results here was that unlike those at the BCCL where the influence motivated persons were found to be conservative and authoriarian, here, i.e., at the RSP, such persons appeared as liberal in social outlook and more democratically committed with greater faith in people.

Another striking result here, with important implications for understanding the functioning of the organization, was the lack of interest in such influence motivated persons for pursuing excellence either in work performance or in life. Such persons appeared to be interested more in pursuing influence as the goal. It was noteworthy because such persons were placed higher in the organizational hierarchy with greater income and a more powerful departmental position. They were required to supervise the work of those placed lower in the hierarchy such as workers, technicians and others who were found here to show a higher need for social achievement. They also felt dissatisfied and alienated in the organization and tended to put a greater value on collective achievement and action. Such workers and others were, therefore, likely to resist the top-down exercise of power. Would such inter-level motivational pattern stimulate inter-group and management-labour conflicts in the organization?

In view of the liberal social attitude of those in higher and leadership position in the organization, they could probably contribute to promoting participation of others at the workplace. In such a case, the two needs, i.e. need for (democratic) influence among the higher placed personnel–managers and others – and the strong need for social achievement among the employees at the lower levels could feed into each other and help promote collaborative and participatory work climate to the advantage of the organization. However, as noted above, employees more or less at all levels of the organization including workers and technicians were high on the need for influence. This factor was likely to create, unless handled positively and democratically, inter-personal and inter-group conflicts in the organization to the determent of its functioning.

Need for Personal-cum-Social Achievement

Table 5.6 shows significant contributors to the variance in this need. The independent variables explained 14 per cent variance which was significant at .01 level. Eight of these variables emerged as significant predictors of this need—three of them positive and five negative. Conservative social attitude was a positive predictor. However, its contribution to the total variance was not much—almost nil. Perceived amenities at workplace explained one per cent and social achievement thoughts five per cent of its variance. Of the negative predictors, age contributed two per cent, length of service nil, sense of political powerlessness, need for influence and needs for social achievement oriented influence one per cent each.

Thus, the need for social achievement emerged as the most important positive correlate of the integrated need for personal-cum-social achievement. Interestingly, the need for personal achievement was not a significant factor in explaining this need. It seemed, thoughts of social achievement were the most important component of this integrated need for achievement and that persons with need for social achievement were much more likely to also think of personal achievement along with it. However, those motivated by the thoughts of personal achievement were not likely to be interested in an integrated achievement with the social component built into it.

Interestingly, the need seemed to diminish with increasing age and stagnation of the employee. These were important findings suggesting that the younger personnel were motivated much more by the thoughts of excellence in performance and productivity in the organization and a better quality of life of which concern for social achievement was an important contributor. However, they tended to

TABLE 5.6 : Significant contributors to variance in need for personal-cum-social achievement
$N = 359$

Positive Contributors				Negative Contributors			
Variable	Change in variance	BETA	F Value	Variables	Change in variance	BETA	F Value
Conservative social outlook	0.00	0.08	1.95	Age	0.02	0.14	3.25
Amenities at workplace	0.00	0.10	2.44	Duration on job (stagnation)	0.00	0.10	2.50
Need for social achievement	0.05	0.20	14.52	Need for influence	0.01	0.11	4.44
				Need for influence oriented social achievement	0.01	0.07	1.76

$R^2 = .136; F = 1.80; P < 01$

lose some of this concern as they grew older in the organization. Non-availability of timely promotion, and denial of greater responsibility in the work organization tended to further weaken this need. There were factors in the functioning of the organization and/or in persons themselves which tended to weaken the need for personal-cum-social achievement. Interestingly, the need for influence and the need for influence oriented social achievement were also negative correlates in this case. The stronger the desire to control and influence and the stronger the desire for influence oriented social achievement, the weeker was the need for personal-cum-social achievement.

Satisfactory working and service conditions were important for promoting the need for personal-cum-social achievement at the workplace. It was also true of the conservative social outlook (giving importance to religion, moral character, military training and some "supreme power"), although it did not contribute anything to the total variance in this case. The finding was interesting as it indicated the importance of traditional thinking and values on social learning of "achievement" including collective achievement thoughts. It indicated that such attitudes and values probably promoted a positive attitude toward work and contributed to developing a concern for excellence in performance and in life.

To sum up, the significant correlates of the need for personal-cum-social achievement (i.e. persons motivated by a desire for excellence in their own individual performance and life as well as in group/social performance) were: youthful age, conservative social outlook, satisfaction with work amenities and promotional avenues (i.e. low stagnation), sense of political efficacy (opposite of powerlessness), high need for social achievement (i.e. strong thoughts for better working condition, higher productivity, etc.) and a low concern for influence and influence-oriented social achievement. It was thus clear that, besides personal variables, organizational variables were very important for boosting or weakening of this important individual need.

Such younger personnel, motivated by the need for personal-cum-social achievement, although satisfied with working conditions, were dissatisfied with reward policies. Politically, they felt efficacious and work-wise not alienated. They were interested in work and performance and not interested in power and influence. Such people, therefore, constituted a source of energy for the organization, provided the elder, higher placed personnel motivated by the need for influence were enable to lead and motivate them.

Need for Influence Oriented Social Achievement (nInf-SA)

The independent variables explained 17 per cent variance in the need for influence oriented social achievement, which was statistically significant at .01 level. Nine individual variables emerged as significant factors in this respect, as seen in Table 5.7. These included education, length of service, length of stagnation, need for social achievement and need for influence oriented social-cum-personal achievement (positive predictors) and age of the employees, their place of birth and upbringing (i.e origin of residence), conservative social outlook and sense of political normlessness as negative predictors of this need. Among these factors, besides the related need for influence oriented personal-cum-social achievement, the employees' place of birth and upbringing emerged as the most important factor.

It was, therefore, interesting that, unlike the need for personal achievement, exposure to urbanization emerged here as a negative correlate of the need for social achievement oriented influence, as seen in Fig. 5.2. This suggested that employees born and brought up in rural areas, although working in the same organization, tended to show a higher need for social achievement oriented influence than those exposed more to urban life. Another interesting finding was, as seen in Fig. 5.1, that unlike the need for personal achievement, this need tended to increase with the length of service. Also, younger, more educated, socially liberal, and those 'satisfied' with the functioning of the political regime showed this need greater.

Such persons, comparatively younger in age, had put in considerable service at the same workplace. Such senior employees felt trapped for want of promotional avenues. They therefore, felt dissatisfied with the organization. They were more educated than ordinary workers and many others in the organization which tended to aggravate their dissatisfaction.

The findings, therefore, indicated that, although there was a significant component of social achievement thoughts, persons motivated by this need were more interested in "our" as well as "my" achievement and in influencing such achievement. They were, behaviourally, unlike those motivated by the need for social

TABLE 5.7: Significant contributors to variance in need for influence oriented social achievement
$N = 359$

Positive Contributors			F Value	Negative Contributors			
Variable	Change in variance	BETA		Variables	Change in variance	BETA	F Value
Education	0.01	0.13	4.21	Age	0.00	0.10	2.00
Length of service in plant	0.01	0.11	2.05	Origin of residence	0.02	0.15	8.18
Length of serivce on the present position (stagnation)	0.01	0.10	2.77	Conservative social outlook	0.00	0.07	1.77
Need for social achievement	0.00	0.11	4.76	Sense of political normlessness	0.00	0.09	2.28
Need for influence oriented personal-social achievement	0.05	0.24	21.39				

R^2 = .170; F = 2.04; P < 01

achievement. The latter showed a sense of political alienation as indicated by their sense of political powerlessness while the former, i.e. those motivated by the need for social achievement oriented influence, did not feel that powerless. They also showed more liberal social outlook. They tended to put a greater value on the actor role and collective assertion for quality of work and life. The findings, therefore, suggested a critical difference in their consciousness as compared to those motivated by the need for social achievement.

Further, persons motivated by the need for social achievement oriented influence were not placed lowly in the organization as probably those motivated by the need for social achievement were. They were placed, probably in between the top and the bottom. Such 'leaders' coming from rural back-ground and placed, as they were crucially, at middle management and senior worker level, were likely to provide leadership in the organization and in unions and staff associations. They were also likely to confront the more powerfully located managers and others in the organization. Such middle managers, technicians and senior workers seemed to present an interesting leadership profile. They were dissatisfied with the organization, particularly its reward and career development policies. They valued collectivism and good quality of work life and were inclined to assert for collective goals. They also seemed to draw some power from outside the work place by their psychological affinity with the political regime. The organization leaders, i.e. top and senior managers, motivated by a strong need for influence, were to interface with such youthful middle management and professional level "leaders" The scenario implied potentially both, conflicts and positive strengths in the work organization, as such leaders harboured a sense of deprivation, showed assertive collectivism for "public" or social interest rather than only for "private gain".

Influence-oriented Personal Achievement Motivation

The independent variables explained only 10 per cent variance in this need which was not significant. Only four variables appeared as significant predictors of this need, as seen in Table 5.8. Of these, three were negative correlates and one, i.e., income, was the only positive predictor. Interestingly, the need for personal achievement emerged as a negative predictor of this need. The more were the personal achievement thoughts, the lower was the fantasy for

TABLE 5.8 : Significant contributors to variance in need for influence oriented personal achievement
N = 359

Positive Contributors				Negative Contributors			
Variable	Change in variance	BETA	F Value	Variables	Change in variance	BETA	F Value
Income	0.01	0.11	2.59	Past satisfaction	0.00	0.12	3.32
				Misanthropy	0.01	0.15	5.71
				Need for personal achievement	0.02	0.15	7.87

R^2 = .096; F = 1.2; NS

influence oriented personal achievement. When personal achievement got integrated with a desire for influence, it became not only a qualitatively different need-state, but a negative correlate for need for personal achievement. The other two variables which were individually significant in deplaning this need were: nostalgia for past (life five years ago) and misanthropy.

The greater the income, the greater was the need for influence oriented personal achievement. On the whole, personnel placed in higher income groups were nostalgic about past life and those having faith in the people, showed a greater need for influence oriented personal achievement. It was not associated with age and or length of service and seniority in the organization. Education and work-related satisfaction were also not important here. Social outlook and political behaviour also did not make any difference. The only organizational variable which made a difference was the income of the employee.

The correlates of this need showed some similarity with the need for influence. Relationship of both needs with income was positive. Both were negative with misanthropy and the need for personal achievement. The differences, however, were that the need for personal achievement oriented-influence was not related to education: such people were not necessarily fresh (shorter length of service) in the organization like those motivated by the need for influence. Unlike the need for influence, this need did not seem to be associated with organization status. It was also interesting to that find this need was in no way associated with work-related satisfaction. They were neither satisfied nor dissatisfied. The fact that, it was stronger among the higher income groups suggested the possibility of such personnel getting either quicker promotions and/or greater income earning positions in the organization.

There was also a possibility of a keen inter-personal competition among such people because of their need for assertion for personal achievement. Such persons in leadership positions may generate inter-personal and inter-departmental conflicts and a hostile work climate for the subordinates. Because of their interest in the pursuit of good performance and excellence, such persons could also contribute to promoting an achievement climate at the workplace, by working as models for others.

Influence-oriented Personal and Social Achievement

The independent variables explained 14 per cent variance in this need which was statistically not significant. Table 5.9 shows that only four independent variables emerged as significant predictors of this need. Of these four, two were positive and two negative. The major source of variance here was the need for influence oriented social achievement. The results here confirmed the earlier result (see Table 5.7) that the two needs were similar in content to a great extent. It was also found more among the younger personnel. Nostalgia for past life and faith in people, however, made important contributions to this need which was not the case with the need for social achievement oriented influence.

Although there was a substantial overlap between the need for influence oriented social achievement and the need for influence oriented personal and social achievement, there were significant differences also. Education, length of service, stagnation, need for social achievement, sense of political normlessness, origin of residence and liberal social outlook were important correlates of the former need. These did not appear as significant in the case of the latter. One of the reasons for a difference in the functioning of the two need-states could be that the latter appeared only in a very small number of stories. The results did, however, suggest the possibility that this need was only somewhat different from the need for influence oriented social achievement.

Sense of Social Efficacy

The findings seemed to establish that, although the need for social achievement and the need for personal cum social achievement oriented influence were substantially different from the need for social achievement oriented influence, the former two were significant predictors, and therefore, correlates of the latter and were highly interrelated. These three needs, more particularly the latter two influence integrated needs, showed a person's sense of social efficacy.

Some characteristics of such a sense of social efficacy are summarized in Table 5.10. For example, such socially efficacious persons at the steel plant were relatively younger, more educated and experienced. They were found more at the lower to middle levels of

TABLE 5.9 : Contributors to variance in need for influence oriented personal achievement-cum-social achievement
N = 359

Positive Contributors				Negative Contributors			
Variable	Change in variance	BETA	F Value	Variables	Change in variance	BETA	F Value
Past satisfaction	0.01	0.09	1.90	Age	0.02	0.19	6.31
Need for influence oriented social achievement	0.05	0.25	21.40	Misanthropy	0.01	0.11	3.14

R^2 = .138; F = 1.8; P < 10

TABLE 5.10: Sense of Social Efficacy : Some Characteristics

Organizational status and personal characteristics		Workplace Integration & Involvement	Motivational and Behavioural Characteristics		Aspirations
Personal	Status		Motivational	Behavioural	
Younger, Educated, Experienced	Lower to middle level	Sense of deprivation and dissatisfaction; alienated	Concern for social achievement and sense of capability, assertion	Socially conscious and democratically oriented; pro-active; vigilant; Hopeful	Better working conditions; Career opportunity; Autonomy; Power; Participation

the organization. They harboured a sense of deprivation and dissatisfaction. They felt trapped. Socially they were liberal and psychologically attracted by the political regime. They felt concerned for social achievement goals and showed a sense of capability and assertion. Such persons were socially conscious and behaviourally vigilant, pro-active and helpful. They also showed faith in people and were democratically-oriented. They tended to aspire for better working conditions, better career opportunities and greater autonomy, power and participation at the workplace. They were aware of the functioning of the workplace and tended to look at the unsatisfactory state of affairs there as structural and organizational factors and not as personal failures. They felt capable of collectively influencing the workplace and the society for improving things. They occupied an important and crucial place in the organization with significant implications for its functioning.

The Emerging Psychological Profile

The obtained data indicated an interesting motivational pattern at the steel plant. Influence emerged as the most important dominant need of the employees. It was present, practically at all levels of the organization. It was, however, much stronger at the top level. The need for social achievement, the need for social achievement oriented influence, the need for personal achievement and the need for personal achievement oriented influence also emerged as important. The first two needs appeared to be stronger in workers, technicians, engineers and medical doctors. Administrative personnel, particularly the office workers, also showed these needs substantially. The latter two needs were more or less equally visible among these various groups.

Both personal action and social action were articulated very substantially by the employees in their fantasies. The former was associated more with the need for personal achievement while the latter with social achievement related needs as well as the need for influence with maximum articulation in stories containing a sense of social efficacy, i.e., the need for social achievement oriented influence. Anticipatory action was the least expressed tendency. Comparatively however, the RSP employees articulated it more than those of the coal undertaking. It appeared to be more a characteristic of persons who thought of an actor and assertive role for either social achievement or personal achievement goals. Articulation of strength was also weak. It seemed more as an achievement related tendency appearing maximum in a fantasy of personal-cum-social achievement and substantially in stories marked by personal achievement oriented influence. Interestingly, the tendency to think in terms of strength—either personal or group—was quite weak in persons motivated by the need for influence. It was an important finding in view of the fact that this was the dominant need of the employees in the present organization.

The same was true of hope of success. Influence oriented persons showed it the least, while those with concern for personal achievement oriented influence showed it the most. This appeared, therefore, more as a characteristic of persons with concern for personal excellence particularly of those who integrated such goals with an actor and assertive self-role. The employees, on the whole, showed substantial social consciousness which appeared to be more a behavioural characteristic of social achievement oriented persons particularly when such thoughts got integrated with the need for influence. The same was true for the sense of vigilance which also appeared quite subsatantially, specially in persons motivated by social achievement oriented influence as well as in those with personal achievement oriented influence.

On the whole, tendencies to think in terms of one's own strength and sense of optimism were articulated less at this workplace, as compared to the coal personnel. The present employees, therefore, tended to be less optimistic than coal-miners and managers. They were, however, socially more conscious, more vigilant as well as pro-active than the coal employees.

Significant Factors

Several organizational, personal and personality variables emerged as significant factors in employees' psychological needs. These included workplace related factors such as the length of service, promotion/stagnation, departmental posting, income, perceived autonomy and influence and work amenities; personal factors like age, education and place of birth and upbringing; personality factors like sense of life satisfaction, social outlook, sense of political efficacy, sense of political normlessness and faith in people. Interestingly, such independent variables tended to affect and predict the employees' needs varyingly.

Organizational Factors

The length of service, for example, tended to depress the need for personal achievement and the need for influence and boost the need for social achievement oriented influence. Lack of promotion and stagnation at the workplace weakened the concern for excellence and enhanced assertion for social achievement. Posting in the main administrative department tended to enhance the need for influence while posting in departments like town planning weakened it, suggesting preference for administrative work over planning and field work. Income tended to boost the need for influence and the need for personal achievement oriented influence and lack of it boosted the need for social achievement. The lower the income of the employees, the higher was this need and the higher the income, the greater were the other two needs. The lower the perceived autonomy, influence and amenities at the workplace, the greater was the need for social achievement. Such employees felt deprived and showed greater interest in and concern for collective achievement goals. On the other hand, adequate amenities (satisfaction) tended to boost the concern for personal-cum-social achievement. Such satisfied employees thought mostly of excellence in their life and work.

Thus, organizational variables emerged as significant factors in employees' psychological needs. Lack of adequate income and reward (promotion), lack of autonomy, influence and amenities created dissatisfaction and a sense of deprivation, boosting employees' interest in collective action and achievement. A sense of collectivism was thus clearly associated with such alienation and a sense of deprivation which tended to shape critical consciousness in them.

Leaders, Achievers and Workers

The various motivational patterns along with their demographic, life related, organizational and work related correlates suggested some distinct group of leaders and workers in the organization. Their psychological profiles were likely to show varying behavioural orientations with implications for functioning of the workplace. Such leadership patterns are briefly described below:

Organization-Leaders: Actors and Pushers

Firstly, there were the organization leaders. These were freshly inducted (recruited probably directly from open market) senior and top managers, with a high status and power; with a very strong need for influence, but rather low achievement orientation; socially liberal; trustful; but unsure and apprehensive about their own future.

Get-Goers

Secondly, there were the get-goers with a high need for influence oriented personal achievement. They enjoyed higher income and higher status in the organization. They were socially liberal with faith in people. However, their concern for their own achievement *per se* was very low. Such persons were likely to compete with each other, within and between departments, contributing to conflicts as well as to achievement climate in the organization.

Socially Efficacious Leaders

Thirdly, there were the socially efficacious and democratically oriented leaders – middle managers, technicians and professionals.

Their need to assert for social achievement goals was very high. They were experienced, relatively younger and educated insiders. They were dissatisfied and felt deprived at the workplace due to lack of career development and promotional avenues. They seemed to have political allegiance and were capable of forging links with powerful forces outside the organization. They were likely to lead collectively oriented workers with a high need for social achievement.

The Achievers

There were also a small number of achievers in the organization with a high need for personal-cum-social achievement. Relatively younger, they were satisfied with the organization for timely rewards and other amenities. They were socially conservative and personally efficacious. However, they were not at all interested in controlling and leading others. They were mostly interested in good performance and achievement.

As the need for influence was generally high, there was likely to be a demand for greater participation at the workplace. In such a context, the top management could utilize the available leadership, achievement and social efficacy potential and move the organization towards greater democratization. Alternatively, they could push it towards a more and more adversial and conflict-ridden situation, thus dissipating the positive resource. In both the situations, the middle managers and professionals, with their high sense of social efficacy, were likely to play a crucial role. They could lead others in generating pressures and demand for greater participation and for better quality of work and life. Thus, they could act and lead others to collectively assert for greater productivity in terms of better quality of life for society.

Differences with Coal Personnel

Case study of the steel personnel brought out some important differences (along with similarities) in their needs and values as compared with those of the coal personnel. We discuss some aspects of conditions of work at the two workplaces in Chapter 6. An attempt is also made to put the emerging value correlates of various needs in a historical and comparative perspective with a view to understanding the obtained findings more meaningfully.

PART THREE

Understanding Organizational Behaviour : Suggested Interventions

Organizational behaviour like other social behaviour cannot be comprehended as a single event. Its understanding has to be grounded in the history of the organization. Social structures obtaining at the workplace also need to be examined in order to understand the inner dynamics of its functioning.

Part Three seeks to put the obtained findings in their historical perspective with a view to uncovering the latent meaning of manifest behaviour. It discusses the importance of work and workplace in human development and suggests some broad areas for interventions.

6

Historical Conditions of Work : Values and Needs at Workplace

SOCAL ATTITUDES and personality tendencies seemed to provide varying content and direction to individual needs in the two work organizations – Bharat Coking Coal Limited (BCCL) and Rourkela Steel Plant (RSP) – as reported in Chapters 4 and 5. This was particularly true of the need for influence. In case of the former, it was associated with conservative-authoritarian beliefs, while at the latter, it appeared to be associated with liberal democratic social outlook. Such findings suggested some important differences in the value systems and norms obtaining at the two workplaces. These in turn reflected their structural conditions of work.

I. THE TWO WORKPLACES : HISTORICAL AND SUBJECTIVE CONDITIONS

The Work Climate – BCCL

The work climate at the BCCL, as discussed in Chapter 4, was perceived as mistrustful, disrespectful to each other, anxiety ridden, insecured and authoritarian. The workers' representatives perceived their managers as dominative, labour leaders as coercive and selfish, and workers themselves as timid and submissive. Further, managers, including senior managers, perceived pressures on them for conformity, inadequate opportunity for taking responsibility and initiative and lack of reward for good work, lack of goal clarity, poor teamwork and, on the whole, poor quality of life (see Mehta, 1989 a : 52).

The Work Climate – RSP

Workers, techincians, foremen, engineers and managers analysed the nature and functioning of their organization, i.e., Rourkela Steel Plant (RSP) in a series of small group discussions. Their perceptions and feelings are summarized in Table 6.1. They perceived their workplace as a modern industrial plant using advanced technology. While analysing the prevailing welfare, they were positive about the management's stress on health, sanitation, safety and prevention of accidents at the plant. They also appreciated the importance given to training and worker-resource and social development. They, however, also felt that the skills, thus developed, were not being used adequately that there were not enough rewards and incentives for good performance; that opportunities for career development were inadequate; that there was increasing bureaucratization; that the management was not very serious about participatory forums and that they were not interested in their success.

On the whole, the employees perceived the work climate as trustful and respectful. Although they perceived efforts for promoting participatory culture, they felt disappointed with the management's indifference. They felt particularly frustrated by the lack of adequate implementation of decisions taken by such formus. Interestingly, they also perceived inadequate orientation for achievement and productivity in the organization.

Increasing Disappointment at Both Places

Thus, there were some similarities in the perceived climate at the two workplaces. Nevertheless, at both the places, the employees showed a sense of disappointment on account of inadequate reward and incentives for good performance. Also, the employees at both the places felt that sincere and adequate efforts were not being made to promote participative forums and to make them a success. At the BCCL, the senior managers felt that the top management discouraged them from consulting workers. At both the places, the

TABLE 6.1 : Managers' and workers' analysis of the Rourkala Steel Plant as an organization

Work Organization		Employees' Feelings	Perceived Work Climate
Organization and Management	Employee Welfare		
Modern plant technology	Improved health and sanitation	Inadequate use of skills	Mutually trusting and respectful
Increasing bureaucratization	Attention to safety and prevention of accidents	Unsatisfactory reward policy and incentives	Inadequate orientation for achievement and productivity
Like to be seen as participatory	Stress on training	Inadequate career development Want participation	Indifferent to participation

* Based on a series of small group discussions in which workers, technicians, engineers and managers participated in 1980 during the period the data for the study reported in Chapter 5 were collected.

employees perceived dysfunctional bureaucratization of their orgnization.

Contrast in two Workplaces

The differences in the perceived climate at the two workplaces were, equally, if not more, conspicuous. For example, the employees at the BCCL saw their work climate as dominative and the leadership as coercive. This was not the case at the RSP where the employees perceived a climate of mutual trust and respect. The leadership was not perceived as coercive, although doubts were expressed about its credibility and sincerity. At the BCCL, there was an all-pervading sense of insecurity whereas at the RSP it was perceived as secured. At the BCCL, the work environment was marked by a sense of helplessness. This was not the case at the RSP, where no such feelings were expressed.

Inculcation and Use of Skills : Sense of Alienation and Sense of Belonging

One of the important elements in perceptions at the RSP was the concern for inculcation and use of skills and promotion of productivity at the workplace. At the BCCL, the people were greatly apprehensive about safety and rarely talked about the work itself. Concern for productivity and improved work performance, which came out clearly in their TAT stories, seemed to have been suppressed in their analyses of the organisation, as they were probably full of feelings about management styles and their own sense of insecurity. On the other hand, the Thematic Apperception Test (TAT) stories at the RSP did not so much reveal their concern for productivity and achievement as they were probably full of thoughts for influencing. Their concern for achievement, productivity and incentives for good performance, however, surfaced in their analyses of the organization.

On the whole, the employees at the BCCL, which included both workers and managers, felt much more alienated. Although they had a substantial need for personal achievement as well as need for social achievement, such needs did not surface in their small group discussions, where they talked mostly of inhibiting factors and their frustrating experience. This was not the case with the RSP, where the employees were positive about the workplace and showed concern for influencing its functioning. They, thus, showed a greater sense of belonging to their workplace.

Reflection of Historical Conditions

Differences in the organizational climate could be due to historical conditions, current conditions of work, leadership styles, management policies and practices, etc. The historical conditions at the two workplaces and the organization of labour process were likely to condition and/or reinforce managerial styles, labour relations and subjective conditions including norms, values, needs, etc. It would be useful to recall some such similarities and differences in order to put the employees' particularly workers; needs, value-system and organizational behaviour in some historical perspective.

The Bharat Coking Coal Limited

The Bharat Coking Coal Limited (BCCL), as reported in Chapter 4, was set up by the Government of India as a nationalized coal undertaking in 1972 by taking oven the interest of a large number of private mines and coking oven plants. A year later, 182 non-coking coal mines in the Jharia Coalfield were also nationalized and handed over to the BCCL. These small collieries were amalgamated to remove the artificial boundary among them in order to facilitate scientific mining operations. Besides slaughter mining, the private mines were characterized by "ruthless exploitation, achieved by the fiercest repression, on the one hand, and widespread corruption, on the other" (Kumaramangalam, 1973 : 31).

Organization-Development Programme

The challenge before the new organization was to move from competitvely exploitative and repressive past to partnership and participation at all levels with emphasis on scientific mining. The new management initiated measures inorder to weave the diverse groups inherited from private coal-mines into a meaningful and cohesive organization. Besides modernizing its plants and collieries, the organization took some steps to energize the various categories of people in order to utilize their talents. It initiated a series of management and workers' development programmes during 1973-74 which sought to sharpen managerial skills, heighten motivation for excellence in performance, and to develop skills and attitudes for participatory functioning. They also initiated modernization of technology at some plants and collieries.

The effects of historical objective conditions, however, were not to wither away automatically simply because the mines were nationalized and brought under the new organization. In fact, such conditions continued to shape thoughts and needs of both, managers and workers, at the new workplace. The attempts at inculcating a new culture were confronted by these historical factors and the continuing socio-economic and structural conditions. Such a confrontation was reflected in the managers and workers' analyses of the organization, as discussed in Chapter 4. Negative images and authoritarian practices and work climate, if anything, seemed to have been further sharpened with inevitable effects on the employees' organizational behaviour (for details, see Mehta, 1989 : 42-44).

The Rourkela Steel Plant

Unlike the BCCL, the Rourkela Steel Plant (RSP) was a new prestigious public sector organization, set up under a professional management right from its inception. It initiated the practice of participatory forums by establishing works committees way back in the early 1960s. The first work committee was set up in 1962, second in 1966, third in 1969 and fourth in 1972. Each one served for a period of three years. Several social measures were also initiated from time to time for providing medical facilities, transport and roads, housing, public conveniences, drinking water facility, shopping centres, fair price shops, schools, employment opportunity for widows and dependents, *Nari Kalyan Kendras* for the welfare of women, etc.

Workers signed an agreement with the management in October 1971, to have Departmental Joint Production Committees and a Central Production Committee at the apex. As a result, the production went up steadily reaching new levels in 1976-77 both in the Steel Plant and the Fertilizer Plant. The rate of accidents came down from 619 in 1964 to 175 in 1975. The network of grievance committees helped in the redressal and reduction of grievances about promotions and rewards, safety conditions and such other issues leading to improved labour-management relationships. Till March, 1983, 44 Departmental Production Committees including the Central Production Committee held 4,198 meetings and made 9,047 recommendations of which 7,484 were reportedly implemented. Such committees reportedly made a significant contribution toward industrial peace and improvement of productivity. Such success experience further reinforced a climate of cooperation, trust and friendship (Mahapatra, 1978, SAIL, 1988).

Historical Comparison of BCCL and RSP

Both the work organizations, i.e., the BCCL and the RSP, were important national public sector undertakings, representing two core sectors of our economy. However, they were differentiated by their history. The BCCL inherited coercive culture of the ruthlessly competitive private coal-mines. There was no such hangover at the RSP. Besides widespread mutual mistrust and negative images, the BCCL continued to be marked by musclemanship. Such a situation persisted despite management development programmes. These things were absent at the RSP. The BCCL suffered from lack of amenities such as housing, drinking water, roads, etc., whereas the RSP was fortunate in having a modern township with other related welfare facilities. The workforce at the RSP was more educated than that at the BCCL. Technologically also, the former was more advanced than the latter, although there also efforts were being initiated for modernization. The objective conditions at the two workplaces were thus substantially different

II. VALUE SYSTEM AT THE TWO ORGANISATIONS

The objective conditions obtaining at the workplace, thus, contributed to inculcating varying subjective conditions as revealed in the employees' perceptions, images and feelings at the two workplaces. The employees showed similarities as well as marked differences in their projected needs. For instance, at both the workplaces, influence was the dominant need. Practically all groups of employees at the RSP, including both, managers and workers, showed a strong need for influence. This was not exactly the case with the BCCL where managers showed a much stronger need for influence than workers. The latter, on the other hand, showed a stronger need for social achievement followed by the need for social achievement oriented influence. While such needs were not that strong at the RSP, there also was a substantial tendency to think in terms of asserting for socal achievement goals.

Another interesting difference in the need-states obtaining at the two workplaces was shown by their thoughts for achievement. The employees at the BCCL, both managers and workers, tended to show some concern for personal excellence in work and in life. Such a concern, as stated above, was more pronounced in workers who tended to think quite substantially about better quality of work and life for themselves as a social group. This was not the case at the RSP where achievement related thoughts, on the whole, were comparatively weak.

The workforce at the BCCL, as stated above, was gripped by a sense of insecurity and personal powerlessness. They seemed to be still under the impact of coercive, dehumanizing conditions of work. They were afraid of musclemen and money-lenders who continued to operate in the coalfields even after nationalization. Such conditions did not exist at the RSP where the employees enjoyed facilities of a good township and other such welfare amenities. They, therefore, felt secured and were not afflicted by feelings of helplessness and apprehension.

Conditions of Work and Values

The value system is not inborn but is acquired under social conditions. It is a learned organization of values and beliefs which helps individuals choose between the given alternatives. The higher the order of significance attached to a given value, the more likely that the value will be activated into action, i.e. behaviour (Kluckhohn and Strodbeck, 1961). Values are preferred modes of orientation, as suggested by Oommen (1990), to specifiable categories of human experience, which define social preferences and choices and provide vision for future action. The objective as well as subjective conditions obtaining at the two work places, as discussed above, were likely to weaken some attitudes and values, reinforce some other values and promote leaning of new values.

As the social conditions were different at the two workplaces, they were likely to show differences in their organizational and individual value system. Such differences were implicit in the employees' perceptions, group images of each other, in need-states and in their socio-political outlook. Such obtained data were subjected to indepth analyses in order to cull out the relevant information.

A multiple regression analysis of the variance in the individual need-states as well as the variance in work-satisfaction and socio-political outlook revealed several important elements of value systems at the two workplaces. Some important conceptual findings of such analyses are briefly described below.

Values Implied in work Satisfaction and Socio-political Outlook

The overall degree of work satisfaction, as discussed in Chapters 4 and 5, was obtained on the basis of the perceived degree of influence and autonomy, availability of amenities, nature of supervisory behaviour and the perceived nature of job. These perceived work dimensions indicated the importance attached by the individual to values of autonomy, comforts and convenience, respectful and trustful human relations, and challenges at the workplace.

Authoritarian (v. democratic) outlook was composed of misanthropy (v. faith in people), sense of political powerlessness (v. snese of political efficacy) and conservative traditional beliefs (v. liberal social outlook). In the positive direction, as shown in Table 6.2, faith in people indicates social value of equality (believing that the rich and the poor in a society are not created by God); value of *self-action* in causing events rather than pre-determination of events by some supernatural power (i.e. believing that death and birth are not in the hands of God and that family planning, i.e. individual's own action in this regard, cannot succeed in controlling population); *tolerance* of others (i.e. believing that good and bad persons can live together. Similarly people of different religions can also live together); *trust* in others (i.e. believing that social interactions would not lead to hatred of each other) and *faith in democratic process* (i.e. believing that elections are important and things can be changed and improved).

A liberal social outlook indicated belief in the goodness of human nature and importance of individual initiative in improving social/national functioning. Similarly, the sense of political efficacy shows value for and belief in citizens sense of competence in

TABLE 6.2 : Democratic and authoritarian outlook

Democratic Outlook	Beliefs	Authoritarian Outlook
All people are born equal	Equality	God has created them unequal
Self-action can cause events to happen	Cause of events	Events are caused by some supernatural power
People of different religions can live together	Tolerance of differences	Different people cannot live together
People are good by nature	Human nature	They are wicked by nature
Citizens are competent to influence political functioning	Efficacy	They are not capable of influencing political functioning
Elections can change governments and improve things	Faith in democratic processes	Elections do not change anything

influencing and changing political sunctioning suggesting commitment to democratic functioning and self-efficacy. Taken together, these constitute a democratic value system giving importance to democracy, secularism, equality, individual autonomy and freedom. (Such beliefs and values are summarized in Table 6.2)

Sense of political normlessness indicated dissatisfaction with the flouting of democratic norms in the functioning of the polity and civic matters, showing interest in democratic functioning. Such dissatisfaction, though an indication of alienation, was functional and, therefore, positive for civic functioning and showed value for norms and standards of excellence in government and political performance.

Learning and Reinforcement of Values and Needs: Role of Workplace Socialization

Our findings indicated the importance of exposure to urban life in the articulation of values and needs at the workplace. For instance, such employees as those born and brought up in urban areas, i.e. those exposed more to urban experience and child-rearing, showed a higher need for personal achievement than others, particularly those born and brought up in rural areas. On the othere hand, the latter, particularly workers, tended to show a greater need for social achievement as well as for social achievement oriented influence.

Educational socialization emerged as another significant factor in some of the needs. For instance, the higher the education of an employee, the greater was his need for influence. This was also true for the need for social achievement oriented influence. Interestingly, education did not emerge as important for the need for personal achievement. Our educational system, particularly higher education, did not seem to inculcate a desire for pursuit of excellence. On the other hand, it seemed more definitive in promoting a craving for influence and control at the workplace. Such findings confirmed the well known fact that education widened the gap between elites and masses with the former conditioned to influence and control those with no or low education.

The workplace experience emerged as the most important factor in learning and reinforcement of values and needs. A sense of work satisfaction or dissatisfaction and the resultant sense of deprivation appeared as a crucial factor in this respect. As Kohn and his associates have shown in a series of studies (1969, 1973, 1983), the nature of the job and its complexity and opportunity available for self-direction at the workplace were vary significantly related to the workers' sense of self-esteem. In other words, occupational conditions of work greatly affected the values and psychological functioning of the workers. Such conditions of work, including the degree of supervision, degree of routinization and, more importantly, substantive complexity of the job, either enabled or inhibited the worker's sense of self-direction. Thus, challenging and stimulating work environment or otherwise greatly affected an individual's values and needs.

Sense of Deprivation, Collectivism and New Values

Such research also suggested that while home and school socialization were important, socialization at the workplace was more important and powerful in this respect. The objective conditions of work were, therefore, vary important for understanding the content of values and needs obtaining at the workplace.

Value System and Need-States

The need for influence, which was rather all-pervading at the RSP, was significantly associated with the domocratic value system, while the opposite was the case at the BCCL where the same need was accompanied by an authoritarian value system. Such value differences seemed to characterize the behaviour of both, managers and workers, at these two places. This was further confirmed by the value correlates of need for social achievement and other needs.

Traditonal Values of Managers at BCCL

The managers at the BCCL, particularly the senior management team, as mentioned above, showed a high need for "dominative" influence. This was confirmed in the workers and managers' analyses of the organization. The managers seemed to attach greater importance to traditional values with lack of faith in the people and lack of respect and trust for each other. They tended to subscribe to beliefs in a supernatural power, fatalistic pre-determination of events and weak moral character as the cause of national problems. They showed attachment to hierarchy and status oriented domination which are integral parts of the traditional value system. The higher the organizational level the higher was the manager's need for influence and also the higher was his attachment to the traditional beliefs and values. Such a value system activated authoritarian behaviour, which greatly contributed to creating an all-round sense of deprivation and resentment in the orgtanization. Such behaviour also contributed to a sense of insecurity among the workers, supervisors and junior managers and to evolving a fear-ridden, mistrustful, fault-finding climate at the workplace.

Democratic Value System at RSP

The managers at the RSP, however, showed a need for "integrative" influence. This was informed by a modern value system. They seemed to attach importance to social equality, respect for others, faith in human nature, trust of others, initiative, self-determination of events and faith in democratic processes.

Historical Differences in Learning Opportunity

Such differences in the managers' value system at the two workplaces were remarkable as all of them came more or less from the same social strata. The experiential background at the BCCL was linked to the erstwhile private coal-mines where managers worked more or less as instruments of ruthless exploitation. There, the organization of labour process was based on mistrust and lack of faith in people. Under the domination of their owners, they used hierarchy, status and coercion for controlling the labour. The BCCL managers seemed to have inherited such work values.

The RSP, on the other hand, was free from such background. It was a new and modern plant based on high technology. It also gave greater importance to the well-being of the workforce including care for housing, education, sanitation, health, etc. Thus, there was greater people-orientation at the RSP which in turn weakened the traditional beliefs among the managers and contributed to promoting a more democratic value system. It was thus interesting to find that different conditions of work gave significantly different value content and direction to the need for influence at the two workplaces.

Organization of Labour Process and Values and Need-States

Did the values and need-states obtaining at the two workplaces vary because of the difference in the organization of their labour process? As stated above, the BCCL inherited a very competitive and nakedly profit-seeking system from the erstwhile privately owned coal-mines. Some such practices and behaviour tended to continue at the new undertaking. The RSP, on the other hand, was organized on the basis of modern technology along with comparatively more modern management.

Such differences in the organization of labour process tend to stimulate different organizational behaviour, even at the same workplace, at two points of time. This was found by Burawoy (1979) with regard to a machine-shop of an engine division of a U.S.-based company. In 1944, the machine-shop was a part, as Burawoy has described, of a competitive capitalist sector where control of the labour process was achieved through firing, wage cuts, close supervision, etc. In 1974, the same machine-shop became a part of a transnational corporation which was marked by decent wages and what Burawoy described as "internal labour market" where preference was given to the employees for filling vacancies and "internal state" with collective bargaining, grievance handling procedure and routine labour management relations. The earlier coercive feature of cutting wages and intensified labour process was now achieved through a technological change and specialisation. The internal labour market tended to generate competitive individualism and the internal state protected the workers from arbitrary authority and gave them some autonomy. Burawoy described the 1944 organization as "despotic" and the 1974 as "hegemonic".

The BCCL seemed to have acquired a coercive organization of labour process. This was not the case at the RSP where the management tended to rely on the consent of workers. The BCCL was also protected by the same labour laws as the RSP, both being Central Government undertakings. The internal promotion policy as well as grievance handling procedures were available at both the places. The workers at the BCCL, however, perceived much greater coercion and tended to think of their management in strong negative terms. The workers at the RSP felt more positive about their management. They also perceived greater autonomy and participation. The workers there showed a greater sense of competitive individualism as indicated by their demand for greater use of their skills and for better opportunity of career development. On the other hand, the workers as well as some junior-level managers at the BCCL thought much more in terms of a respectful relationship at the workplace. They also showed a greater sense of collectivism for improving their conditions of work.

The findings suggested that there was a greater ideological consent and legitimation of control at the RSP. Although the organization tried to secure labour surplus, it was, as Burawoy has call it (1978), more "obscured". It was not so at the BCCL where the workers not only perceived but openly resented their coercive exploitation. In this sense, the organization of labour process at the RSP was different from the one obtaining at the BCCL which in turn contributed to the inculcation of values and needs at the two workplaces.

Another important difference, as mentioned above, was between the managers and workers' value system and needs, which at the BCCL was not that sharp as at the RSP. For instance, the managers at the BCCL showed greater attachment to authoritarian beliefs and values than the workers who showed an emerging sense of democratic beliefs and values. Such differences were also reflected in their need-states in as much as managers showed a much greater need for influence whereas the workers showed a greater need for social achievement oriented influence. Such a clash of motivation and behaviour was clearly evident in the perceptions and images of the BCCL workers and managers. At the RSP, no such apparent conflicts were perceptible. In fact, both workers and managers showed a strong need for influence accompanied by democratic beliefs and values.

New Sense of Collectivism: Social Efficacy and Emerging Democratic Aspirations

Workers on the whole, along with some dissatisfied engineers and middle managers at both the workplaces, tended to show a substantial need for social achievement. Such employees showed a sense of alienation at the workplace accompanied by feelings of deprivation on account of lack of autonomy, influence, adequate work amenities and meaningful jobs at their respective workplaces. Such employees also showed a sense of political powerlessness, i.e. a belief that "own hehaviour cannot determine the occurrence of the outcomes or reinforcements they seek" (Seeman, 1972 : 46). They probably tended to evaluate and show their discontent with the prevailing political conditions along with dissatisfaction with their conditions of work. They, thus, felt alienated at the workplace, as well as, to some extent, outside it. This was accompanied by a sense of deprivation and aspiration for a better quality of life and work for themselves as a social group. This was indicative of their emerging critical social consciousness.

Such persons seemed to value autonomy, participation, self-defined standards of living and working conditions along with a strong sense of collectivism. They tended to question the traditional values associated with organizational hierarchy and social staus. It was interesting to find that such was the case at both the workplaces in-as-much as their work dissatisfaction was concerned. The findings suggested that a sense of alienation and deprivation at the workplace tended to promote democratic aspirations among the workers. It was particularly discernible at the BCCL where there was also a deeper sense of deprivation. Such a sense of deprivation and discontent seemed to promote resurgence and reinforcement of collectivism.

Discussing issues pertaining to state and society in India, Oommen has suggested that a process of re-sacrilization of primordial ties is taking place partly as a 'quest for community' and partly as a response to the process of marginalization – actual or imaginary – the peripheral communities are threatened with". He further suggests that such a quest "is likely to crystalize more easily among the deprived". As long as the mainstream, i.e. powerful and peripheral communities are weak, a "coercive equilibrium" would exist. He suggests, that, once the cumulative dominance is dispersed, "the tension between the centre and the periphery becomes visible and gets articulated" (Oommen, 1990 : 45).

A similar process seemed to have been taking place at the micro level at the BCCL, not between communities but between the workforce and the management. The "coercive equilibrium" obtaining at the competitite private coal-mines was disturbed by the nationalization. The workers' sense of deprivation and the tension got clearly articulated at the new state undertaking. They were no longer prepared to, unquestioningly, accept the values and practices associated with coercive hierarchy and their subordination. The new social conditions, brought about by the nationalization, facilitated articulation of social values of democracy and equality. The managers, traditionally being part of the dominant group, continued to adhere to the *status quo* related authoritarian beliefs and values. It was interesting to find that the workers tended to assert for better distribution of resources, for better productivity and welfare and for equality of opportunity and autonomy at the workplace.

The emergence of collectivism among the workers at the BCCL as well at the RSP was not a "primordial quest for community". Their quest was for democratic values and for fulfilling their interest as workers. Thus, the release of such collectivism was not primordial but a sense of social efficacy and was democratic in content. It was informaed by new social consciousness including tolerance of all religions and castes and a keen desire for a better quality of life for society.

Individual Assertion for Personal Achievement

Need for influence oriented personal achievement, implying an assertive/actor role for obtaining personal excellence, was found more among the educated and those placed in higher income groups at both the workplaces, i.e. more among the managers placed at a higher level in the organization. Such persons were also satisfied with their influence and autonomy at the workplace. Such individualistic managers valued an assertive and active role for themselves. They were not interested in only personal excellence per se but in asserting and acting on the environment for such personal achievement goals, giving importance to individual initiative, autonomy and excellence. Work-wise, they were influential and seemed integrated at the workplace.

There was, however, a difference in the value system of such managers at the two workplaces. At the RSP, their need for an assertive role for personal excellence was clearly tempered with faith in people and tolerance of others. They attached importance to social equality and mutually respectful and trustful relations. This was not the case at the BCCL were they did not show such a value system although they also did not clearly show traditional and conservative values like those with a high need for influence. It was found much more in managers than workers at the BCCL, who were also more educated, who earned more and enjoyed better housing facilities. At the RSP also, such persons earned more but there was no difference between the managers and workers as far as this need was concerned

The BCCL managers, motivated by the need for assertive and actor role for individual excellence, were yet not ready for democratic values like their conterparts at the RSP. Those, mostly managers, motivated by this need at the BCCL were more self-centred and interested in personal gain, may be at the cost of other people, whereas at the RSP, they clearly showed concern for other people. They also attached a greater value to social equality and tolerance of others. Such persons were, therefore, less likely to be aggressively competitive with each other than those at the BCCL

Collective Assertion for Social Achievement: Sense of Social Efficacy

Persons motivated by the need for social achievement oriented influence showed several important similarities with those motivated by the need for personal achievement oriented influence. However, they also showed certain very important differences. The latter were found more at the higher organizational level, i.e. among the managers, while the former were found more among the lowers levels of the organization. This was the case at both the workplaces. Edcuation-wise, both the groups of employees were relatively more educated than others, particularly so at the RSP. This contrasting picture was sharper at the BCCL, where the managers showed a greater need for personal achievement oriented influence while the workers showed a greater need for social achievement oriented influence, i.e. greater sense of social efficacy. Unlike the former, the latter harboured a strong sense of deprivation at the workplace. They felt alienated and dissatisfied with their degree of influence and autonomy, quality of working conditions as well as with the nature of their job.

The picture was different at the RSP, where those motivated by the need for social achiever ient oriented influence were comparatively younger and expe ienced. They, however, tended to stagnate on their respective jobs. They are found among both managers and workers.

Both, i.e. managers with a need for personal achievement oriented influence and workers with a need for social achievement oriented influence and a sense of social efficacy, attached importance to democratic values with belief in equality, trust and respectful human relations, faith in self-action and in human goodness. However, the former seemed to be more individualistic while the latter were clearly more collectivistic. It was, thus, interesting to note that the upper strata—mostly managers—were individually assertive for personal excellence while the lower level of employees, mostly workers, particularly at the BCCL, tended to be collectively assertive for group/social achievement, at the workplace and in life.

It was clear that a sense of deprivation and alienation at the workplace was an important factor in such differentiating democratically oriented social efficacy. While the managers felt relatively more integrated and contented at the workplace, the workers felt alienated and dissatisfied. Their rural background, occupational and organization status, education, emerging social consiousness, democratic aspirations and values and marginalization at the workplace accompanied by a strong sense of deprivation all seemed to inculcate and reinforce a sense of new collectivity, solidarity and assertion in them. These were important behavioural characteristics of those with a sense of social efficacy. It was particularly so at the BCCL where the system was more coercive and the workers experienced a greater sense of deprivation and resentment.

Pursuit of Collective Excellence including Excellence for Self

Individuals found to value excellence in work and quality of life for the people as a whole, including themselves, showed a high need for personal-cum-social achievement. Such personnel were found to be highly dissatisfied at the BCCL. They showed a strong sense of deprivation because of a low degree of autonomy and influence. They were also not satisfied with their supervisors' behaviour and perceived their jobs as not interesting and challenging. Such persons were found more among the higher income group who were also relatively more educated. Interestingly, such persons also felt politically alienated. They seemed to have a feeling of powerlessness vis-a-vis political decision-making and functioning of the system.

Persons with a similar need orientation, i.e. those wanting social as well as personal achievement, showed a different, almost opposite, picture at the RSP. They were relatively younger and quick promotees. Work-wise, they were satisfied. They were also found at all levels of the organization and not necessarily concentrated among the higher income groups as was the case with the BCCL. Unlike the latter, they felt politically more competent and showed no sense of deprivation on this count.

Emerging Value for Individualism

The workers at the BCCL also seemed to show an emerging value for individualism, particularly autonomy, along with a sense of collectivism and assertion for social achievement. At the BCCL, therefore, socially efficacious workers showed an overlap of individualism and collectivism with a significantly greater need for personal-cum-social achievement. It was interesting that, on the one hand, they tended to collectively resist their coercive organization and, on the other, showed readiness to work hard and improve individual as well as group performance. They talked much more about the need for improving productivity for a better quality of life for society than the workers at the RSP. The workers' mixed response was due to the change in the organization. After their bitter experience at the private mines, they expected the nationalized undertaking to be more democratic and just. They, therefore, welcomed nationalization and gave a positive response to the call for greater productivity.

Their hopes, however, seemed to have been belied. Their factasy for hard work could have been due to internalization at the private mines as well as the positive response to nationalization and their ideological readiness which was not adequately reciprocated by the management.

At the RSP, however, there was a more visible sense of individualism. They showed greater intergration with the organization, hoping for an effective participation, autonomy and better career opportunity for themselves. They were individually more competitive for a better status. Such a desire for better individual careers did not surface at the BCCL, they did, however, talk about better incentives and rewards. This was accompanied by a sense of collective assertion and negative perception of the organization.

The findings tended to suggest that such persons who valued good performance, implying standards of excellence, liked to work under congenial, interesting and challenging work situations. This was the difference between the two workplaces. At the BCCL. They were largely denied such an opportunity and, therefore, felt alienated and deprivated. This was not exactly the case at the RSP where they felt more satisfied. Such a situation promoted a sense of competence at the RSP as well as in the wider society. The conditions of work at the BCCL tended to greatly inhibit autonomy and the value for achievement.

Sense of Security and Survival

There was another significant difference in the subjective conditions at the two workplaces. At the BCCL, workers, and some managers also as stated above, showed a sense of insecurity and apprehension about future. Their imagery, as discussed in Chapter 2, contained an elements of self-doubt and apprehension regarding payment of wages, implementation of assurances, retrenchment, police atrocity, children's education, day-to-day hardships, etc. They were concerned with their own very survival. Their experience of life was bitter. They, therefore, valued the public distribution system and orderly and disciplined behaviour as against lawlessness and musclemanship prevailing in their environment. They also hoped that their sons' education would usher them into a better life. Their rising sense of collectivism and democratic aspirations for a better life have to be understood in such a historical, social and work context. They tended to shift in a psychological space characterized by both conservative moral values and emerging democratic values with an aspiration for a better quality of life.

Many of them had rural and tribal backgrounds which probably taught them the holistic value of submerging personal interest for the sake of collectivity. However, their present sense of collectivism was not the same as the traditional holistic type. Its content was more modern and democratic. They seemed to be fighting a battle for survival, and at the same time valued the democratic system social equality, tolerance of different religions and castes, trust of other people like themselves, and a concern for autonomy and better quality of life. They saw their problems as not personal but common with other people which they could overcome only by uniting with others in collective action.

The workers' experience at the RSP was different as the conditions of their work were different. They did not feel so insecured and there was no such struggle for survival. They seemed to enjoy a somewhat higher level of living and felt respected. Their dominant concern was for more power at the workplace in pursuance with their democratic value system. The objective and historical conditions made a major difference in the subjective conditions at the workplace.

Power Distance: Questioning Hierarchy and Inequality

The difference in the objective and subjective conditions was marked by another important organizational dimension, i.e. what Hofstede (1980) has described as power-distance. Rigid hierarchy and inequality seemed to have been the principles on which most work organizations have been based and designed. Hierarchical workplaces are thus marked by large power differentials at various levels of the organization. As mentioned above, the BCCL management tended to demand conformity which was resented by skilled workers and junior managers. They wanted greater planning, greater autonomy and initiative, greater equality, trust and tolerance at the workplace. They seemed to question the traditional values associated with hierarchy. This showed their growing sense of individualism which is associated with democratic values. However, they also showed militancy for common causes and a sense of collectivism in this regard.

The picture at the RSP was different in this respect also. The workplace there also was organized on the basis of hierarchy. It was, however, not that authoritarian as was the case at the BCCL. Some participatory forums had been introduced here with some success. This had created and enhanced a sense of team spirit and togetherness among the workforce driving them to ask for further weakening of hierarchy and for greater democratization. They were unhappy not because of a rigid hierarchy so much as for want of real participation. They tended to ask for a substantial say in decision-making and in the affairs of the organization.

III. SOCIAL STRUCTURES AND ORGANIZATION-BEHAVIOURS NEEDS AND VALUES AT THE TWO WORKPLACES

Thus, the two case studies, as summarized in Table 6.3, highlighted the importance of objective historical conditions in understanding individual values and needs in work organizations. Subjective conditions obtaining at the BCCL were correlated with the historical background of the new organization. For example, the employees showed a deep sense of insecurity mixed with feelings of helpelessness. Under such an unsecured environment, survival became their most important need. Surviving under such conditions was itself a difficult task. They learnt to doubt their own capacities, and internalized a negative self-image. Such learning was based, as suggested by Elias and Scotson (1965) on a realistic assessment of the power of thieir adversaries but in the process they accepted their exploitation. Such internalization was reflected in their moralistic thoughts about themselves and the society, as revealed in their TAT stories.

Although workers were forced to adjust with the circumstances, they were not happy with such conditions. Contradictions, therefore, emerged in their conditions of life and work. Nationalization provided the greatest boost to the emergence of a new consciousness in the workers. Sharing the same goals and the same feelings, they

TABLE 6.3 : Conditions of Work, Needs— and Dominant Values—Summary

	BCCL	RSP
Objective conditions	Despotic and bureaucratic	Hegemonic and bureaucratic
Subjective conditions	Insecurity; work dissatisfaction primarily due to lack of autonomy, influence and work amentities; deprivation at the workplace	Sense of security; dissatisfied due to lack of reward, career opportunity and effective participation; sense of self-worth/esteem
Workplace climate	Mistrustful, unfriendly, dominative	Trusting; friendly, caring; integrative
Dominant needs of workers	Social efficacy, need for personal-cum-social achievement	Need for influence; social efficacy; high personal-cum-social achievement orientation in some workers
Managers	Need for influence, need for personal achievement oriented influence	Need for influence, very high at the top level, with low achievement orientation; social efficacy at the middle management level
Dominant Values of Workers	Productivity in terms of QOL for society; democratic-collectivism; autonomy, participation	Democratic-collectivism; autonomy; participation
Managers	Personal gain oriented QOL; misanthropic individualism; conservative-social outlook	Liberal social outlook; individualism; democratic-collectivism at middle managers level for QOL and participation

were emboldened to think in terms of collective action in order to improve their conditions of life. They were hard working and desired to improve the situation for themselves. The new organization failed to provide them with adequate work satisfaction. Their sense of deprivation and anxiety about future motivated a new sense of collectivism in them. They became more vigilant and saw the need to cooperate with each other and act collectively to face the situation. They were able to overcome some of their traditional beliefs and to imbibe social values of equality. Such learning was reflected in their need for social achievement and for social achievement oriented influence.

Such findings lent credence to the hypothesis, as mentioned in Chapter 1, that socially conscious and disadvantaged people with a sense of deprivation and some anxiety about future show an urge to improve their condition, i.e. a need for social achievement.

Thoughts of Managers and Workers: Two Sides of the Same Reality

The work climate at the BCCL was very widely perceived as negative. This view was shared by both workers and junior managers. The managers' strong need for influence and for personal achievement oriented influence motivated them to aggressively compete among themselves which further strengthened the coercive work climate in the organization. They were interested mostly in their personal gain and manipulated others for this purpose. The workers, on the other hand, showed a need for social achievement and collective assertion for improving the conditions of life and work. They also showed a new emerging cocial consciousness of equality, trust, tolerance and democratic values. Subjective conditions and consciousness of managers and workers seemed, therefore, to be shaped by two sides of the same objective dialectival reality. On one side the managers showed a strong tendency for dominative influence and authoritarian individualism, and on the other, the workers showed cooperative and democratically oriented collectivism and a sense of social efficacy for resisting such domination and for improving their situation.

Values and Needs Obtaining at RSP

The historical background of the RSP and the perceived work

climate there were quite different. Although the employees were not altogether happy with their climate, they perceived it as more congenial, caring and participatory. Here, the need for influence was accompanied by an integrative leadership style. Unlike the BCCL, the workers at the RSP also showed a strong need for influence. They showed a sense of social efficacy and assertion. Along with workers, the middle managers also showed a need for social achievement oriented influence, i.e. a sense of social efficacy.

There was, therefore, more sharing of goals among workers and managers at the RSP, who probably desired to obtain a greater say and participation at the worklpace. They showed greater faith in people; were more liberal in social outlook; valued a sense of equality and desired to have greater autonomy and influence in the organization. Their sense of collectivism was accompanied by an emerging sense of individualism. They seemed to value autonomy and initiative along with a sense of collectivism.

Thus, with a different, somewhat contrasting, structural background, while the two organizations showed a number of similar needs and values, they also showed several contrasting values and attitudes.

Importance of Structural Variables

The above findings underlined the importance of structural variables in understanding organizational behaviour. The results provided confirmation for the proposition put forth by Mills (1959), while discussing sociological imagination, that social structures affect human consciousness and motivation. Discussing the need for rekindling sociological imagination in social psychology, Gecas (1989) has traced the importance of several classical studies in this connection. For example, Weber's analysis showed the importance of Calvinist theology of personal salvation for economic motivation and the rise of capitalism in western Europe. Durkheim's study of suicide brought out the importance of social structural bases of anomie.

Marx had pointed out the alienating consequences of capitalism on the basis of a socio-historical analysis of the psychological consequences of economic relations. In another related review, Rosenberg (1979) has shown the importance of structural variables for self-esteem. Such variables include an individual's class position, position in the social system. A series of macro studies also showed importance of the workplace, family and peer group in social learning of psychological modernity (Inkeles and Smith, 1974; Inkeles, 1978; 1969). Kohn and his associates have provided insights into the importance of occupational conditions and conditions of work in the psychological functioning of workers (Kohn, 1969; Kohn and Schooler, 1983).

The present research, thus, highlighted the importance of structural variables in studies of motivation and organizational behaviour. It is necessary, therefore, in this connection, that we move from the surface, i.e. the observed behavioural event , to the depth in a "logue duree" manner. "The hour-glass must be turned over both ways from event to structure and then from structure and model back to event" (Braudel, 1988 : 98). It is important, therefore, to use sociological imagination to "understand the larger historical scene in terms of its meaning for the inner life" and to enable us "to grasp history and biography and the relations between the two in society" (Mills, 1959 : 5-6). Such an approach would be helpful in understanding the meaning of the obtained values, as discussed above, and the need-states, as discussed in Chapters 4 and 5.

7

Understanding Organizational Bahaviour

The two case studies reported in Chapters 4 and 5 and discussion of historical conditions, values and needs at the work place in Chapter 6, suggest the need for paying adequate attention to conditions of work and the history of the given organisation in studies of organisational obehaviour. In this chapter,`we discuss some such pertinent issues.

I. ALIENATION, SATISFACTION AND PSYCHOLOGICAL FUNCTIONING

The workers as well as junior-level supervisors and managers at the BCCL, as discussed in Chapter 4, showed a sense of insecurity and helplessness. They perceived their organization as coercive and management practices and behaviour as dominative and unfriendly. They were largely dissatisfied with their work situation in which Iack of autonomy and influence was the most important factor. Other significant factors included lack of responsibility, initiative and challenge on the job, lack of respect (for them) in supervisory practices and behaviour and lack of dignity and comfort in working conditions. Such conditions of work fostered a deep sense of deprivation and frustration in them.

The picture was, at least somewhat, different at the RSP, as discussed in Chapters 5 and 6. There was no such sense of insecurity and helplessness. On the contrary, the workers showed a greater sense of efficacy and self-esteem. They also showed greater faith in the people and a liberal social outlook. The managers were, comparatively, more democratically oriented the workers were more assertive and wanted greater autonomy. They were also more consious of their skills, wanted greater opportunities for skill-utilization and for individual career development. And though the workers were not as clearly dissatisfied as those at the BCCL, they were, nevertheless critical, of the management for lack of interest in promoting and sustaining an effective participation. Influence was their most dominant need.

The two organizations, as discussed in Chapter 6, seemed to play an important role in personality development among their respective members. Their historical conditions also contributed to development/reinforcement of values, needs and attitudes of the people working there. The case studies underlined the need for a historical understanding of organizational behaviour and in designing and implementing interventions in organizations.

Work and Human Development

In developing countries such as India, where the bulk of the people are engaged in agriculture, industrial work has its own distinctness. Jobs with a decent pay and security of employment are not easily available. In a study of aspirations (Mehta, 1979a) rural youth tended to project imagery of lathe and factory work for themselves. With widespread unemployment, factory work is vary attractive and desirable. It may also mark a significant break in their traditional work and life-styles. As research has shown, experience of factory work seems to play a crucial role in inculcating psychological "modernity" in workers (Inkeles and Smith, 1974; Inkeles, 1978).

Personal qualities which tended to develop as a result of factory work experience and which were selected to define modernity in workers included the following: (i) Openness to new experience, (ii) Readiness for social change, (iii) Disposition to hold opinions, awareness of opinions around him, i.e. tolerance of others' opinion, (iv) Information seeking and sharing, (v) Autonomy, i.e belief that man can learn to have control over his environment, confidence in one's ability, (vi) Trust in others, (vii) Valuing technical competence, (viii) Aspirations both educational and vocational, (ix) Respect for others, (x) Understanding of production process (Inkeles and Smith, 1974:19-25).

Participation in Non-factory Autonomous Work

Personal qualities of modernity, such as the above, tend to flourish not because of factory experience alone. Poor tribal people, not much exposed to urbanization and "modernization", showed similar qualities and attitudes as a result of their participation in self-action socio-economic projects (Mehta, 1983; Mehta and Chandra, 1984). They learnt to favour new methods of irrigation and cultivation; qulifications, special knowledge and skills as the basis for appointment to a high office; and hard work, and not grace of god and luck, as an important factor in progress. Many of them also showed an awareness of local events and appreciation for different ways of living. They were keen to learn more and to acquire new skills. One of the remarkable findings of the above participatory development was that women showed such social development, equally, if not more.

The village community (in the above projects) was initially very backward, with almost total illiteracy and fear-ridden dependency on money-lenders and petty government functionaries. The key factor in their subjective development was their participation in decision-making and involvement in organized individual and collective action for their own development. Such participation and activism resulted in their economic, socal as well as psychological empowerment – releasing their self-esteem and efficacy for autonomous work and in social learning of new attitudes, skills, needs and aspirations.

Stimulating and Challenging Environment

Inkeles argued that factory was a school in modernity. Although, it showed a strong linkage with exposure to urban living, there was no evidence that urban experience, as such, was the determinant of modernity. Education showed highly significant correlations with modenity in all countries. However, urban schools were not necessarily more modernized than rural schools. It was concluded that an effective stimulating environment in adulthood can do a great deal to compensate for the slow start. The same limited amount of village schooling can have different personal consequences when it is linked to adult engagement in the urban industrial millieu rather than being followed by work in traditional village agriculture (Inkeles and Smith, 1974: 247).

The people in the above mentioned participatory projects, as people in several similar grassroot level social action projects (Mehta, 1994) organized themselves and initiatied several innovative activities in order to solve some of their pressing problems. They, thus, created a challenging environment and a process of social learning for themselves. By acting on the objective socio-economic reality, they enhanced their subjective development, which in turn helped them, in a way, to transform their world. Their participation and experience, thus, worked for them as a school of social development and psychological empowerment.

Conditions of Work

The nature of work experience, not only at an organized place like a work organization, but also in a rural setting, thus, emerges as a crucial factor in shaping members' personality and their consciousness. As Inkeles showed by his studies of factory work, "it is not consciousness of men that determines their existence but on the contrary, it is their social existence that determines their consciousness" (Inkeless and Smith, 1974: 11). His studies (Inkeles, 1969, 1978) brought out the cognitive consequences of various institutional and organizational contexts – at the societal level such as family and peer groups and at the workplace. His work particularly suggested the importance of workplace in learning and reinforcement of democratic values.

At the micro level, as our findings discussed in Chapter 6 showed, and as Kohn and his associates (1969, 1973, 1983) have reported, occupational conditions of work greatly affect the values and psychological functioning of workers, particularly their sense of self-direction and self-esteem. Such long term studies confirm the importance of work environment and autonomy in development of a creative and flexible mind. Such findings from the workplace are congruent with Piaget's theory of mind which stresses the importance of challenging and stimulating environment. Such studies also show the value of the hypothesis put forth by Swanson (1974) that reflective intelligence was more likely to develop in families which institutionalize and encourage diverse points of view in decision-making. As Khandwalla (1987) has argued, people's productive potential could be released only by inculcating and allowing different points of view, and by promoting creativity and innovativeness at the workplace. Such accumulated body of knowledge firmly establishes the importance of freedom of opinion and enriched environment at the workplace in development projects and in society in general for members' human development.

II. WORK STRUCTURES, SATISFACTION AND ALIENATION

Our findings, as reported in Chapters 4 and 5 and discussed in Chapter 6, also suggest the importance of structural variables in explaining the sense of dissatisfaction and alienation at the workplace. Over the years, a large number of studies (Likert, 1961; Argyris, 1964; Blauner, 1964) have shown that satisfaction and conflict at the workplace are linked to its structure and control mechanism. Decentralized and informal structure, where surveillance is infrequent and enforcement mild, is conducive to higher satisfaction and lower conflict. Alternatively, a mechanistic structure alienates the employees. Under such a situation, group members may feel powerless and, as a consequence, will not experience psychological success associated with their own goals and objectives (White, 1959; de Charms, 1968). Rigid formalization gives the message that the participants are unable to think for themselves leading to low satisfaction and a climate of indignation. Such was the case with the rigid structures and the organizational climate prevailing at the BCCL, as discussed in Chapter 4.

It was Karl Marx who first presented the concept of work-alienation and self-estrangement (Marx 1844/1974). Discussing the labour process in industry, he said, "it is true that labour produces for the rich wonderful things, but for the worker, it produces privation. It produces palaces but for the worker, hovels. It produces intelligence but for the worker, stupidity and cretinism" (p. 65). "Conditions of work and production structures not only create a sense of dissatisfaction but may also affect workers' mental development. They perceive their own labour as external to them, which does not develop freely his physical and mental energy but mortifies his body and ruins his mind" (p. 66).

The 'Forced' Labour and Self-Esteem

Excessive control and surveillance under an "alien" ownership of labour promotes a feeling in the worker that "his labour is not voluntary but coerced, it is *forced* labour" (Marx, 1974; 66; emphasis in the original). Under such a labour process organization, the worker tends to lose his individuality. Instead of affirming himself, he denies his self. His own labour does not belong to him but to some "alien" force. "The worker's activity," as Marx says, "is not spontaneous activity. It belongs to another; it is loss of his self" (1974: 66).

The "alienated" worker is not only a dissatisfied worker, but he feels he is a slave at the workplace. "If he treats his own activity as unfree activity, then he treats it as an activity performed in the service, under the domination, coercion and yoke of another person" (1974 : 71).

Thus, the workplace, such as factory, represents new social conditions, under which individuals develop a new consciousness and learn "modern" values as against traditional values. However, structures at the same workplace, where "modern" manufacturing takes place, may cripple the workers' mental development, sense of self–direction and self-esteem by restricting their freedom and autonomy. The routine, repetitive and simple nature of job and coervice controls may thwart the workers' human development. In a comprehensive study on work in America, O,Toole (1973) found autonomy at the workplace as the key variable in work satisfaction and development. Reviewing more than 100 studies, he came to the conclusion that, "what the workers want most is to become masters of their immediate environments and to feel that their work and they themselves are important–the twin ingredients of self-esteem" (1973 : 13).

It was found that workers with jobs high on variety, autonomy and use of skills were found to be low on measures of both–political and personal alienation (O'Toole, 1973 : 31). In the present case study, Rourkela workers, as dicussed in Chapter 6, could be placed higher as compared to the BCCL workers on the nature-of-job scale. In the organizational hierarchy, unskilled workers were placed at the bottom. Such workers were less educated and earned less. They also showed a greater sense of powerlessness. Such workers tended to lose their skills as well as self-esteem.

Middle Management Alienation

It is not only the workers who are adversely affected by unsatisfactory conditions of work and nature of their job. There is now growing evidence of middle management alienation in Indian work organizations (Mehta, 1976c; Sharma, 1990, 1991; Ramaswamy, 1985; Iyer, 1991). Such sudies show that personnel and reward policy, lack of autonomy and participation, authoritarian top management, changing socio-economic conditions and some other such factors contribute to their alienation from the organization. The lower levels of management, particularly engineers and other technical personnel, are likely to be affected more by such conditions. Such conditions tend to develop a high sense of relative deprivation among middle managers which in turn contributes to the rising trend of officers' activism (Sharma, 1990, 1991). Changing values also contribute to such a sense of deprivation and growing unionization among the white–collar employees. Socially liberal and democratically oriented "officers" tend to show lower job satisfaction. They tend to feel more aggrieved and frustrated by the nature of their work and the degree of influence and autonomy available to them at the workplace (Mehta, 1976; Sharma, 1991). Similar tendencies were observed in the present case studies, as discussed in Chapters 4 and 5.

Alienation of middle managers and of technical officers/experts has been widely observed elsewhere in the world. Middle managers were once considered the bulwark of company loyality in the USA. During the 1960s and 1970s, one in every three of them showed willingness to join union. It was found that "the inherent quality of the job of middle managers was the prime source of their dissatisfaction" (O' Toole, 1973 : 40).

Similar alienation was observed and documented in the erstwhile USSR. Review of studies of work organization in the former USSR highlighted the crucial link between democracy and workplace control (Ray and Sundaram, 1990 : 1599). "Authoritarian" controls over the workplace and repetitive nature of jobs which denied challenge and autonomy led to a "negative control" on the part of workers as well as their managers. It was thus interesting that managers and officers tended to join the workers in exercising such negative control resulting in wastage and poor quality of production with far-reaching implications for the functioning of production as well as society (Smith, 1983; Arnòt, 1988).

In the present case studies, the middle managers at the BCCL, as reported in Chapter 4, also showed (along with the workers) a sense of insecurity and helplessness. They were highly critical of both their supervisors and top management, on the one hand, and the workers, on the other. They were particularly angry with the workers' representatives and leaders, who seemed to exercise greater power in the organization. Such alienated and powerless managers, as found in the BCCL case study (Chapter 4), and in the USA and the erstwhile USSR, as mentioned above, tend to bureaucratize the organization and frustrate reforms and changes at the workplace.

Such managers tend to establish a culture and cycle consisting of inflexible rules and procedures resulting in discontent and anger among both managers and workers. Such a situation is detrimental to both the organization and the employees. A general feeling of obsolescence also, sometimes, overtakes middle managers. Such feelings are often related to technical and managerial competence and an inability to cope with the changing situation at the workplace. Sometimes, older managers cannot cope with the changing values and technical competence of their younger subordinates.

Expanding work organizations are usually marked by induction of young workers, engineers and other technical personnel. With new products and younger personnel, an organization's internal dynamics begins to change. Sections of middle managers find it difficult to cope with such changing situations. They continue to behave in their old, historically learnt ways, with disastrous consequences for both productivity and people's welfare as was found in a case study of multinational company (Iyer, 1991). A similar situation seemed to obtain at the BCCL, as reported in Chapter 4. With the coming of nationalization, workers acquired new democratic aspirations and values. The middle managers, conditioned to feudal and authoritarian practices, found it difficult to cope with the changed situation and with the new goals set before them, resulting in a feeling of frustration and insecurity in them as well as workers and in the release of dysfunctional elements in the functioning of the organization.

Contradictions at the Workplace

The social costs of managerial obsolescence (O'Toole, 1973 : 42) can be seen in Tayloristic or other outmoded philosophy that these managers instil through companies. Such "authoritarian" controls, inherent in design of work based on one-man-one-job, and the concept of tight supervision and control (Taylor, 1911) inevitably result in authoritarian practices which directly contradict emerging democratic aspirations for greater autonomy and influence at the workplace. Thus, the gap and conflict between the changing consciousness among the people at the workplace and outmoded design of work with coercive controls greatly contribute to workers and middle 'managers' sense of deprivation, alienation and dissatisfaction.

Interaction of Needs and Values

Understanding of values held by members along with employee needs has now been attracting greater attention in studies of organizational behaviour. For example, commitment to quality and service has emerged among the most important values in the culture of successful contemporary enterprieses. Where the choice is between quality and good service, on the one hand, and short-term profits, on the other, the former is the consistent choice. There is also now an increasing stress on values of creativity through people. Respect of the individual is a central belief in such values (Peters and Waterman, 1982).

As mentioned above, conditions of work tend to contribute to social learning and reinforcement of values at the workplace. As our two case studies show (Chapters 4 and 5), there is an intimate relationship between the conditions of work and learning of values at the workplace. There was a significant and qualitative difference in the value system operating in the two work organizations. In one, influential persons, particularly the managers, showed lack of faith in people and authoritarian beliefs and values. They tended to use coercive methods of control. On the other hand, similarly placed persons in the other organization showed greater faith in people and democratic beliefs and values. They were more participative and friendly. Interestingly, such key persons, at both the workplaces, tended to show a strong need for influence. However, this need assumed a qualitatively different meaning in the context of and in combination with their value system. Thus, in one case, it was the need for "authoritarian" or dominative influence and in the other, it was the need for "democratic" or integrative influence. If one were to go by the information on needs alone, it could result in a very misleading inference about the organizational behaviour. Such a comprehensive understanding is, thus, important not only for empirical research, but also, probably more, for proper interventions in organzations such as organization development, etc.

Reciprocal Behaviour: Two Sides of the same Reality

Managers and workers, as members of the same work organization, work under the same objective conditions which may, however, affect them in different ways. Many a time, as argued by Hill (1981), the interests of these two groups are structurally opposite to each other. With improved education, technical skills and social consciousness, workers tend to become more assertive, as found in our two case studies and in studies elsewhere in the world. For example, workers were found to challenge the established authority of management in several European countries (EEC, 1975).

Managers may or may not be able to accept and cope with such a changing reality and workers' rising expectations, as briefly stated above. In such a situation, as reported in the case study in Chapter 4, they may show a strong need for "authoritarian" influence and the need for influence oriented personal achievement. On the other hand, the same social reality tends to reinforce democratic values and the need for social achievement oriented influence among the workers. In such cases, managers' and workers' needs and values may reflect two sides of the same objective reality. As managers resort to coercive mothods of control and the related manipulative practices, the workers respond by collectively resisting them. They (managers and workers) thus tend to show reciprocal behaviours. It is, therefore, imperative that we study the needs and values of both workers and managers in order to correctly comprehend the total reality and to understand both the objective and subjective dimensions of such a reality.

Leadership Styles and Influence Strategies

Our two case studies suggested yet another important aspect of organizational behaviour, namely, the nature of influence and leadership styles. For instance, some of the senior and top managers, relatively younger than their subordinates, tended to be "actors" and "pushers". They may or may not give importance to excellence in their own performance but would like to influence the organization for targets and such other goals. Some others among the top and senior manager, may behave as "get-goers" for quality. They show a strong need to influence the organization for excellence. They would rather promote competition for excellence within and between departments, which may contribute to inter-personal and inter-departmental conflicts, on the one hand, and the achievement-oriented climate in the organization, on the other. There may yet be another kind of leaders at the workplace, more likely to be found among the middle managers, engineers and other professionals. They may be described as socially efficacious leaders who may assert for collective achievement and common gains. They may be able to motivate workers and others for common achievement goals, such as better conditions of work and quality of life. They may, therefore, exercise considerable influence at the workplace. The nature of leadership and influence may, therefore, vary among the various levels at the work organization, with varying implications for its functioning.

The leaders may also vary in their leadership styles commensurate with their dominant needs and values. Some influential members, particularly managers and union leaders, may exercise a "dominative" influence strategy and others may use "integrative" or democratically oriented influence strategy as discussed above. Such leadership styles and influence strategies play a very significant role in promoting and reinforcing an organizational climate and various management practices at the workplace. Such styles and strategies could either facilitate or inhibit autonomy and the related subjective development among other members of the organization.

Understanding of organizational behaviour thus requires understanding of conditions of work, structures and policies operating at the organization and the historical experience of the members. Such an understanding is particularly important for getting at the meaning of psychological needs and values of managers, workers and others and of social interactions at the workplace.

8

Energizing Workplace for Human Development

Some Suggested Areas for Interventions

THE PRESENT research is not designed to suggest and discuss an elaborate design of interventions for improving the functioning of the workplace. However, our findings do suggest some important areas in which suitably designed interventions are required. Some such areas are briefly mentioned below:

I. DEMOCRATIZATION AND WORK REDESIGN

A brief review of research in Chapter 7 suggests the importance of structures and policies at the workplace. Studies show the importance of control, supervision, authority, flexibility in jobs, autonomy and challenging work environment for human development. Work redesign and similar movements for humanizing the workplace are important for obtaining such crucial human goals as development of mind.

Efforts at democratizing the workplace by restructuring organizations are informed by the need for joint work-design in which knowledge and expertise could be de-elitized (Thorsurd, 1972). His studies and several others (O'Toole, 1973; Rice, 1958; Herbst, 1962; Trist, 1976; Kanawaty et al, 1981; Emery and Thorsrud,

1970; Maccoby, 1975; De, 1984) show some promising results as reflected in a reduction in the rigid rules and regulations and in absenteeism in an increased work satisfaction and a positive change in the workers' attitudes and motivation.

Redesign of work shows a positive impact on the employees' work outside the plant. "It has been long observed that workers in dull and 'routine' jobs seldom participate in community affairs, but it is the first instance where it has been shown that redesign of work can have positive effects on community participation (O'Toole, 1973: 99). As discussed elsewhere (Mehta, 1992) work democratization and political democratization are significantly interrelated.

Need for Security and Income

As a part of improving the workplace, job enrichment methods have been tried out for challenging workers for higher productivity. Such enrichment may not always be welcomed by workers (Simonds and Orif, 1975). It was found that the majority of the enriched jobs to which workers were moved were also the higher paid jobs. Where the jobs shift did not provide a pay increase, the workers tended to prefer the less enriched but higher paid job. In the context of such economic development, where the real wages fall and unemployment and cost of living increase, enriched jobs unaccompanied by an increased income are not likely to be favoured. Workers and also managers may look at such experiments with mistrust and perceive them as a mechanism for extracting more work without adequate compensation. In such cases, job redesign and job enrichment may prove to be counter-productive. Workers (and other members of the work organization) have an overpowering need for security and income.

Importance of Work and Social Structures

As part of their strategy to improve job challenges, the American business has been called upon to focus attention on developing a positive institutional culture, as a dominant force for a forward looking organization (Ouchi, 1981 : 71-72). It recognises the importance of structures and systems but seems to give greater importance to culture, based on collective decision-making, individual responsibility, integrated evaluation and promotion of and concern for people. While such institutional culture is very important, experience in India shows that this will not last long without appropriate structural changes (Roy, 1969). In the context of education, for example, it was found that motivation of teachers and pupils and an integrated and challenging instructional culture were very productive in the short run. However, the effects of such changes began to taper off in two to three years' time. The traditional institutional structure remained intact which inhibited and weakened the effects of motivation development (Mehta , 1976, 1989a: 16-42).

A similar situation was found in the case of some government departments (Chaturvedi, 1988). Inter-departmental dynamics made it difficult for the public officials to cooperate. Each of them was supposed to serve the same people with their respective inputs. The administrative system, however, gave greater importance to individual departmental functioning and rewarded their little goals. Such a system, therefore, came in the way of inter-departmental team functioning by forging linkages and mutual cooperation. The same was observed with regard to a modern process plant. Here, despite a series of managment and motivation development programmes, the various departments continued to show entrenched negative images of each other. They found it difficult to cooperate as the reward and promotion policy of the company favoured inter-departmental competition (Mehta, 1989 a : 85-104).

In the context of European countries, it has been argued that the pursuit of goals like improvement in the quality of life requires the differential distribution of power and influence in organizations, subject to different types of industrial democracy systems (IRG, 1981). With improved education, workers tend to be more assertive and to challenge the established authority of the management. The company structure, therefore, required change with a more "broader democratic base" (EEC, 1975). Our case studies (Chapers 4 and 5) also showed the changing profile of the workforce. They desired greater freedom and autnomy and better work environment at the workplace. Autonomy and challenging work could, however, last only in an appropriate work-redesign along with necessary restructuring of the organization, including labour process, reward policies and management practices.

II. EMPOWERMENT : CAPABILITY DEVELOPMENT

Human resource development has been getting increasing attention in India in industry as well as elsewere. In this connection, studies suggest the following (i) Freedom to project different points of view, as mentioned in Chapter 7, helps members develop reflective intelligence. Such capability in turn helps them to critically examine various matters which facilitate release of their creativity; (ii) Sometimes, there is a tendency to blame the ordinary workers for lack of skills, motivation, etc. Such a tendency is like blaming the victim (Ryan, 1976).

Most often, environmental conditions and conditions of work contribute to their disempowerment including the loss of their skills and motivation. It is, therefore, necessary to devote attention to developing appropriate enabling conditions at the workplace for empowering the members, for development of their skills, motivation an involvement.

Autonomous Action and Empowerment

There is now a growing body of knowledge about the processes and inputs for people's empowerment. Studies show that their involvement in initiating self-action and their participation in such projects facilitate their human development and in improving their quality of life (Mehta, 1983; Chandra and Mehta, 1984; Agashe, 1992; DGSM, 1982; Behera, 1992; De Silva *et al*, 1979; Mitra, 1992; Wiganaraja, 1989). In such autonomous projects, people take initiative for acquiring literacy, voluntary prohibition, wells and irrigation, primary education, vocational training, social and political awareness and for fighting against money-lenders and corrupt public officials. A review of several such participatory projects in different parts of the world (Rahman, 1987; Wiganaraja, 1989) shows that people are not only able to improve their skills and access to productive resources but they also succeed in enhancing dignity and status of their labour. They, thus, move away from being pawns in the hands of their superiors and dominators to becoming actors in improving and managing their lives (Mehta, 1994).

Participation and Empowerment

Conger and Kanungo (1988) have suggested a multi-stage model from promoting empowerment of people at the workplace. Their suggested interventions include an analysis of the conditions leading to a sense of powerlessness; implementation of suitable managerial strategies; information-sharing with subordinates for enhancing their self-efficacy; providing subordinates with empowering experience such as strengthening their personal efficacy; and activization of behaviours like initiative and persistence for accomplishing basic objectives. As our case studies show (Chapters 4 and 5), it is important to pay attention to historical experience for understanding organizational behaviour. As experience of participatory projects shows, it is not only sharing of information but their active participation in self-initiated programmes that contributes to their empowerment. In this sense, participation and empowerment are very important for human development (UNDP, 1993) where both objective and subjective conditions interact for promoting the well-being and happiness in life as well as in work.

Influence, Autonomy and Activism

As our case studies show, there are important contextual factors which contribute to lowering of self-efficacy at the workplace as well as elsewhere. These include organizational factors like competitive processes, bureaucratic work culture, dominative supervisory styles, reward system and job design including nature of job. Similar factors have been identified in other studies of employees' sense of powerlessness (Conger and Kanungo, 1988). One factor which has consistently emerged as important in this connection is the availability of influence and autonomy at the workplace as well as in development and other social situations. Organisations which deny members influence and autonomy heighten a sense of powerlessness among them. Initial success experience with autonomous work help prepare them for subsequent complex tasks. They, thus, become more capable and, therefore, more empowered. As Anand and Sen have stated, capability development is the core of human development (UNDP, 1993 : 104-112). As members participate, gain success experience, enhance personal and social efficacy and acquire new skills, they also learn a new sense of hopefulness (Zimmermann,

1990).

There are now several examples in India, where empowered employees have taken things in their hands, in order to cope with and solve problems. For instance, in one sick plant engaged in the manufacture of engineering equipment. The management was unwilling to restore the sick factory while the workers were keen to begin production. The workers then took initiative in this case and prepared an action plan to achieve a growth rate of 10 per cent. They succeeded in putting the plant in proper operation and in getting profit in the first year of its operation itself (Srinivas, 1989).

Thus, while human development and people-empowerment are important as terminal values and ends in themselves, these are also powerful means of dealing with industrial sickness, fighting absenteeism and stoppages and of releasing creativity of people for greater productivity.

III. QUALITY OF LIFE FOR ALL : PROMOTING SENSE OF COOPERATION

An increasing body of empirical as well as theoretical research shows that common people possess adequate internal resources for obtaining good life for themselves as well as for society. Competitive profit-seeking corporations, high-powered advertising and various other such institutions tend to vitiate the natural human tendency to cooperate with each other for achieving such social goals. As pointed by Mead (1934), and reviewed later by Turner (1988), people have a fundamental need for cooperation.

As discussed in Chapter 7, structural conditions that fail to meet such needs create pathologies at the workplace. Such a violation of basic needs as Turner has argued (1988) raise important ethical questions about retardation of human potential by creating a dysfunctional competitive situation. As Fitzgerald (1986) has argued, some of the motivational theories did not work at the workplace because they tended to underestimate the seriousness of the problem. Some of the management techniques, in this respect, tend to increase hostility and indifference and distrupt work-group solidarities. Some such efforts are based on pleasure-pain and input-output calculations. In such a situation, a worker tends to ask "what is in it for me". The competitive attitudes of the managers and supervisors create the situation of one-against-all resulting in a self-perpetuating cycle of suspicion, blaming and reprisal.

Such a situation, further buttressed by all-pervading and utopian advertising as Reich (1970) had discussed, encourages self-aggrandisement, populist hedonism and compulsive accumulation. Under such competitive and individualistic situations, as Bell (1976) has shown, people find it difficult to think of collective solutions and of readily accepting the idea of public interest as against private gain. Our case studies (Chapters 4 and 5), however, suggested rather a strong sense of collectivism motivated by the need for social achievement oriented influence among workers and other members of the organization. The same need is reflected in the workers' takeover of sick plants as mentioned above. Such challenges motivate members at the workplace to act on the environment for social achievement. Such tasks facilitate the release of "collective creativity" (Khandwalla, 1984 : 30-32).

Such needs, for cooperation, collective action and social achievement could be usefully activated for obtaining readiness for public good, better quality of life for the society, for environment protection and sustainable development and for raising productivity for the benefit of all. "Acting in collaboration with each other beyond the states' reach", as Friedmann (1992 : 70) has argued,"they can work for collective self-improvement". Learning to work together, with each other rather than against each other, is not just important for productivity at the workplace. In fact, it is "one of the essential elements for survival (of human civilization)". It is essential that people develop a "greater sense of cooperation, of community, ability to work together for the common good, not simply for personal aggrandisement" (Bowen, Miller and Rogers, 1979 : 15).

IV. LEADERSHIP DEVELOPMENT AND SOCIAL RESPONSIVENESS

Theory and Practice

The above requirements for improving effectiveness in work organizations, namely, work redesign and democratization, empowering members of the organization, conditions of work for improving quality of life, sense of cooperation and team work, all these and more such goals indicate the importance of promoting social responsiveness in managers and others at the workplace. It is imperative that, managers and may be, union leaders, internalize their responsibility for creating enabling conditions for challenging environment and autonomy in order to promote and sustain human development at the workplace.

It has been argued in various studies of industrial democracy that there is nothng so practical as a good theory. Application of organizational theory and behavioural science to workplace functioning implies matters of national importance. Such issues have to be viewed from societal rather than merely organizational or magagerial points of view (IRG, 1981). Managers and other leading members have, therefore, to be sensitive and responsive to theoretical and practical implications of their policies and practices at the workplace.

The Need for Pluralist Frame of Reference

We have a long tradition of plural thinking in our cultural heritage in India. Various beliefs and points of view, sometimes contradictory to each other, have existed side by side for centuries. In the Western society, people are also taught to tolerate pluralist ideology including respect for different points of view.

However, contrary to such heritage, there is a tendency to impose a "unitary frame of reference' at the workplace. This is particularly true of labour relations. Such an approach needs to be avoided as it has been argued, "conflicts of interest are inevitable in all societies. There are rules for their adjustment, there are no rules for their elimination (Fox, 1973:17). Such conflicts were clearly perceptible in our case studies, particularly the one discussed in Chapter 4. All conflicts at the workplace are not dysfunctional. Many a time, these are "ortho-functional" i.e curative like orthopaedics (Finifter, 1972). Such conflicts could become ortho-functional provided managers are able to view them positively and are socially responsive to the needs of aspirations of the members.

In a comprehensive study in a large number of countries, it was found that the countries which enjoyed greater political and civil liberties also performed the best in terms of the growth in national income per head. They also showed greater improvement in life expectancy at birth and in the infant survival rate (Dasgupta, 1990). The same is true of the workplace. For example, as mentioned in Chapter 7, freedom of opinion has been found as very important in the development of mental faculties and reflective intelligence. Managements, therefore, need to develop adequate sensitivity to such issues and readiness to allow such liberties as this would facilitatate human development and general well-being of the employees and happiness in society in general. In an action research programme, Passmore and Fridlander (1982) showed that there was a significant reduction in work injuries and enhancement of safety and health at the workplace when employees were involved in various ways in problem-solving and decision-making by promoting new working arrangements. Denial of such freedom and involvement, on the other hand, could prove disastrous for the health and mental development of the members. It is here that the managers need to show social and ethical responsiveness to issues associated with such matters.

Life Satisfaction

Life satisfaction and work satisfaction have been found to be inter-related in Indian context (Mehta, 1978), as also has been shown by various studies stated above. Income and amenities at the workplace such as housing, canteen, proper sanitation and drinking water facilities, medical care, amenities for women, environment and safety, etc., have emerged as very significant predictors of life satisfaction. Such objective conditions are also found to be highly correlated with satisfaction with influence and autonomy, trust and support, nature of job, supervisory behaviour, and peer-relations at the workplace. Such subjective factors interact with objective factors at the workplace for promoting general well-being and happiness in life.

Civic Participation

It is clear from both experience and a large number of studies that involvement of people in decision-making at the workplace works as an important means of their civic education and social awareness. People develop aspirations for a better quality of life and readiness to participate in related political and civic matters. Such wider participation, i.e. at the workplace and in civic matters helps develop physical and positive mental health including a sense of efficacy and self-esteem.

Thus, an increasing body of experience and knowledge shows the social responsibility of corporations and work organizations. They also underline the importance of a sense of social responsiveness in managers and policy–makers at the workplace so that they become more sensitive to human needs and to issues pertaining to environment, sustainable development, women, mutual cooperation, and to societal implications of a wider and effective participation of memebrs in various activities and processes at the workplace.

Ethical Issues

As Kanungo has argued, work is inextricably bound with human existence. It is a means of self-development as well as development of society. The content and context of work should, therefore, promote rather than damage human dignity. Every human being has a right of access to and use of resources of nature–common property of humanity. Historical experience confirms the priority of labour over capital which is acquired through work in order that it may serve work in future. Workers, therefore, have certain rights including the right to work whose content and context, including the superior-subordinate relationship, do not treat employees as an "instrument" of production but accord to them their due right as the primary efficient cause of production with the right and duty to take such initiative which one would, if one were self-employed (Kanungo, 1992). Managers, therefore, have the moral obligation to empower his/her subordinates and thereby promote their growth and development. Such responsibility is grounded in human values and morality of work. They need to analyse work norms and conditions to see whether such practices promote productive behaviour, higher job satisfaction, and overall improvement of work life and are consistent with the dignity of the employees as human beings (Kanungo, 1992).

Dominative v. Integrative Leadership Styles

As mentioned in Chapter 7, managers with a high need for dominative/authoritarian influence tend to create an inter-personally aggressive and competetive work climate in their organization. They also tend to use coercive control over work which contributes to developing hostility in the organization. On the other hand, managers with a high need for democratic/integrative influence tend to promote team-work, participation and cooperation at the workplace. Integratively oriented managers also show a higher sense of social responsiveness to democratic values and beliefs and to human needs at the workplace. Suitable interventions are required to develop and sustain socially responsive integrative leadership at the workplace. Such leadership is also important for work redesign, democratization and empowerment.

V. NEED FOR COORDINATED INTERVENTIONS

The above suggested areas of interventions are highly inter-related with overlapping dimensions and practices. There is, therefore, a need for coordinated and comprehensive interventions for a better work design effective organization structures, empowerment of members, curbing the tendency for perosnal gain at the cost of public good, promoting the need for cooperation for improving the quality of life for all, and for fostering socially responsive leadership at the workplace. All such interventions have one common goal, i.e., to empower people at the workplace for general well-being and happiness as well as for improving productivity. Otherwise, as has been repeatedly argued, alienated labour would affect the development of mind and other psychological consequences such as cognitive and affective aspects of personal functioning (Schwalve, 1986).

The Need for Integrated Efforts

It is, therefore, an ethical question, as denial of such opportunities would adversely affect the development of mind and mental health of the employees. Such socially crucial human development goals require integrated efforts as borne out by the functioning of social services like health programmes, housing, employment, education, etc., which shows that one activity alone is unable to make an impact on the poverty syndrome. Workplace reforms are also not very effective when implemented piecemeal. Systematic, well planned and coordinated efforts are required for improving the members' capability and for boosting their morale and sustaining their motivation.

Such coordinated efforts and interventions are likely to facilitate human development at the workplace including development of : (i) Personal and social efficacy and self-esteem, (ii) Liberal social attitudes which could be designated as "psychological modernity", (iii) Faith in people, (iv) Sense of security, (v) Sense of collectivism and cooperation, (vi) Flexible, as against rigid, hierarchy. (vii) Concern for improving the quality of life, safety, working conditions and mutual trust at the workplace for both general well-being and higher productivity.

Workplace as Multi-purpose Institution

Some thinkers (Harman, 1977) have argued in the context of Western civilization, that their survival requires transfiguration of man, his motives and values. Toffler (1980) sees a corporation towards becoming a multi-purpose institution being accountable for its performance, environment, social information and for political, moral as well as economic products. Such a view transforms the workplace into a multipurpose institution which should seek to promote an appropriate human development of its members. The coordinated interventions should, thus, address to such crucial goals.

PART FOUR

Manual for Scoring Stories

As discussed in Part I, a set of six pictures was selected following a series of try-outs and analysis of the obtained stories for eliciting the need for personal achievement, need for social achievement, need for influence and other related needs. Part I also reports research undertaken for developing a system for scoring relevant imageries in the stories.

Based on the above research, a detailed manual was prepared for scoring the obtained TAT (Thematic Apperception Test) stories. Part IV provides this manual for researchers who would like to use the TAT pictures. Three sets of practice stories along with the expert scoring are also provided to facilitate the learning of the scoring system.

APPENDIX I

Analysing Imagination for Motivation

1. Development of Pictorial Cues

2. Content Analysis of Imagery

2.1 Personal Achievement Imagery (PAI)

2.2 Social Achievement Imagery (SAI)

2.3 Influence Imagery (Inf-I)

3. Scoring for Sub-categories

3.1 Personal Action (Ap)

3.2 Social Action (As)

3.3 Anticipated Action (Aa)

3.4 Strength (S+)

3.5 Hope (H)

3.6 Personal and Social Awareness (PSA)

3.7 Vigilance (V)

3.8 Thema (Th)

4. Some Ground Rules

5. Practice Scoring

5.1 Further Rules for Scoring

5.2 Reliability of Scoring

5.3 Individual Needs : Range of Scores

5.4 Specimen Scoring of Stories : Need Profile

1. Development of Pictorial Cues

A series of pictorial cues were tried out on various groups to test their suitability for evoking motive-related imagination. Finally, a set of six pictures (see Appendix III) was selected on the basis of related research data (see Chapters 2 and 3 for details). These pictures have been used in a variety of situations and with a veriety of respondents for research and for training over the past several years. The present scoring manual has, thus, evolved over such experience.

The Ss are given the usual instructions and the pictures presented in the usual way, individually as well as in a group, depending on the situation. Slides can also be used to project pictures on a screen. (A set of pictures and instructions, etc., can be obtained separately.)

The obtained TAT type stories are scored here for thoughts containing three main needs, namely, concern for some standard of excellence in one's own work and/or in living conditions; concern for a standard of excellence in group work and/or in quality of life of society and a desire to assert and act on the given environment, including people's socio-economic conditions and the workplace in order to influence them and/or the ongoing situation. The following criteria are used specifically for analysing the content of a given story for presence of the related imagery.

2. Content Analysis of Imagery

2.1 *Need for Personal Achievement (nPA)*

Concern for some standard of excellence and quality in performance (work) related situations has been identified as need for achievement. The concept has been enlarged here also to include concern for standard of excellence and quality in one's own living conditions. Thus, whenever there is evidence for the presence of such a concern for quality in personal performance (work) and/or for quality of life, the story is scored for personal achievement imagery (PAI). The following criteria are used to identify such imagery in a given story:

(i) *Competition with a standard of excellence*

(a) One of the characters in the story is engaged in some activity where wishing or doing as well or better than others is actually stated as the primary concern; (b) evidence of an emotional concern over goal attianment and/or some intense activities indicating a concern for standard of excellence (the achievement goal itself may not be stated explicitly); (c) evidence of standard of excellence involving self-imposed requirements of good performance.

(ii) *Unique accomplishment*

One of the characters is involved in accomplishing more than a daily task. Inventions, artistic creations and other extra-ordinary accomplishments fulfil this criterion.

(iii) *Long-term involvement*

One of the characters is involved in the attainment of long-term achievement goal: becoming a doctor, a lawyer, a craftsman, are examples of career involvenment which permit the inference of competition with some standard of excellence.

(iv) *Desire for excellence in life*

When any one character in the story shows a concern for improving the quality of one's life indicating a desire for some standard of excellence in life conditions for self and immediate family.

Examples:

(i) Whatever work one may do should be done in a techincal and scientific way;
(ii) The engineer wanted to do his work in a perfect way;
(iii) His son will become a famous doctor;
(iv) He wants to become an engineer; and
(v) He. is dreaming for a *pucca* (strong) house and education for his children.

The story is scored as personal achievement imagery (PAI) when at least one of the above criteria is present in the story.

2.2 *Need for Social Achievement (nSA)*

A story is scored for social achievement imagery (SAI) for the same criteria as mentioned above for personal achievement with one major difference. Here the concern for standard of excellence is expressed in relation to community/group's work and life condition. Thus, when any character in the story shows a concern for success in relation to standard of excellence in some group work/activity or for improvement of quality of group/social/community life, it is scored for SAI. In the case of personal achievement, the goal relates to one's own personal work and life, while in the case of a social achievement, it relates to group work and group/community life.

Examples:

(i) We can improve our lot by increasing production in mines, factories and fields;
(ii) He thinks, by working as a good team, they can improve performance of their department;
(iii) He thinks that his village needs drinking water, good teachers and better housing facility; and
(iv) We are definite that the working and living conditions in this factory need improvement.

2.3 *Need for Influence Imagery (nInf)*

Influence imagery is scored when any one character in the story or the story as a whole shows a desire, overt or covert, for influencing other persons upwards or downwords or an ongoing situation. It is found when there is a desire to assert over other people and/or on a given situation in order to change them. The specific criteria for scoring influence are:

(a) *Actor role*

Whenever a person or a group of persons shows an *actor role* in a given situation. This is shown when someone in the sotry asserts in a given situation by taking initiative, by leading others; when someone in the story as a whole shows a tendency to come to grips with a given problem in order to solve it.

Examples:

(i) Emphasizing this the yound man said he would continue to struggle for his rights;
(ii) We would force them to pay minimum wages;

(iii) The managment is determined to control the problem of absenteeism; and

(iv) There has been a scarcity of supply and disorderly behaviour. The administration has enforced this arrangement and given ration cards to all.

(b) *Help downwards*

When someone with fame, prestige or position gives help/advice or instructions in order to influence and direct thoughts, opinions and behaviour of others downwards.

Examples:

(i) He is discussing with each member of his department to find out the reasons for shortfall in production;

(ii) The father was supervising his son to ensure that he works hard;

(iii) The engineer has come to inspect and he tells the workers to come on time; and

(iv) The leaders are making arrangements for everyone to come to the meeting to discuss their common problems.

(c) *Influence upwards*

When some person or persons in the story try to influence another person or persons in a superior position by questioning, persuading, arguing and/or joining with others in order to influence such persons/situations and/or form associations and carry out activities designed to influence decisions upwards.

Examples:

(i) They have gone in deputation to convince the managment;

(ii) He is trying his best to convince the policeman of his innocence;

(iii) The workers are trying to explain to the shift officer that the accident was caused because the machine was very old; and

(iv) They are tyring to form organization from village to village to seek justice for themselves.

(d) *Counter-action/argument without self-deprecation and fear*

When strong feelings are aroused in a person by arguments, discussions, and/or by forceful actions such as attacks, insults, etc., without any self-deprecation; when counter arguments given/actions are taken to safeguard one's repuation, without fear, dread, apprehension, etc.

Examples:

(i) The worker is angry because the money-lender has cheated;
(ii) The union leaders are giving facts to counter the managements' arguments and the wrong decision;
(iii) He is upset by his supervisor's behaviour and wants to sort it out at the earliest; and
(iv) They are annoyed because of discrimination against their community.

3. Scoring for Sub-categories

In scoring a given story for sub-categories, presence of at least one of the three imageries, i.e. for personal achievement (PAI), social achievement (SAI) and influence(Infl) is first established. Thus, the given story is scored further for sub-categories only when at least one of the three main imageries is present in the story.

Sub-categories

A person with the concerned goals is likely to think and/or act in some way in pursuance of the stated goal. Such an activity could be by the person herself/himself and/or it could be an activity by a group of people. There could also be some activity in anticipation of some problem or difficulty. Persons with such concerns or goals may also think about their strength, assets and resources; they may anticipate, or hope for success in attaining their stated goals.

They may also anticipate difficulties and problems both from within themselves and/or from outside world and show vigilance about such problems. They may also show awareness of causes and/or consequences of various difficulties or problems which confront them and others. Such awareness helps them to plan actions appropriately and to more toward success in their stated goals.

Lastly, all goals may not be equally strong in one's imagination. Some individuals think only of *one goal exclusively* and only this theme appears in their thoughts. Such a single-minded thought about a goal gives added strength to it.

Thus, a story, which qualifies for further scoring, i.e., the one which has been found to have *at least one* of the three main imageries/goals, namely, personal achievement imagery (PAI), social achievement imagery (SAI) and influence imagery (Inf-I), is scored further for sub-categories. Some stories may contain more than one, i.e. two or three imageries at the same time. Such stories are also scored further for sub-categories.

3.1 *Personal Action (Ap)*

Personal activities undertaken in pursuance of some stated goal or for dealing with a problem related to such goal (PAI, SAI, Inf) are to be scored as personal action (Ap). However, not all activities mentioned in the story are to be scored. For example, in the context of voting, counting of votes and such related activities are not to be scored here. On the other hand, a boy is working hard (for some stated achievement goal); he is talking to the manager (for the stated goal) or he will become a member of the credit society (in order to get rid of the money-lender) are examples where Ap is to be scored.

3.2 *Social Action (As)*

Expressions stating collective action, mental or overt, for dealing with stated problems or in pursuance of some stated scorable goals are scored as social action. This is different from personal action where some one person is engaged only himself in some action in pursuance of the stated goal. The emphasis here is on collective or community action, which is different from individual action.

Examples:

- (i) We are forming a credit society to avoid the money-lender;
- (ii) They are taking steps to enrol members in the organization;
- (iii) The committee is meeting to arrive at a collective solution; and
- (iv) They are meeting to discuss ways of improving safety

and productivity.

3.3 *Anticipated Action (Aa)*

Ap and As, i.e. personal and social actions respectively are scored when statements indicate tendencies to act in response to certain problems and situations. Anticipated action takes place in anticipation of some problem or difficulty with a view to dealing with it. This is a pro-active tendency which anticipates some difficulty and, therefore, an advance action is contemplated or taken.

Examples:

- (i) Worried that if he remains sick for long, his son's education be affected, suddenly gets an idea that he should meet his old friend for help;
- (ii) Similar statements made in the past meant trouble in future. Ram, therefore, asked his co-workers to join him and stage a demonstration;
- (iii) If water is not rationed now, there would be a serious shortage in three months' time; and
- (iv) If this machine is not replaced immediately there may be a serious safety problem.

For all the above three action categories, statements indicative of mental and/or overt activities are to be scored. Thinking about or planning some course of action is also to be scored for the respective action categories.

3.4 *Strength (S+)*

Expression of personal strength and personal resources as well as those of social strength and resources including skills, abilities and assets are to be scored here. Statements indicative of internal resources are also to be scored here.

Examples:

- (i) He is a brilliant boy;
- (ii) He is a good helper;
- (iii) They have the determination; and
- (iv) They have shown excellent unity and solidarity.

3.5 *Hope (H)*

This is in anticipation of success in the stated goal or in dealing with the expressed problem. This is indicative of optimism.

Examples:

(i) We will certainly raise production;
(ii) They will get the right to own and cultivate their lands;
(iii) He will pass the exam. with credit; and
(iv) Unitedly they would win.

3.6. *Personal and Social Awareness (PSA)*

Awareness regarding cause-and-effect relationships about events (which have already happened) and facts of life. Such events or facts could be personal and/or social. Awareness about one's own shortcomings and about social/environmental difficulties/blocks consequences of certain actions may also be scored here. Such awareness, however, has to be understood and scored in relation to the stated goal.

Examples:

(i) The village was suffering as there was neither a tank nor a well;
(ii) He could not succeed as he was lazy;
(iii) They did not succeed because they were disunited; and
(iv) We are poor because the system is unjust.

3.7. *Vigilance (V)*

Awareness of certain consequences if the problem is not tackled in advance; anticipation of problems, setbacks and difficulties indicate vigilance. However, scoring will depend not only on the expressed words or sentences but also on the *context* of the story.

Examples:

(i) He may fail because he is lazy;
(ii) He is afraid, management may take advantage of their disunity;
(iii) His memory is short and he may forget facts while arguing; and

(iv) The management made the same promise last year and it was never fulfilled.

Both personal and social awareness (PSA) and vigilance (V) show a certain amount of awareness. The difference, however, is that PSA is scored for the past and present events and facts, whereas V is scored when the statements/words indicate a certain amount of anticipation of some future setback/possible difficulty and some kind of future problems.

3.8 *Thema (Th)*

When a story contains just only one theme (any one of the three imageries or goals) it is scored for thema. This additional score is given to the story for its single-minded theme which indicates the strength of the relevant imagination. When a story contains more than one theme, for example, both influence and social achievement or all the three concerns, it is not scored for thema.

4. **Some Ground Rules**

There are certain ground rules for scoring the TAT stories. Some such rules are:

1. When in doubt about imagery or category, don't score that story for that category. Doubtful categories are not to be scored.
2. The same word or sentence cannot be scored twice, except in some cases where action tendencies and goals are mentioned together. This should also be scored with caution and only when there is no doubt about their presence.
3. As a rule, only the explicit statements are to be scored; no influences are allowed.
4. The statements can be scored for any one of the characters in the story. The sequence and the meaningfulness of the story should be kept in mind while scoring. One good example when statements in the story cannot be scored is expressions of such activities on the part of the characters which are not related to the goals mentioned (and scored) in the story. In this sense, unrelated to goal(s) statements are not to be scored.

5. **Practice Scoring**

Three sets of practice stories and expert scores have been provided to help learn the scoring method. Persons without an adequate experience of TAT scoring would be benefited by following the scoring procedure systematically. Some steps found useful in this regard are stated below:

The scorer should first examine all the stories in the set for the presence of each of the three main categories. For instance, one should score all the 30 stories in a given set first for the presence of personal achievement imagery (PAI). In case a story contains this imagery, a right mark (✓) is entered under the relevant column against the given story in the scoring sheet (as shown in the specimen on page 209). This is done for all the stories one by one. The same procedure is followed for social achievement imagery, for influence imagery and for stories which show integrated imagery, i.e. any two or all the three imageries. Stories which show none of these imageries are marked under UI (Unrelated imagery).

Thus, the 30 stories are examined, all at a time, first for the presence of PAI, then once again all of them for the presence of SAI, thereafter all of them for the presence of influence imagery. Some of the stories would show more than one of these imageries, thus, showing integrated imagery. Such a procedure enables the scorer to compare one story with another in a perspective and in evaluting them according to the criteria laid down in the manual.

After the stories have been scored for the presence of the main imageries or categories, the appropriate ones, i.e., those found with at least one of these three imageries/categories, are taken up for further scoring for sub-categories. For the sake of practice, it is helpful to examine all the stories in the set at a time, for the presence of each of the sub-categories. Some ground rules for scoring sub-categories have been indicated above. Some further ground rules for practice scoring are given below:

5.1. *Further Rules for Scoring*

(1) While scoring the set of stories for practice, the scorer should not consult the expert scores. This should be done only after the scoring of the entire set is over.

(2) However, the scorer may like to consult the rules and criteria

of scoring various categories and sub-categories whether scoring for practice or afterwards. This helps in practising as well as in maintianing objectivity in scoring.

(3) Remember that categories or sub-cateogies have to be present explicitly. No influence should be drawn from in between the lines/words.

(4) Once some sentence is used for scoring action sub-categories, the same cannot be used again for scoring the main categories.

(5) At the end of scoring for each categoy, the scorer may like to check the reliability of his scoring by consulting expert scores. This would be done separatley for PAI, SAI and Influence and then for each of the sub-categories. The inter-scorer reliability, i.e. reliability of the practice scoring as compared with the expert scoring and/or with other scores cane be obtained as follows:

5.2 *Reliability of Scoring*

The scorer compares his scores for a given category/sub-category with those given by the expert scorer or by another experienced scorer in order to check objectivity and reliability of his scoring. A set of stories is thus scored by the practice scorer as well as by another scorer independently without any knowledge about each othr's scores. For example, they score a set of 30 stories for the presence of personal achievement imagery (PAI). At the end of such independent scoring, it is found that the practice scorer has scored 18 out of 30 stories for PAI, whereas the experienced/expert scorer has scored only 12 stories for the same category. It is further found that in the stories thus scored, 9 stories are common, i.e. these have been scored for PAI by both the scorers. Thus, the reliability of the practising scorer can be calculated in the following way:

$$\frac{2\,(9)}{18 + 12} = \frac{18}{30} = 0.60$$

The agreement of the practice scorer with another experienced and/or expert scorer thus comes to 0.60. Usually, reliability of 0.80 (and above) is considered necessary in this regard. The scorer then compares his scores with those of the expert and examines the differences. He scores further sets of stories in order to attain acceptable reliability. He may also like to score the same stories again after some days (without looking at the previous scores) and

Specimen Scoring of Stories for Individual Needs

Person's Code	Story	UI	PAI	SAI	Inf-I	AP	As	Aa	S+	H	PSA	V	Th	Total
	1				✓	✓	✓	—	—	✓	✓	–	✓	6
	2	✓												0
01	3		✓	✓	-	✓	✓	-	-	-	-	✓	-	5
	4	✓												0
	5	✓												0
	6		-	-	✓	✓	-	✓	✓	-	✓	-	✓	6
	1			✓			✓		✓		✓	✓	✓	6
02	2	✓												0
	3	✓												0
	4			✓			✓			✓			✓	4
	5			✓	✓		✓				✓		✓	5
	6			✓	✓	✓		✓					✓	5
	1	✓												0
03	2	✓												0
	3		✓	-	-	✓	-	-	✓	✓			✓	5
	4	✓												0
	5		✓	-	-	✓	✓			✓			✓	5
	6		✓	-	✓	✓			✓					4

then obtain score-score reliability in the same way as explained above.

5.3 *Individual Needs: Range of Scores*

A given story may contain none, any one, or any two or all the three i.e. PAI, SAI, Inf-I, imageries. The eligible stories may also contain all the seven sub-categories (excluding thema, which is scored when a story shows *only* one of the imageries). In such a case, the story gets a score of 10 if it has all the three imageries and all the seven sub-categories, 9 if it has any two imageries and all the 7 sub-categories; and also 9 when it has only one of the three imageries and all the sub-categories. Similarly, a story may contain none of the imageries and is, therefore, scored as UI (unrelated imagery and assigned zero (no score). Theoretically, therefore, the score on any one story could range between 0 and 10.

The relevant scores for imageries (categories) and sub-categories present in a given story, as mentioned above, are entered on the scoring sheet. This is repeated for all the six stories of the given person. As illustrated in the *specimen scoring of stories for individual needs*, the obtained total scores indicate the individual's need profile. Thus, as seen in the specimen scoring, the person, coded as 01, obtained a score of 12 for the need for influence (*n* Inf) and 05 for the need for personal-cum-social achievement (*n*PSA) and none for the rest of the five needs. The second person scored 10 each for *n*SA and *n*SA-Inf, while the third got 10 for *n*PA and 4 for *n*PA-Inf. The scores, therefore, show individual differences in these persons' needs.

The total score for each need is obtained by looking at the scoring sheet. In some cases, more than one story may contain the given need. For example, the second person, as seen in the specimen scoring, showed *n*SA in two stories and *n*SA-Inf in another two stories. In sush cases, the total scores of the relevant stories are totalled to obtain the final score, and recorded in the table, as shown in the specimen scoring. The scores obtained by the three persons are only hypothetical and are used here to illustrate the scoring procedure.

The scores thus obtained for the given seven needs are to be used only for research and training purposes. The data cannot be used for any normative or evaluative purpose, as no norms have been provided in the manual.

Individual Need Profile

Needs	Score		
	Persons		
	01	02	03
Personal Achievement (*n*PA)	0	0	10
Social Achievement (*n*SA)	0	10	0
Influence (*n*Inf)	12	0	0
Personal-cum-Social Achievement (*n*PSA)	05	0	0
Social Achievement Oriented Influence (*n*SA-Inf)	0	10	0
Personal Achievement Oriented Influence (*n*PA-Inf)	0	0	4
Personal-cum-Social Achievement Oriented Influence (*n*SPA-Inf)	0	0	0

APPENDIX II

ANALYSING CONTENT FOR NEED PROFILE

Practice Stories : Set A

Three sets of practice stories are given below to facilitate learning of the scoring system. These stories have been randomnly picked up from a pool of stories wirtten to the TAT pictures (as shown in Appendix III), by groups of workers, managers, organisers of rural poor, social activists, development functionaries etc.

A1: A labourer going on duty meets with an accident. His family is sitting and worrying at home, thinking that steps be taken cautiously otherwise consequences to be faced.

A2: Honesty can make a man more prosperous – Ramu was a great smuggler. He was enjoying a very happy life with his family. On the other hand, there was an honest man who was passing his days according to his status and income. A day came when the smuggler was caught red-handed. Policemen came to arrest him. His son was crying. At that time the son of the honest man came and gave his consolation. The son of the smuggler realized the fact and became an honest man and carried on a happy life in the long run.

A3: Today in the country wherever you see, you will find people standing in queues. It may be the bus stand, ration shop or any other public place. This is symbolic of the disturbed economic situation in the country. We get such things to see. But this is also indicative of a sense of discipline. This is a good symptom. It shows that the country and its 80 per cent workers have a bright future.

A4: Today in the country there is such an inequality that lakhs of poor hungry mothers are begging on the roads for food for their children. This inequality can be removed only by socialism. We all the workers should take a pledge to do every

---

Some of the stories contained in Sets A, B and C were originally written in Hindi. These have been rendered here in English. The original style, grammar and spellings have been maintained.

thing to fulfil this task.

A5: Some people were found in a queue in a public office for having something. They were very peaceful and doing their business decently without any hesitation.

A6: A poor woman with her baby sitting near a railway station was begging from the rich people passing by in their cars and were overlooking her. She was very disappointed. The baby was sleeping. Her husband might have died for some reason.

A7: Shri Ram was a labourer working in a steel factory. But he was very careless. Once, due to his carelessness many materials were spoiled. But he never paid any attention to the work. Once he was looking at somebody else and was doing his work. Due to this his hand was cut severely. He tells everyone, "brothers, do your work carefully otherwise you may get the same condition like mine." Carelessness can bring hazards in life.

A8: Ram's wife Veena is a mother of six children. He did not pay attention to family planning in the beginning. Therefore, in this time of rising cost of living he is in great difficulty. He begins to get sick and Veena's health also is spoiled due to producing six children because due to low income they could get only one meal a day for the entire family. Ram could have avoided all this by having two children. His family would have been happy. Due to Ram's sickness, there was no income in the family. Whatever was there was spent on his treatment. Helplessly, Veena had to start begging. Children also were loitering here and there eating others' left overs. "We should, therefore do family planning from the very beginning. We two our two, this will lead to happiness. Both in the family and also for the country's prosperity."

A9: One poor woman due to her poverty is begging on the road with the child in her lap. She is requesting the passers by for something. People do not even turn and look at her.

A10: One late worker prepared something and gave. This was not enough. He is now talking to someone about the things lying there. The other person is telling him that this thing cannot be used. Some other people are standing and looking at them.

A11: This is a picture of a family. These people are talking among themselves that they should live and work together and contribute for the progress of the country. "We have to understand all the people of this country and think the wealth of the whole country as our own."

A12: The fourth picture tells us that all of us are countrymen. All of us together should think the good of the country. More work and labour at less and less expenditure and prepare everything in the country so that we do not have to look to other countries for our things.

A13: The sixth picture shows that whatever work we do should be done in a technical and scientific way so that in the shortest possible time and minimum capital we can do the maximum possible production. Whatever may be the industry, everyone should do his job with responsibility and honesty. One major thing for everyone else is that we should be honest, strong and peaceful.

A14: In the picture a gate meeting is going on. These are the workers and the union leader. The management has locked them out and stopped their work. These people are raising slogans that give us our work and take back the lockout order.

A15: Police has come at the instance of the management. They are arresting the union leader. Some people are running away. This was an illegal strike because some workers were dismissed from their jobs. The leader is thinking what would happen now, whether the workers will be given back on work.

A16: What is wrong and right? This education is being given through the police. In some way we all know what is good and correct and what is wrong. Still mostly we commit a mistake even knowingly. We should always walk on our left while walking on the road, i.e., we should work after thinking what is right so that we don't have to repent later. This way the results are good.

A17: Here the workers of some undertaking are thinking about the results of the production for the company and they are being reprimaded by one big officer. Something wrong must, have happened previously about which they are now being told by the officer that such things should not have happened. This was the carelessness of the workers of this undertaking. They are now thinking why it happened like this. They all want production and good name. Now they will decide they should deliberately try to work in a proper way so that no blame comes on them and they should do work with honesty and sincerity.

A18: Some people are collected. It seems they belong to the same party. One of them seems to be the leader. Some of them are seen speaking and others are listening. The tone of their speaking is critical. It seems some special event has taken place as they are now collected here. Or they are now trying to solve some mutual dispute. Many of these persons are not agreeing to the decision. This is the guess. May be after some time they may reach some decision. May be they may agree to the new point of the officer or the leader. Or may be they may not agree to their decision and the situation may take a violent turn.

A19: These three are students. It seems they belong to a fascist party. One of them is the leader who is telling them to do wrong things. These persons have made a plan to create disturbance against the present government and against progress. There after one of them will be caught by the police red-handed. Other two are trying to escape. The person who has been caught red-handed is giving his explanation. A police constable is keeping a watch over the other two also. The person caught red-handed will have to undergo punishment and the other two also will be traced out. In this way the fascist elements try to put obstacles in our democracy and follow a policy of sabotage.

A20: Raju was employed as a welder. He had one son and his wife had expired after giving birth to the child. Raju used to remain in the plant quite late at night and he did not see how his son was studying. His ambition was to educate him well and make him a big man. One evening he returned early and found his son playing. He got annoyed and slapped him and asked him to study. The son went and started studying but Raju felt quite repentant as to why did he slap his only child whom he loved so much.

A21: The police recognized the culprits. In this way the police controlled the situation. In this way, they helped the people.

A22: Babu (the son) is studying preparing for his exam. His father is listening to what his son is reading. He is feeling rather sorry, as he is unable to guide his son. This has happened because Hari's father was very careless in his own study and he is repenting today. However, he is determined to give his son the full opportunity of education even if he has to engage private tutors at a great cost. This will definitely yield good result and Hari will prosper in his life through his son's education.

A23: The workers are in the workshop working on a machine. The injury caused to the worker has made everyone look at him to help him. It is being thought to take him immediately to hospital. They want assistance to carry him to hospital for treatment. He will remain in hospital for treatment. He will remain on the accident roll for some days.

A24: There is a union leader addressing the workers. The leader is an outside leader and has come to the colliery on his weekly visit and is talking and listening to the grievances of the workers to discuss the same with the management. The situation has arisen due to non-payment of wages on time. The workers were expecting wages on last Saturday as it was the pay day, but since the payment could not be made so this situation. Also the workers are expecting to present their grievances. They are discussing and thinking on the line of action they intend to take in case the talks fail. The workers want payment. Strike or *gheraos* will take place if the payment is not made.

A25: Ramu is sitting in his verandah while his son Rajesh is reading a book inside the room. Rajesh is very good in studies. His school master was saying that he will be a big man if he continues his studies. He is a brilliant boy. He should be sent to town for further studies. Ramu is thinking that with his meagre salary how he will educate his son. Sending him to town for further studies will mean a lot of expenses.

He would have lived there and his son could have helped him in farming as he was growing old. But when he thinks of the words of the school master his thoughts change. He is thinking of going to the village landlord to arrange for money so that his son can go to town for further studies.

A26: The leader is giving a thought to a problem and the child is reading. He is deeply involved with that dispute. The same dispute of the parties has led to this situation. He is thinking over the problem—that a police case has been instituted. He is thinking to solve it by compromise and donesn't want litigation, by going to court.

A27: In a workshop fitters and others are engaged in the manufacturing of iron materials. They are all workers connected with the work. Recently many breakdowns and deterioration in quality has been reported and a special drive has been launched to speed up the work.

A28: Ram approached the workers of his community after being dissatisfied with the decision of his boss. He told them that all the demands put forward by him have not been conceded. The management though prepared to take up welfare work are not prepared to do the repair, etc., in phases. In the past also similar assurances have been given but the programme has not been implemented. As such Ram ask his co-workers to be with him to launch an agitation.

A29: He is a poor father worrying about the future of his young son. He wants that his son should rise in his career. He is planning how to save money for the higher education of his son. He is not happy with the present state of affairs and wants that the same fate should not be fall his son. He was high hopes for his son.

A30: The employee appears to have been very sorry for what has happened in the past. The boy is his son. For the fault committed by the employee he appears to be repenting. The employee is seriously thinking as to how to get rid of the rut. He is visualizing the bad days ahead. He is contemplating about the future of his family.

Practice Stories: Set B

B1: At some place 10 to 15 *Sanyasis* had collected. They wanted to give *diksa* and convert one young man to *Sanyas*. According to them the world is untrue and unreal. Therefore you should adopt *Sanyas*. The youngman gave the example of the *Bhagavadgita* and said that he would never do it as to work is the teaching of Lord Krishna, work is supreme. Emphasizing this, the young man said that he would continue to be in the world and continue to work. While working he would complete his *Sanyas*. The *Sanyasis* were silenced by this reply.

B2: A father was paying attention to his son's studies but the boy was only acting to study. It was only an excuse. The father said, "Son, you are not deceiving me but deceiving yourself because in the beginning you have to do some hard work but then you can enjoy the whole day. This education appears useless now but later the life becomes good and prosperous. Son, do as I say and do as I do." The son agreed to do so and started working hard on his studies and also started coming first in his class.

B3: In the village the *Chowkidar* came and asked Mohan to come to the police station. He refused to go saying that he was not the leader. On seeing the Chowkidar two other persons were going ahead. The Chowkidar went and also explained to them that they should not have any fear. Don't run away because of the fear of one person.

B4: Before this, Ram and Shyam, the two brothers, used to live in this house. After the death of these two brothers, their children, instead of dividing this property among themselves, handed over the property to the government. They did so because in this country nobody should have such properties. All should work together, think together and live together.

B5: There was a famine in our country. What will happen now? What will be done in future? We should solve this problem by increasing production in factories, mines and fields, arrange for ration at different places so that nobody in the country dies of starvation. By increasing production and by sending our things to other countries, getting the things from them which we need. In this way our problem of food is to be solved.

B6: On seeing the fifth picture, we find that workers work hard for 8 hours, perspire for the defence of the country and for increasing the production. In this way factories run in the whole country. All of them work, still they do not have a small hut for living and there is no medicine for their small children. The boy is lying sick but there is no medicine to cure him. Our own carelessness can also make our children unhappy. When we work in danger our conditions, we should take proper care for our safety. Otherwise my danger can also put my family into danger. Therefore, if we are not careful, we can meet with an accident.

B7: Now workers have understood that we should follow all safety methods. If we do not do so the future of our children will become dark. We should, therefore, be very careful while doing things in dangerous circumstances. We should be careful so that our children and others in the family are also happy.

B8: These people are in a poor condition. This is because they don't understand their own responsibility. They have been going in wrong ways. They are not able to understand this and now they also feel weak. Because of somebody's wrong advice they are now in such a bad shape. We should, therefore, do everything after a careful examination so that no complication arises in future. We should act according to the requirements of the time.

B9: One poor woman is passing her days in difficulty. The society criticizes her and also ridicules her. But this society cannot find a solution for this problem. This is because the society has not been able to produce the right atmosphere. If one person has followed, a wrong path, he should be corrected. This is the duty of all of us. I am not talking of the principles of myself but the principles of the entire society. A person who is fallen down should be helped to rise up.

B10: There is a policeman and a person in the picture. These persons are labourers. There has been some accident in the past. This happened because of carelessness. The labourers are thinking whether they will get adequate compensation. Therefore, these workers are asking for full compensation and also good arrangement for work. Nothing should happen like this. We should, therefore, come forward and strengthen our organization.

B11: In the picture, one worker is sick. He is thinking and a leader is explaining something to him. We are all workers. But before this there was an accident. This happened because of carelessness. The leader and the workers are thinking whether they will get compensation, if so, how much and when? Nothing will happen and people have to come forward and organize themselves.

B12: This is a morning of a cold day. People have come out after putting sheets on their bodies to protect against the cold. The workers' leader, Ramu Chacha, is calling them. People have come out from their homes. People are anxious. They want to know what is the matter. Why has Ramu Chacha called them? Ramu Chacha then removes their curiosity. He tells them, brothers, now our turn has come. The government has decided to invite us to participate in the management. We are now about to get our rights. This work has now started.

B13: Oh, what a time has come! Everywhere there is a crowd. Whether you have to buy a ticket or you have to take the bus or at a ration shop. Why such long queues everywhere? What can the government do? What is the way out? Everyone has an answer. And this is family planning. Let's help the government so that in our neighbourhood people are advised to have only two or three children. This is enough. This will lead to a good life.

B14: In the picture a policeman is talking to a person. Two other persons are passing by. One of them is having an attache. They are walking fast. These persons appear to be thieves. Their porfession is to indulge in mischiefs. In the picture it is clear that after doing something wrong they are entering into some kind of an understanding with the police. Now this happened that they are doing all these mischiefs in collusion with the police. Two persons want to run away but the third has decided with the police that in future they will do their work.

B15: In the picture people are standing in a queue. They are standing in front of a ration shop. In the past someone broke his leg because there was no system of a queue. This happened because people did not follow the rules and stood in a line. People are thinking that this is the right way to take things. The person who has been injured in the leg is thinking that he got the injury because of his own mistake. Other people are thinking that they should take ration in a proper way.

B16: A pedestrain while walking along the street has noticed some article which has dropped from somebody quite unknowingly or through carelessness. The article may be of value. The person very rightly goes to the police constable on duty and reports the matter. The constable in his turn asks him to go to the police station and deposit the article. The police man may also accompany him if required.

B17: They assembled, they are villagers and workers. They had to assemble to tackle, the situation which has arisen due to some theft in one of the villages. Theft has occurred in the name of the persons in the middle of the assembly. The situation, cause and finding the culprit is the subject of their thought. They want to catch the thief. They will find out the culprit, they will sent the culprit to jail and his goods will be recovered.

B18: All the persons are standing in the queue for giving their vote. They are the voters of municipality. The situation has arisen. To elect a member of the municipality. The term of office of the last board him expired. They are thinking of casting their voters for the right person and according to whatever image they had been given of the candidates. They want to elect the right persons for the municipality, and then they will form the committee and the committee will elect their chairman and they will run the municipality effectively.

B19: The workers are working in a workshop, and the engineer has come to inspect the performance of the workers. They are the workers of the workshop. As it is an inspection by the engineer, the co-workers are looking towards the worker whose work is being inspected. The worker has made some mistake in his trumming. The work has been hard and he is being pulled up by the engineer. The engineer wanted the work to be perfect by the worker. The worker will be punished for bad work. The material which has been spoiled will be rejected.

B20: In the morning the son has got up and is reading his class book. The father has some problem worrying him and he is engrossed in the same. He has been trying to get his problem solved but so far he has failed. He is thinking of how to do the work. He wants that the study of his son should not suffer and he should be able to fulfil his ambitions. The man is unable to solve his financial problem and will not be able to educate and bring up his son as he wants.

B21: People have formed a queue outside a ration shop to get their ration and other consumable items. As there has been scarcity of supply and also disorderly behaviour, this arrangement has been enforced and all have been given their ration cards. All workers are thinking how soon they will get their ration. An adequate supply of stores is needed by all workers. After proper checking, the ration will be given to all the workers.

B22: A long queue at the ration shop: Madan has to procure ration for his family and then board a bus for his new job assignment. Seeing the long queue he thought by the time he reaches to the counter, the bus would have left, so he has to make up his mind—either to procure ration or to go for the job. But both are equally important. So he decides to jump the queue and go right in front to get the ration quickly and hence quickly for the bus. However, he was detected by others and there was resentment and thrown out of the queue. He will be referred to the Mukhia for action.

B23: At the pay counter workers are collecting payment and one man is sitting at the feet of another man. In the queue they seem to be workers. But the other man is a money-lender. This money-lender is taking money from a worker forcibly. In the past the man had taken a loan from the moneylender. The man then thought he would return the money but coult not. Money-lenaing should be stopped and loans given to workers to buy extra goods they need. If this is not done the worker will be more and more involved in borrowing and interest paying and ultimately he will run away.

B24: A worker coming out of the factory has been searched at the end of his shift, some company material has been found in his possession which he intends to take home dishonestly. Other workers are seeing it. Dishonest intention to take home company property has led to this situation. This man was in the habit of committing thefts and the management had confidential reports about it and a watch had been kept on him. The co-workers are apprehensive that the management would definitely take a drastic action. The management wants disciplinary action if theft proved.

B25: A job service holder getting a poor salary is thinking about his son as to how to provide better education to him, who is quite sincere in his studies. He think on the problem deeply because the mother of the child is no more, and hence how to provide him affection is another point of thinking in the mind of the gentleman sitting. The gentleman is very serious about his future programme of providing proper facilities to the son for his better development.

B26: A group of workers is talking to the trade union leader. It seems the management has taken some strict disciplinary action on which the workers are agitated. The Union leader on hearing the workers is getting excited and he is trying to excite the workers. He wants to retaliate to this action of the manager and take some action. The leader may take out a procession to make soure demand.

B 27: A man is sitting on a cot, a boy is reading. It seems they are related to each other as father and son. The father is watching the son's study most steadily. The son is not intelligent and not interested in study. Hence the father is keeping a constant eye on the son. The father is thinking that his son will become a good boy after study and will be a good earning member of his family and then he will leave work. If the son read in his presence he will become a good boy.

B28: The persons are son and father. The son is reading a novel in the corner of a room which the father may not see. The father watching his son quietly. At last the boy was caught red-handed. It is being thought that the son should read his school books. The father wants that the son should read his course books.

B29: This is law and order problem. Two persons were found walking along the railway line. Anyone walking on a raliway line is committing a criminal act in as much as it is a trespass. This would endanger the life of the trespasser and also create a problem for the railway administration. The railway police is explaining to the trespasser that it is dangerous. The other persons who were doing the same thing stood there. What had happened? The police did not notice the other end. When they came to know of the fact others tried to slip away.

B30: Prakash is a coal-miner and Sohan is his son. Sohan was reading in a school and was very intelligent. Tomorrow is the last day for depositing the exam. fee of Sohan. There is no problem for Prakash as today is his pay day. He drew his wages in the office and started coming back to home. On the way money-lenders caught him and took away all his wages. He was penniless on his pay day. He came back to his house and sat on the cot despondent. He saw his son deeply engrossed in his studies. This aggravated his despondence. How will he disclose this to his son that he has no money. He suddenly decided and determined that this time he would take a loan from his friend but in future he would not do anything wrong.

Practice Stories: Set C

C1: In order to promote happiness in families and of other people and to develop the country and achieve progress, an organization was formed of villages. This organization carried on a successful campaign for rehabilitating the unhappy poor, illiterate, unemployed families and to reduce the number of such people. Initially, in order to make unhappy homes happy, the social workers and intelligentsia explained this to Ramesh that he should go ahead by his own hard work and that they are with him and that every help in the society will be given to him.

They are all with him. He was assured not to be disheartened.

C2: Ramesh has come back from the hospital. He wants to show to society by his hard work and honesty can enable one to go ahead in society. He went to work in a workshop. He was working there. Luck was not with him there, and his finger was injured. What the God has done to him? The unhappy Ramesh like a water-spring going up and down but in the end his honesty and determination helped him to go ahead. In spite of his finger being injured, his courage helped him and he got success.

C3: One sincere and honest person has gone to a group of people and tells them things of wisdom. By this he is trying to take them and the society and workers away from bad thoughts and to the right path. In this way groups of people do progress and understand their duties collectively. In this way our own welfare as well as of the country also improves. Sitting together and imagining things and thinking of concrete activities and paying attention to them is our duty.

C4: A son, in order to make his own future and the country's welfare bright, is reading his book with keen attention. In this way everyone should send his promising boys to school or to library so that such boys can improve their future and also being to understand their country and society as their own so that we continue to always make progress. In my country every person will understand his responsibility.

C5: Many years ago, man was uncivilized. But gradually he started understanidng how to live, eat, react and in this way everything changed. Today man has made so much progress that he has even walked on the Moon. In the past man did not know how to live and how to eat but today he has made great progress.

C6: There are many people in the picture. We understand from the picture that in the past people used to go everywhere in crowds. They used to on together. Now there is nothing like this. The reason is that now for going to any place, we have trains, buses and other means of journey which can take us to any place in a very short time. Now the man by his intelligence will find out ways so that he can go to any place even in seconds.

C7: In the picture, a woman is sitting with a child. She is looking after her. These persons are from the labour class. Before this, the man was like a child and gradually he started standing and made progress. Now he is learning to work becuase he had no other means. The man always wanted to make progress. He always thinks that what kind of education should be given so that the nation makes progress and also that our own life standard can be improved.

C8: On the road, two persons are going and also one policeman. The policeman is talking to one person and walking. They both are looking at other two persons who are walking on the road. The policeman and the person talking to him become suspicious of the other two persons walking on the road. The other two persons walking on the road want to know what the third person is talking to the policeman. They guess that the policeman might be asking something, although such behaviour on the part of the police is not right.

C9: Many people are standing in a line. In the country, standing in such lines has become a matter of daily routine. It is as if we cannot live without such queues. There is shortage of things in the ocuntry. Population is increasing. In proportion to the increase in population, the rate of increase in production is not enough. In this way things in shortage. People cannot get them easily. When they don't get things easily people give up all kinds of ideas and only try to procure them in whatever way possible. In this way people also do all kinds of wrong things and repent later. In order to save the country and oursleves from such queues, we should put a brake to the growth of population.

C10: A car came out from the gate of a bungalow. After seeing the car go a person reaches the gate. A woman beggar with a child in her lap comes and extends her hands and says, "Malik, the child is hungry, give something, some money. God will give you something much more than you will give to the poor." The young man stops at the gate. He thinks why such a difference between man and man. There could be no happiness and peace as long as everyone does not get something. Some people have so many things, others don't have anything.

C11: In the pricture, there is a woman and a child. She has got some kind of punishment. From this picture everyone should get a lesson. After doing something wrong, we have always to face the consequences. The police may take us again and again to jail and we shall have to face all kinds of difficulties. Every man should do his duty well so that good things can lead to good and right ways. We get the lesson from the picture that we should keep to the right way. We should give good treatment to everyone.

C12: Who is thinking what? Every person should get a lesson from this picture that everyone should be educated and we should show such a way to our children that they also get educated and make progress. Along with this we should try to give education to each and everyone in society so that society also makes progress.

C13: We get the lesson from the picture that all of us should work together in a united way. Here is a machine which can show any picture quickly and there is a well which is used by every animal. Animals, birds, etc, drink water from this well. Therefore, every person should work like a machine. We should think of the ways of achieving peace of the soul like this well. And we should think of ways and means of working together so that we can do good work together.

C14: Always follow the law because any violation of the law will do harm to the country. A policeman or an officer, who are the custodians of law, should be helped by us. Their morale will go up only when we together will help them. We should not support anyone doing any wrong thing or taking a bribe because this is not in the interest of the country; it will only harm. We should not encourage any wrong thing. We should try our best to stop it and we should look after the country as our own property.

C15: People working on machines should always be alert and careful. While working they should not divert their attention here and there because there is a danger to life and also a possibility of damage to the machinery. People working in factories and/or on machines should try to see that they do not cause other people inconvenient. They should not divert their attention. They should not wear loose clothes and should not talk to people here and there so that nobody is harmed. We should pay adequate attention to the machines so that they work properly.

C16: A conspiracy is going on. There has been a serious setback to the man who is talking something to the audience most of whom belong to his group. The audience is always kept as a gang by the orator. The orator got a message that tomorrow he is going to be attacked by his rival group. The information has excited him as the time at his disposal to prepare for the counter-attack or defence is very short. There has been old enmity between the two rival groups. They are thinking to gather arms and ammunition, and also lodge an early FIR with the local police so that the onus of all the consequences will lie on the rival group. It is expected that some onslaughts, serious injuries or even more may take place. Hence this preparation is being made.

C17: Ram is very sad. He has resigned his job and is thinking how to continue normal life at his home. His child's education will be disturbed, etc. Ram had some differences in the past with his supervisor. The management charge-sheeted him and an inquiry has proved his guilt. So before getting dismissed, he has resigned as the Union also does not back him. He is thinking of some alternative job or business. He will discuss with his wife and relatives and finalize it. He will soon find out another job and establish his domestic life in a normal shape.

C18: While two workers are working in the workshop two are simply wasting their time. They are wondering why these people are working so hard when at the end of the day they all get the same wage. The two persons working on the lathe are involved fully in their job and want to do an excellent job. All along they have performed jobs with perfection and so they are eager to maintain their record and keep the bosses fully satisfied. The involvement and keenness of these two persons is inducing the other two to start working. The two are having second thoughts about wasting their time.

C19: Shyam is a brilliant student in his class and is very hard-working, always standing first in the examination. His father Ram Lal is a poor man, who is sweating it day and night for the betterment of his family. Sometimes, he thinks how can he afford higher studies for his son Shyam on such a low income of his. His son must continue his studies throughtout and he has to think of ways and means to fulfil this. He is thinking of a determined hard work to get his son all the education, so that his son can really prove his mettle, for the benefit of the country and his family.

C20: Gopi Lal comes to take ration from the Government controlled shop. There is a long queue and he has no place to stand. He also does not want to stand there for long, because he is afraid of Khan, the money-lender, who had been asking for money since the last pay day. Gopi knows if the money is taken away by Khan, he will not be able to take ration which in turn would mean long days without food for his three sons and wife. He tried his best to hide in the queue but Khan found him and beat him and brought him out of the queue and asked for money. Gopi is in tears and begs of Khan to release him as he is in real trouble.

C21: Mohan is a new recruit as a worker and is very sincere and hard-woking. His supervisor Sohan is very happy that he picks up work in a short time and carries on the work for more production. Today, he is learning a new job and the eyes of all the workers including of the supervisor are on him. They are wondering how quickly Mohan has picked up the job and is doing expertly. Sohan knows Mohan's problem and wants to help him to earn money for his studies, which are interrupted now because his father cannot afford. Sohan being a community leader thought of training him up as his worker for his studies.

C22: It is the house of a villager who looks worried; the child is studying in the room. The villager is very much worried about some wrong. He is thinking to find out a solution.

C23: A large number of persons are standing in a queue to ontain something. It seems they are ration takers. It seems that the thing they are standing for is in short supply in the market. So many people are standing in the queue shows that the shortage is great.

C24: It is a scene slightly away from the market. There is a case of pick-pocketing and the policeman has caught a man who actually is an innocent man. He is trying his best to convince the policeman of his innocence. The man shows to have nothing on him, and will be allowed to go. But the real culprit has gone away without any trouble.

C25: The father is worried and is busy thinking as to how to make the two ends meet, and the son is busy in his studies. How innocent the childhood is, free from all worry! He is busy in the studies, preparing for exams which are near, and the father is worried about tomorrow – about food, clothing and also possibly how to arrange the examination fee. He will have to work hard.

C26: The poor woman. Her husband was a well-to-do man, earning about Rs. 500 a month. Unfortunately, the he fell is bad company and started drinking and gambling. He lost both his money and job. Ultimately, because of his drinking habit he died leaving behind an unhappy widow and a child who are forced to beg because of non-availability of a job. She looks at the rich man who is moving towards her, but he pays no attention to the beggar. She must find some job and leave begging.

C27: Some persons are talking. It seems that there is one union leader and some are workers. It looks like they are planning for future. In the past they might have faced some trouble. How to avoid it? In future trouble may arise again. They will try to solve the problem themselves or through the union.

C28: Ram is sharpening a tool to manufacture nut bolts. He has been slightly injured. His middle finger received a slight bruise. His co-workers are looking on. He was a little unmindful today due to a domestic quarrel with his wife. The co-workers are thinking to give his first-aid. He will be cured and start working properly. They safety officer will be able to arrive at the root cause of the accident, caution him against it, which will be duly followed.

C29: People are standing in a queue. These are the people of ordinary status, and they are lining up for casting their votes. In the past they have not elected good people to look after their interests. They are now thinking to elect good people. The aspirants are both good and bad. The man standing is consoling the other. He would come back in the queue.

C30: The poor woman has kept her son in her lap and the car with a right person is standing at his door. This leads the poor woman to think about her poorness and imaging that her son after growing into an adult will enjoy all the facilities of life. The woman wishes to have a better life for her son. This will all be dependent upon the education of her son.

EXPERT SCORING

Scoring Practice Stories: Set A
Personal Achievement Imagery (PAI)

A1: Unrelated Imagery: The story contains imagery neither for personal achievement nor for social achievement nor for influence. This is not taken up for further scoring for sub-categories.

A2: No PAI. "The son of the smuggler realized the fact and became an honest man." Doubtful whether it involves any standard of excellence in life and work.

A3: No PAI.

A4: No PAI

A5: No PAI. "They are very peaceful and performing their business decently." Doubtful whether it involves any standard of excellence.

A6: No PAI.

A7: No PAI. "Never paid attention to this work; due to this his hand has been cut severely." Doubtful.

A8: PAI. "Veena's health also was spoiled in producing children, because due to low income they could get only one meal a day." This implies some standard of excellence for personal life and concern for a better life.

A9: No PAI.

A10: Not scored. It is merely a description of a situation.

A11 and A12: No PAI.

A13: PAI. "Whatever work we do should be in a technical and scientific way." It implies standard of excellence in work. Some other words in the story also indicate PAI.

A14 and A15: No PAI.

A16: No PAI. There is a moral tone in the story but concern for improvement or standard of excellence in living conditions not explicit.

A17: PAI "They should do work with honesty and sincerity" and try to work in a proper way", clear indication of some standard of excellence in work. The use of words like "we" and "they" does not make it social achievement imagery.

A18: to A19. No PAI.

A20: PAI "His ambition was to make his son a big man and well educated".

A21: Not scored. "Police controlling the situation" is not enough for scoring story for PAI.

A22: PAI. "Determined to get his son the full opportunity of education", indicates standard of excellence. Some other words also indicate the same thing.

A23: Not scored. The story is mostly a description of a situation.

A24: No PAI

A25: PAI. "His school master was telling that he will be a big man if he continues his studies." Some other sentences also indicate PAI.

A26: No PAI.

A27: PAI. "Recently a lot of breakdowns and deterioration in quality has been reported." It is a case where no character is specifically mentioned. However, the story clearly contains imagery for personal achievement based on some standard of excellence in performance.

A28: No PAI.

A29: PAI. "Planning how to save money for the higher education of his son." Other sentences indicating dissatisfaction with the state of affairs also suggest some standard of excellence in life.

A30: No PAI.

Social Achievement Imagery (SAI)

A1: No SAI.

A2: No SAI

A3: SAI. "This shows that the country and its 80 per cent workers have a bright future." Clear indication of a concern for improvement in community life.

A4: SAI. "Lakhs of poor hungry mothers are begging on roads for their children", a concern for better life for the community.

A5 to A7: No SAI.

A8: SAI. "We two our two, this will lead to happiness, both in the family and also for the country's prosperity." There is a clear concern for superordinate achievement – the country's prosperity.

A9: and A10. No SAI.

A11: SAI. Do progress for our country.

A12: SAI. "More work and labour at less and less expenditure and prepare everything in the country." Intense activities also suggest achievement concern.

A13: SAI. "In the shortest possible time, we can do the maximum possible production" – a superordinate achievement goal.

A14 to A16: No SAI.

A17: SAI. "Thinking about results of production for the country" shows concern for high production – a superordinate achievement goal.A18: No SAI.

A19:No SAI. No clear mention of social achievement goal. "Create disturbance against the present government and against progress" may have some implicit concern. The goal has to be stated explicitly.

A20 to A30: No SAI.

Influence (Inf)

A1: No If.

A2: Inf. "A day came when the smuggler was caught red-handed and the policeman came to arrest him."

Here the policeman is not doing the routine job of apprehending some offender. He is arresting a smuggler who is clearly looked down upon in the story. This shows a desire for control over social evils like sumggling.

A3: No Inf.

A4: Inf. "We all workers should take a pledge to do everything to fulfil our task." This is a statement of intense social activity reflecting a desire for collective action to influence the fulfilement of the goals.

A5: No Inf. It is not scored for influence altough the sentence "some people are found in a queue in a public office for having something" seems to indicate influence.This is indicative of some action but whether they are there to influence some decision is not clear.

A6: No Inf. Begging comes as description.

A7: Inf. "Now, therefore, he tells everyone to do his work carefully; otherwise you may get the same condition as mine." This is not merely a talk. This talking here implies influencing others' behaviour.

A8: Inf. "We should, therefore, do family planning from the very beginning." This statement about the need for family planning may not always be scored for influence. However, in the context of the story it is scored as influence as it clearly indicates a desire for control over the situation and an intervention in order to remedy a bad situation.

A9 and A10: Back largely descriptive – no Inf.

A11: No Inf. "People are talking among themselves that we should live and work together." Taking is an activity from which the concern cannot be inferred (unless the activity mentioned is very intense). There is no explicit influcence goal.

A12: Inf. "Prepare everything in the country so that we don't have to look to other countries for our thing." *Actor role criterion* indicates a desire for influencing situation and not merely sitting as a spectator.

A13: No Inf.

A14: Inf. "A gate meeting is going on; these are the workers and the union leader." It is an example of acceptance of inflence from others like leaders and also imagery indicating desire for influencing others' opinion. Other works like "these people are reising solgans that give us work and take back the lock-out" indicate intense activity showing the presence of influence.

A15: Inf. "The leader is thinking what will happen now and in future. Whether the workers will be given back the work." Scored in the context of the story. By itself, it may not clearly indicate influence.

A16: Inf. "Education is given through police." An example of teaching or advice giving about right and wrong implying influence on others' opinions and ideas.

A17: Inf. "Being regrimded..."

A18: Inf. "One of them seems to be the leader." The other words also like "speaking is critical" indicate the desire to influence the situation and people. The other words also like "they are now trying to solve some mutiual dispute" indicate influence toward problem-solving. However, the story is scored only once for any category.

A19: Inf. "Therefore one of them will be caught by the police red-handed." Police arresting a person scored for influence in the context of the story. There are several other sentences which indicate influence.

A20: No Inf. "Slapped him and asked his son to read", an example of anger and frustration.

A21: Inf. "Controlled the situation".

A22: Inf. "He is feeling rather sorry for he is unable to guide his son." This is an example of inference from father's desire for influencing son's behaviour. There are several other statements and words which indicate influence. However, each category is scored only once.

A23: No Inf. "Help him" and will be taken to hospital and will be "given treatment". These are not intended to change or influence behaviour.

A 24: Inf. "A union leader addressing workers." Other statements also indicate influence. A good example is where the story is full of influence imagery.

A25: Inf. "He will be a big man" indicates desire for influence.

A26: Inf. "He is thinking to solve by compromise and don't want to go for litigation." This indicates a desire to influence the situation toward problem-solving.

A27: No Inf.

A 28: Inf. "He told them, all the demands put forward by him have not been considered." It indicates a desire to influence the opinions and ideas of others. There are other sentences also which indicate the same desire.

A29: Inf. "He is planning how to save money for higher education of his son." Some other sentences also indicate the same.

A30: Inf. "Seriously thinking about how to get rid of the rut." Indicates desire to influence the on-going situation by problem-solving.

Personal Action (Ap)

A1: No Ap

A2: No Ap

A3 to A6: No Ap

A7: Ap. "Tells everyone" shows personal activity for influencing.

A8: Ap. "Should, therefore, do family planning." An indication of personal activity for improving one's own life.

A9 and A10: No Ap.

A11: Not scored for personal activity. There is no personal activity to support the goal.

A12: Mention of more work and labour indicates a suggestion for collective activity. Nothing to suggest the personal activity. Not scored.

A13: Ap. "Everyone should do his job with responsibility and truth" indicates mental activity and also guideline for overt activity.

A14: No Ap.

A 15: Ap. "The leader is thinking what will happen now in future", an example of mental activity.

A16: Ap. "Education is being given through the police." Scored for personal activity. Other sentences like "we should work after thinking what is right" also indicate personal activity. The use of words "we" or "they" does not make such activities social. The emphasis here is on individual activity.

A17: Ap. "Now they will decide that they should deliberately try to work in a proper way." An example of metal activity.

A18 and A19: No Ap.

A20: Ap. "Asked his son to read." "Slapping him" may also indicate personal activity.

A21: No Ap.

A22: Ap. "Father listening to what his son is studying." "Determined to give full education even if he is to engage private tutors" also indicate an activity.

A23: No Ap.

A24: Ap. "On his weekly visit" and "his talking and listening to the grievances of workers" scored for personal activity. The story opens with a description of an activity, "addressing the workers", but not scored for it as the opening statement is not scored for activity. "Thinking on the line of action" also indicate, mental activity on the part of workers.

A25: Ap. "Ramu is thinking that with his meagre salary." "Thinking of going to the village landlord. Studying a book". These indicate personal activity.

A26: Ap. "He is thinking over the problem", "thinking to solve", examples of mental activity.

A27: Not scored for personal activity. The opening sentence does indicate some activity but is not scored as the first sentence is not to be scored for activity.

A28: Ap. "He told them that all the demands put forward by him have not been considered." Personal activity on the part of the leaders.

A29: Ap. "He is planning how to save money", an example of mental activity.

A30: Ap. "The employee seriously thinking", an example of mental activity.

Social Action (As)

A1 and A2: No As.

A3: As. "People standing in queues". Other words such as "indicative of sense of discipline" also suggest the presence of social action. Social discipline is a good example of social action.

A4: As. "Workers should take a pledge."

A5 to A7: No As.

A8: "We should do family planning." Despite the use of word "we" family planning is essentially a personal activity. Not scored for social action.

A9 and A10: No As.

A11: As. "People are talking among themselves that they should live and work together." This is a mental activity indicative of social thinking.

A12: As. "All of us together should think the good of the country." Another example of social thinking indicative of a mental activity. "More work and labour" indicate social action.

A13: No As.

A14: As. "People are raising slogans."

A15 and A16: No. As.

A17: As. "They all decided that they should deliberately try to work", indicative of a collective action.

A18: As. "They are now trying to solve some mutual dispute." A clear indication of a collective activity.

A19 to A23: No As.

A24: As. "They are discussing and thinking on the line of action," clearly suggest the presence of a collective activity. The reference to strike and *gheraos* also indicates social activity. However, each category is scored only once.

A25 and A26: No As.

A27: As. " A special drive has been launched" indicates a group activity hence scored for social activity.

A28: No As. This is a good example where workers are mentioned int he story but all actions relate to the leader. Hence not scored for social activity.

A29 and A30: No As.

Anticipated Action (Aa)

A1: No Aa.

A2: No Aa. There are activities mentioned in order to deal with a smuggler but no advance activities are metioned.

A3 to A6: No Aa. It is a good example where there could have been a sense of carefulness before things went wrong. Therefore, no pro-active orientation or anticipated action.

A8: Aa. "We should, therefore, do family planning from the very beginning." Another example where a clear lack of pro-active orientation has led to serious difficulties. The story actually mentions need for a pro-active or anticipated activity.

A9 to A11: No Aa.

A12: Aa. "Prepare everything in the country so that we don't have to look to other countries for our things." Preparedness indicates anticipated activity and pro-active orientation.

A13 to A15: No Aa.

A16: No Aa. A good example where there is some kind of a sermon. This does not suggest actual activity, hence not scored for anticipated activity.

A17: No Aa. There is some kind of determination in "now they will decide and deliberately try to work in a proper way". This, however, comes only after the reprimand by the officer. The thinking, therefore, has appeared in response to some proble. This is not scored ia Aa.

A18: No Aa.

A19: No Aa. Action follows only after a plan to create disturbances.

A20: No Aa. "Getting annoyed and slapping the child" are negative actions in anticipation of a failure in the desired goal. Not scored for anticipated activity.

A21: No Aa.

A22: Aa. "He is determined to get his son the full opportunity for education even if he has to engage private tutors at his cost," suggests clear determination and anticipated action-orientation for the fulfilment of the goal.

A24: No Aa.

A25: Aa. "He is thinking to go to the village landlord to arrange for money so that his son can go to town for further studies." It is a good example where borrowing of money also suggests anticipated action tendency as far as directed toward a scorable goal.

A26 and 27: No Aa.

A28: No Aa. "As such Ram asked his co-workers to stage an agitation" suggests an anticipated action against the managment. However, the context in the story suggests this in response to the pbblem created by the management's refusal to accept all the demands. As such not scored for anticipated activity.

A29: Aa. "Planning how to save money for higher education of his son." Clear example of an advance activity for the education of his son.

A30: No Aa.

Strength (S+)

A1: No S+

A2: S+ "There was an honest man". A positive quality of the man is mentioned.

A3: S+. This is also indicative of a sense of discipline. A positive quality of the groups as a whole is mentioned. Good examples to illustrate that the positive qualities mentioned for an individual or a group as a whole, both are to be scored.

A4: No S+.

A5: No S+. "They were very peaceful." A positive quality, but may not be a strenght.

A6to A16: No S+.

A17: No S+. A good example where honesty, sincerity are mentioned as qualities of work. These are, however, not mentioned as the qualities possessed by the people mentioned in the story. Therefore not scored as S+.

A18 to A24: No S+.

A25: S+. "He is a brilliant boy," a positive quality mentioned definitely.

A26 to A30: No S+.

Hope (H)

A1: No H.

A2: H. "The son of a smuggler realized the fact and became an honest man and carried on a happy life in the long run." This shows a hope that honesty and honest life will prevail over smuggling.

A3: H. "The country and its 80 per cent workers have a bright future." A clear statement of hope in the country's future.

A4 to A7: No H.

A8: H. "We two our two; this will lead to happiness." The hope that family planning will lead to positive results is clearly mentioned.

A9 to A17: No H.

A18: No H. "May be after some time they may reach some decision; may be they may not agree." Success anticipated as doubtful.

A19: H. "Thereafter one of them will be caught by the police red-handed." Expresses hope that the police will be able to apprehend the fascist elements. The other statement, "the other two also will be traced out" shows some hope.

A20 and 21: No H.

A22: H. "This will definitely yield results and Hari will prosper in his life through his education."

A23 to A30: No H.

Personal and Social Awareness (PSA)

A1 and A2: No PSA

A3: PSA. "This is symbolic of the disturbed economic situation in the country." Awareness of socio-economic causation of social problem.

A4: PSA. "Today in the country there is such an inequality that lakhs of poor hungry mothers are begging on the roads for food for their children." "This inequality can be removed only by socialism." Awareness of the problem as well as some way out.

A5 to A7: No PSA.

A8: PSA. "He did not pay attention to family planning in the beginning, therefore, in this time of great distress he is in great difficulty." Other sentences like "Ram could have avoided all this by having two children," "His family would have been happy" also suggest awareness of the problem of growing population.

A9 to A11: No PSA.

A12: No PSA. "All of us together should think good of the country" indicates a good sentiment. It, however, does not suggest any clear soical awareness.

A13 to A16: No PSA.

A17: PSA. "This was carelessness of the workers..."

A18 to A21: No PSA.

A22: PSA. "This happened because Hari's father was very careless".

A23: No PSA.

A24: No PSA. "The workmen were expecting wages last Saturday as that being the pay day but the wages could not be paid because of this situation." Suggest resentment and anger but no clear expression of awareness.

A25: No PSA. "Ramu is thinking that with his meagre salary how will he educated his som, sending his to town for further studies will mean a lot of expenses." Some appreciation of the proble but not clear awarness of the social situation.

A26 to A29: No PSA.

A30: PSA. "For the fault committed by the employee, he appears to be repenting."

Vigilance (V)

A1 to A6: No. V.

A7: V. "Due to this his hand has been cut severaly." Clearly expresses a personal shortcoming and carefulness for future.

A8: No V. Certain sentences indicate awareness and have been scored for PSA.

A9 to A15: No V.

A16: V. "We should always walk left while walking on the road," shows vigilance in cicic behaviour.

A17: No V. "They are now thinking why it happened like this." Vigilance may be implicit, but cannot, however, be inferred.

A18: No V.

A19: V. "These persons have made plans to create disturbances...." Anticipation of a problem.

A20 to A27: No V.

A28: V. "In the past also similar assurances have been given but the programme has not been implemented." Awareness of some anticipated difficulty, so shows vigilance.

A29: V. "He is not happy with the present state of affairs and he wants that the same fate should not be repeated with his son." Desire for the removal of some present difficulty with future orientation, so shows vigilance.

A30: No V.

Thema (Th)

A1: No Th
A2: Th
A3: Th
A4 to A10: No Th
A11: Th
A12 and A13: No Th
A14: Th
A15: Th
A16: Th
A17: No Th
A18: Th
A19: Th
A20: No Th
A22 and A23: No Th
A24: Th
A25: No Th
A26: Th
A27: Th
A28: Th
A29: No Th
A30: Th

PRACTICE STORIES : SET B

Expert Scoring

Personal Achievement Imagery (PAI)

B1: No PAI. There is a talk about work. But the standard of excellence of concern for improvement is not explicitly mentioned.

B2: PAI. "...the life becomes good and prosperous and started working hard on his studies and stared coming first."

B3 to B9: No PAI.

B10: No PAI. "...This has happened because of the carelessness." Doubtful whether the perception of accident due to carelessness shows standard of excellence in work or a concer for personal safety.

B11 to B18: No PAI.

B19: PAI. "The engineer wanted the work in a perfect way."

B20 : No PAI. "Father wants that the study of his son should not suffer and he should be able to fulfil his ambitions." Doubtful.

B21 to B24: No PAI.

B25: PAI. "How to provide him better education." A clear indicatio of a standard of excellence for education.

B26: No PAI.

B27: PAI. "Father thought that his son would become a good boy Some other words also indicate a standard of excellence for th upbringing of the child and his education.

B28 to B29: No PAI.

B30: PAI. "He saw his son deeply engrossed in his studies." A intense activity permits an inference for the person's standa of excellence.

Social Achievement Imagery (SAI)

B1 to B3 : No SAI.

B4: No SAI. "They did so because in this country nobody sho have such properties." It may be a superordinate goal but presence of a standard of excellence or a concern improvement in community life is not clear.

B5: SAI. "We should solve this problem by increasing productio factories, mines and fields."

B6: SAI. "Workers work hard for 8 hours; shed their perspiration the defence of the country and for increasing production."

B7 to B12: No SAI.

B13: SAI. "The people are advised to have two or three child This is enough, this will lead to good life." The statement l implies some standard of excellence for personal life but imagery is geared to the concern for social achievement h scored for need for social achievement.

B14: No SAI.

B15: No SAI. "Right" and "proper" ways are mentioned but standard of excellence in community life is not clearly state

B30: No SAI.

Influence (Inf)

B1: Inf. "Emphasizing this, the young man said that he would continue to be in the world and continue to work." This is a good example where a person refuses to be influenced by some other persons and tries to influence others.

B2: Inf. "A father was paying attention to his son's studies." Other sentences also indicate father's desire to influence son's development.

B3: Inf. "He refused to go saying that he was not the leader." A good example where refusal to get influenced by others indicates one's own desire for influence. The mention of the word "leader" also suggests influence of imagery in the story.

B4: No Inf.

B5: Inf. "We should solve this problem." A desire to solve problems shows a desire to influence the ongoing situation.

B6 and B7: No Inf.

B8: Inf. "Because of somebody's wrong advice, they are now in such a bad shape; we should, therefore, do everything after a careful examination. Clearly implies a desire not be influenced by others in a wrong way as well as for influencing things in a correct way.

B9: Inf. "A person who has fallen down should be helped to come up." An example of help becoming a source to influence the other person.

B10: Inf. "Therefore, the workers are asking for full compensation. Other words like "strengthen our organization" also show influence.

B11: Inf. "He is thinking and a leader is explaining something to him."

B12: Inf. "The workers' leaders Ramu Chacha is calling them." Other words such as "he tells them that, brothers, now our turn has come" also show influence. Here influcene is involved in influencing others' opinions and ideas.

B13: Inf. "Let's help the government so that in our neighbourhood people are advised to have two or three children." A clear example of a desire to influence the on-going situation as well as to have a say in what the government is doing.

B14: No Inf. No clear influence concern mentioned.

B15: No Inf.

B16: Inf. "The person very rightly goes to the police constable on duty and reports the matter." This indicates a tendency to act in a given situation, hence scored for influence.

B17: Inf. "They had to assemble to tackle the situation which across due to some theft in one of the villages." Clear indication of the tendency to act in a given situation in order to control it.

B18: Inf. "To cast their vote to the right person..." Merely casting a vote at some election may not indicate concern for influence. Here several other words also show concern for influence.

B19: Inf. "The engineer has come to inspect the performance." Inspection is indicative of influence and control.

B20: No Inf. "Father has been trying to get his problems solved but so far he has failed." This does not clearly indicate influence. The activity also is not so intense as to warrant inference of influence, hence not scored for influence.

B21: Inf. "There has been a scarcity of supply and some disorderly behaviour; this arrangement has been enforced and all have been given ration cards." Scored for influence, although there is no particular character involved in the imagination. Still the thoughts indicate a desire for influence over the disorderly behaviour.

B22: No Inf.

B23: Inf. "Money-landing should be stooped and loans should be given to the worker." Shows a desire to influence the practice of money-lending.

B24: Inf. "This man was in the habit of committing thefts and management had the confidential reports about it." Shows a desire to influence the situation and control the problem.

B25: No Inf.

B26: Inf. "The union leader on hearing is getting excited and trying to excits the workers." Other words also indicate influence.

B27: Inf. "Father is watching son's study most steadily." Intense activity showing father's desire to influence son's behaviour. Other words such as "keeping a constant watch on son from behind also indicate influence.

B28: No Inf. "Father wants that son should read his course book." A doubtful indication of father's desire to influence son's behaviour.

B29: Inf. "The Railway Police is explaining to the trespasser that it is dangerous." The imagery here indicates that the policemen is trying to influence the behaviour of the trespasser.

B30: Inf. "He suddenly decided and determined that this time he will take loan from his friend." In the context of the story this shows a desire to influence the son's studies. It can also be out of the father's affection for the son. But there is obviously a desire for influencing the son's future studies and also for avoiding the money-lender.

Personal Action (Ap)

B1: Ap. "While working he could complete his *Sanyas*." Other sentences also indicate personal action orientation.

B2: Ap. "The father said,'Son you are not deceiving me but deceiving yourself'." A clear example of activity designed to influence.

B3: Ap. "He refused to go." Example of personal action orientation for influencing the other person. The chowkidar's coming and asking Mohan to "come to the policed station" also indicates personal action orientation.

B 4 to B7 : No Ap.

B8 to B10 :No Ap.

B11: Ap. "The leader is explaining to him:" Personal activity on the part of the leader.

B12: Ap. "The workers' leader Ramu Chacha is calling them."

B13 to B15: No Ap.

B16: Ap. "The person very rightly comes to the police constable on duty and reports the matter." The same words/sentences can be scored for more than one category. This clearly involves a personal action.

B17 to B18 : No Ap.

B19: Ap. "The engineer has come to inspect the performance."

B20 to B23 : No Ap.

B24 to Ap. "A guard has been laid on that."

B25: Ap. "He thinks on the problem deeply."

B26: Ap. "He is trying to excite the workers."

B27: Ap. "Father is keeping a constant eye on son."

B28: No Ap.

B29: Ap. "Police is explaining to the trespasser."

B30: Ap. "He suddenly decided..."

Social Action (As)

B1 to B4 : No As.

B5: As. "We should solve this problem by increasing production in factories, mines and fields." Clear emphasis on a collective activity.

B6 to B9 : No As. It is necessary to distinguish between personal and social activity. A mere use of a plural pronoun like "We" does not make an activity a social activity. It has to be clearly mentioned as a collective action or activity.

B10: As. "We should therefore come forward and strengthen our organization." A clear emphasis on collective action and organization.

B11: As. "Nothing will happen and people have to come forward and organize themselves."

B12: No As.

B13: As. "Everyone has an answer, this is family planning." The emphasis on collective action for the good of the society.

B14 to B16 : No As.

B17: As. "They had to assemble to tackle the situation which arose due to some theft in any of the villages." An indication of a collective activity for common good.

B18: As. "They are thinking to cast their vote for the right person." Indicates group activity. Voting itself is an example of social behaviour for certain common goals.

B19 to B30 : No As.

Anticipated Action (Aa)

B1 to B4 : No Aa.

B5 : Aa. "Arrange for ration at different places" indicates action orientation in order to prevent some serious problem.

B6 to B11 : No Aa.

B12 : Aa. "He tells them that, 'brothers, now our turn has come'." This is anticipated action. There is no problem as such but the activity here aims at some forthcoming programme.

B13 : Aa. "...and this is family planning, let us help the government so that in our neighbourhood people are advised to have two or three children." Suggests an activity in anticipation of the seriousness of the growing problem.

B14 to B22 : No Aa.

B23 : Aa. "If this practice is not stopped then the worker will be more and more involved with the interest and ultimately he will run away." "Money-lending should be stopped and loans be given to workers." It is an example of action in anticipation of aggravation of a problem and to prevent the workers from running away. This shows a pro-active orientation.

B24 to B30 : No Aa.

Strength (S+)

B1 to B15 : No S+. No words to indicate the presence of strength.

B16 to B24 : No S+.

B25 : S+. "He is quite sincere in his studies." Clear example of personal quality.

B26 to B29 : No S+.

B30 : S+. "Sohan was reading in his school and was very intelligent."

Hope (H)

B1 to B15 : Hope (H) is not present.

B16 : No H.

B17 : H. "They will send the culprit to the police station and his goods will be recovered." Clear anticipation of success in the stated goal.

B18 to B26 : No H.

B27 : H. "He will be a good boy." Clear hope for success.

B28 to B30 No H.

Personal and Social Awareness (PSA)

B1 to B9 : No PSA.

B10 : PSA. "This happened because of carelessness."

B11 : PSA. "This happened because of carelessness."

B12 : No PSA. "The story mentions about some new programmes. However, there is no explicit mention of problem and its social causation . Merely talking about some new programme is not to be scored as social awarness.

B13 to B17 : No PSA.

B18 : PSA. "To elect the right person by the people, they will elect the members of the Municipality." Several other words show awareness about election, their funtions and consequences of right voting.

B19 to B30 : No PSA.

Vigilance (V)

B1 : No V.

B2 : V. "Son, you are not deceiving me but deceiving yourself. because in the beginning you have to do some hard work but then you can enjoy the whole day." Clearly implies a personal difficulty and vigilance about it.

B3 and B4 : No V.

B5: V. "... so that in the country nobody dies of starvation."

b6: V. "When you work in danger, you have to give proper care to safety." Clear perception of difficulty and vigilance.

B7 to B9 : No V.

B10: V. "Nothing will happen like this..." Perception of some block and difficulty showing vigilance.

B11: V. "Nothing will happen..." Perception of some future problems.

B12 : No V.

B13 : V. "Everywhere there is a crowd where you have to take a ticket... answer is family planning."

B14 to B22 : No V.

B23: V. "If this practice is not stopped then the worker will be more and more involved in interest and ultimately he will run away." Shows understanding of consequences of a problem in future, if not tackled, hence scored for vigilance.

B24 to B28 : No V.

B29 : V. "This would endanger the life of the trespasser and also it creates a problem for the railway administration." An example of an anticipated problem.

B30 : No V.

Thema (Th)

B1 : Th.

B2 : No Th.

B3 : Th.

B4 : No Th.
B5 : Th.
B6 : Th.
B7 to B12 : No Th.
B13 : Th.
B14 to B18 : No Th.
B19 : Th.
B20 to B30 : No Th.

PRACTICE STORIES : SET C

Expert Scoring

Personal Achievement Imagery (PAI)

C1 : No PAI.

C2 : PAI "Today in society, determination, hard work and honesty can enable one to go ahead." Suggests the presence of standard of excellence and life.

C3 : No PAI.

C4 : PAI. "He is reading his book with keen attention." Inference from an intense activity. Other words also indicate presence of personal achievement imagery.

C5 and C6 : No PAI.

C7 : PAI. "The man always wanted to make progress."

C8 to C11 : No PAI.

C12 : PAI. "Everyone should be educated-make progress." Suggests presence of a standard of excellence in life.

C13 and C14 : No PAI.

C15 : PAI. "We should pay adequate attention to the machines so that they are not spoiled." Some standard of excellence in work.

C16 : to C18 : No PAI.

C19 : PAI. "A briliant student in his class and is working hard."

C20 : No PAI.

C21 : PAI "Picks up work in short time and carries on the work for more production".

C22 : to C27 No PAI.

C28 : PAI. "...Start working properly."

C29 : No PAI.

C30 : PAI "...Expresses that her son after being adult also will enjoy the facilities." The woman wants to have a better life for her son. Presence of standard of excellence and desire for improvement in life conditions.

Social Achievement Imagery (SAI)

C1 : SAI. "To develop the country and achieve progress." A super-ordinate achievement goal.

C2 : No SAI.

C3 : SAI. "...the country also progresses."

C4 : SAI. "...begin to understand their country and society ...that we continue to always make progress."

C5 and C6 : No SAI.

C7 : SAI. "So that the nation makes progress."

C8 : No SAI.

C9 : SAI. "The rate of increase in production is not enough." Shows a clear standard of excellence for group production, other words also indicate SAI.

C10 : SAI. "There can be no happiness and peace as long as everyone does not get something." An example of super-ordinete achievement goal and a concern for improvement in the community's life conditions.

C11 : No SAI.

C12 : SAI. "So that the country also makes progress." Other words also indicate social achievement imagery.

C13 : SAI. "...so that we can do good work together."

C14 : to C18 : No SAI.

C19 : No SAI. "Such that a son can really prove his mettle for the benefit of the country." Concern for social achievement is hot clearly stated.

C20 : No SAI.

C21 : SAI. "Carries on work for more production." An example of superordinate achievement goel.

C22 to C30 : No SAI.

Influence (INF)

C1: Inf. "An organization was formed in village to village." Suggests a desure to influence the on-going situation. Other words also indicate this desire for influence.

C2: Inf. "He wants to show to the society by his hard work." An examlpe of his desire to influence the thinking of society toward him.

C3: Inf. "By this he is trying to take them, the society and the workers away." Suggests desire to influence the behaviour of others.

C4: No Inf. "Everyone should send his promising boys to school or library." Doubtful desire to influence.

C5 to C8 : No Inf.

C9: Inf. "...should put a brake to the growth of population."

C10 and C11 : No Inf.

C12: Inf. "We should show such a way to our children." Desire to influence children's behaviour.

C13 to C15 : No Inf.

C16: Inf. "The man is telling something to the audience." Clear example of an activity to influence others.

C17 to C18: No Inf.

C19 : Inf. "He is thinking of determined hard work to get his son all the education." An intense activity and desire to influence the son's development.

C20 : Inf. "Khan beat him... for money." Clear evidence of concern to influence and control.

C21 : Inf. "Sohan being a community leader thought of training him as his worker."

C22 and C23 : No Inf.

C24 : Inf "He is trying his best to convey the policeman of his innocence." An intense activity suggesting a desire to influence the other person's ideas.

C25 and C26 : No Inf.

C27 : Inf. "There is one union leader and some are workers. They are planning for future. They will try to solve the problem." Shows a desire to influence problem-solving.

C28 : Inf. "The shift officer will be able to arrive at the root cause of the accident, questions him against it." Problem-solving and influencing others' idea and behaviour.

C29 : Inf. "They are thinking to select good people." Suggests desire to influence elections in a desired way.

C30 : No Inf.

Personal Action (Ap)

C1 : Ap. "Special workers and intelligentsia explained this to Ramesh." It is a case of personnel activity carried out by social workers.
C2 : Ap. "He wants to work in a workshop."
C3 : Ap. "He is trying to take them away." Indicates personal action tendency.
C4 : Ap. "Reading his book with keen attention."
C5 to C15 : No Ap.
C16 : Ap. "Telling something to the audience." Personal action on the part of leader.
C17 : No Ap.
C18 : Ap. "The two persons working on a lathe are involved fully in their job."
C19 : Ap. He is working very hard."
C20 : No Ap.
C21 : Ap. "Today he is learning a new job."
C22 and C23 : No Ap.
C24 : Ap. "He is trying his best,"
C25 and C26 : No Ap.
C27 : Ap. "They are planning for future." Thinking and planning are mental activities.
C28 and C29 : No Ap.
C30 : Ap. "Thinking about her poorness." An example of mental activity.

Social Action (As)

C1 : As. "This organization carried on successful campaign." An example of a collective action by the organization.
C2 to C4 : No As.
C5 : As. "Started understanding how to live, eat and read," and "...he has even reached the Moon." These activities indicate collective action orientation.
C6 : As. "Now the man, by his intelligence, will make such ways." Emphasized social action of men.
C& : As. "Man was like a child and gradually he started standing and made progress." Another example of collective/social activity on the part of man. Although the activity is connected

personally by an individual the emphasis here is on a similar collective activity.

C8 to C30 : No As.

Anticipated Action (Aa)

C1 to C8 : No Aa.

C9 : Aa. "In order to save the country and ourselves from such queues, we should put a brake in the growth of population." Population control methods are an example of anticipated activities.

C10 to C15 : No Aa.

C16 : Aa. "It is expected that some onslaughts and serious injuries or even more may take place; hence this preparation is being done." Action suggested in advance of a serious problem.

C18 to C30 : No Aa.

Strength (S+)

C1 : No S+.

C2 : S+. "Honesty and determination," clear examples of personal qualities.

C3 : S+. "Sincere and honest person."

C4 to C18 : No S+.

C19 : S+. "Brilliant student."

C20 and C21 : S+. "Very sincere and hard working."

C22 to C30 : No S+.

Hope (H)

C1 : No H.

C2 : No H. A statement of an actual success is not indicative of hope for future success. Hope is scored only for anticipated success.

C3 : No H.

C4 : H. "In my country every one will understand his responsibility."

C5 to C23 : No H.

C24 : H. "Will get away." Hope of success in influencing.

C25 to C30 : No H.

Personal and Social Awareness (PSA)

C1 to C8 : No PSA.

C9 : PSA. "In correspondence to the increasing population the rate of production is not enough." Some other words also show awareness of an important national problem.

C10 to C30 : No PSA.

Vigilance (V)

C1 to C13 : No V.

C14 : V. "We should not support any one person doing any wrong... it will harm." Perception of a possibility of a problem in relation to the goal.

C15 : No V.

C16 : V. "...expected that some onslaughts, injuries or even more may take place."

C17 and C18 : No V.

C19 : V. "Sometimes he thinks how he can afford to make his son do higher studies with such a low income of his." Perception of a difficulty suggesting vigilance in relation to the goal.

C20 to C30 : No V.

Thema (Th)

C1 and C2 : No Th.

C3 : Th.

C4 to C12 : No Th.

C13 : Th.

C14 : No Th.

C15 : Th.

C16 : Th.

C17 : Th.

C18 and C19 : No Th.

C20 : Th.

C21 to C23 : No Th.

C24 : Th.

C25 and C26 : No Th.

C27 : Th.

C28 : No Th.

C29 : Th.

C30 : Th.

APPENDIX III

THEMATIC APPERCEPTION TEST (TAT) PICTURES

TAT pictures for obtaining stories for understanding of the need for personal achievement, need for social achievement, need for influence and other related needs.

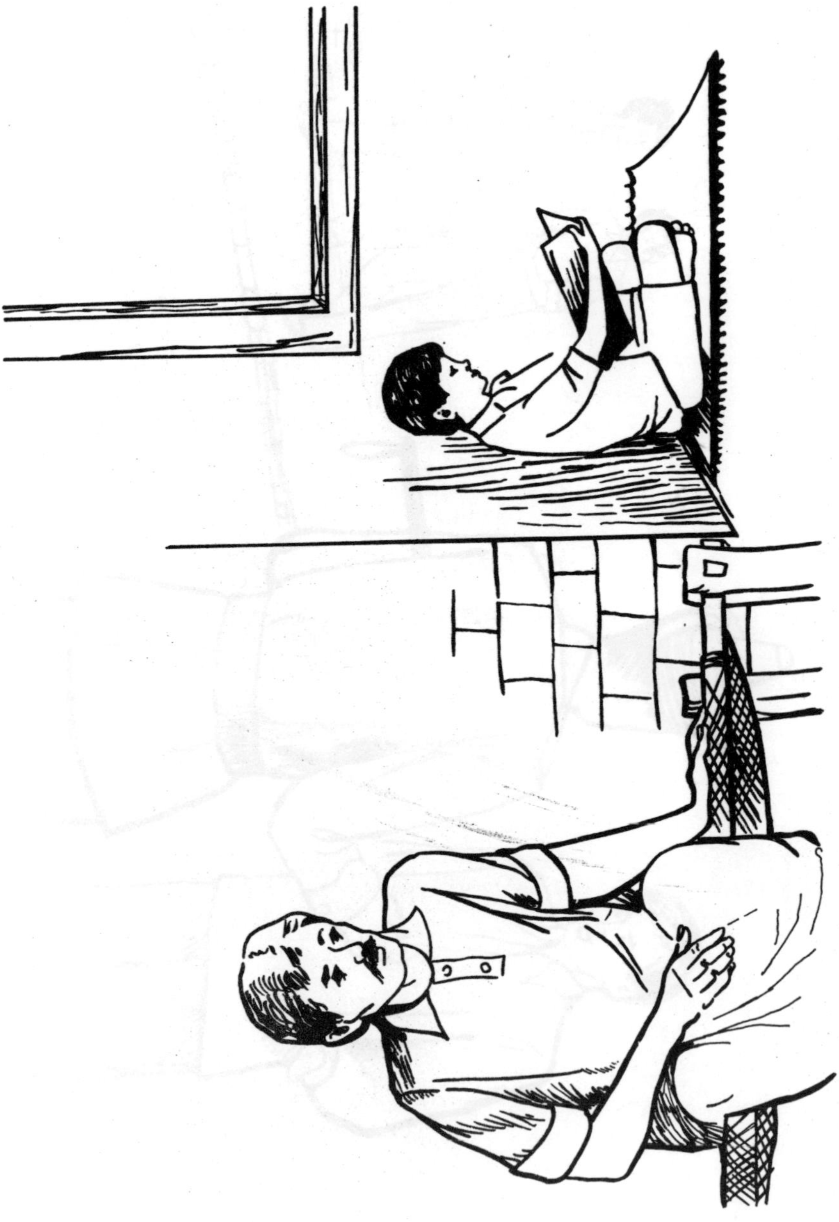

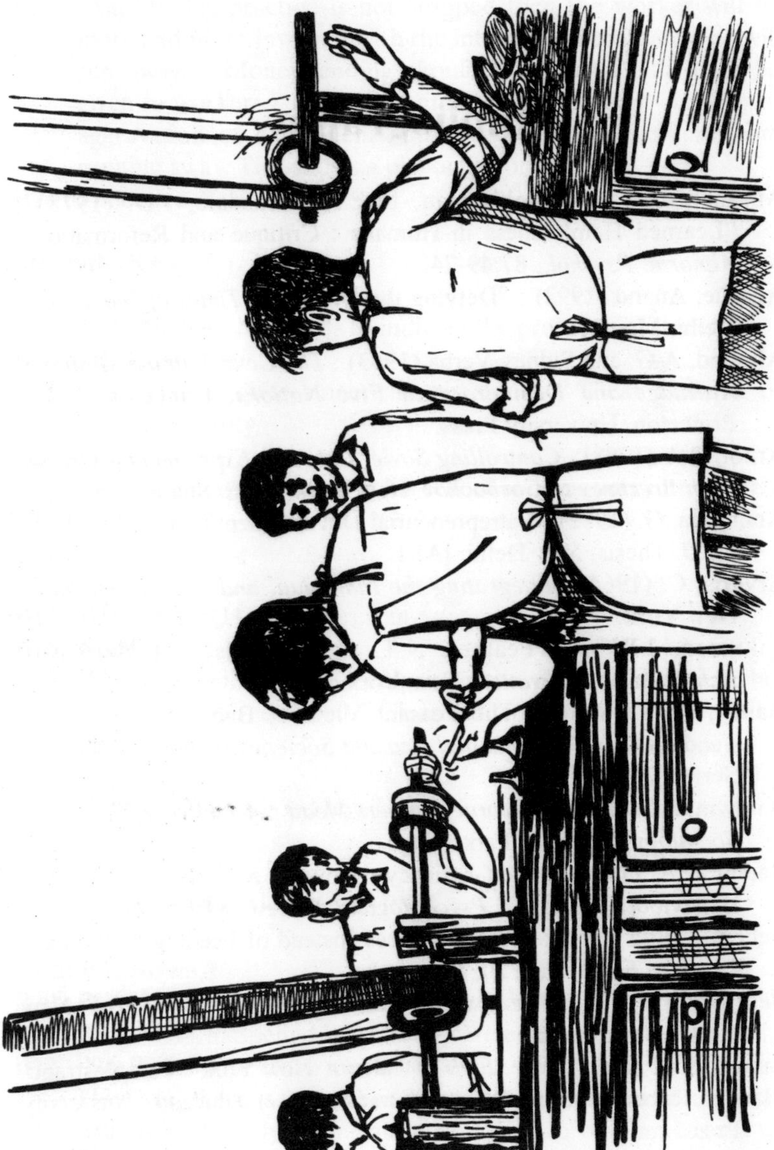

Bibliography

Abrahamson, L.Y., Selingman, M.E.P., Teasdale, J.D. (1978) : "Learned Helplessness in Humans : Critique and Reformation", *Abnorm. Psychol.*, 87:49-74.

Agashe, Anand (1992) : "Defying the Drought," *Times of India*, New Delhi, May 31.

Almond, A.G. and Sidney Verba (1963) : *The Civic Culture : Political Attitudes and Democracy in Five Nations*, Princeton, N.J. : Princeton, University Press.

Arnot, Bob (1988) : *Controlling Soviet Labour : Experimental Change from Brezhnev to Gorbachov*, New York : M.E. Sharpe Inc.

Anuradha, G. (1982) : Entrepreneurial Development under TRYSEM : Ph D. Thesis, New Delhi, IARI.

Arygris, C. (1964) : *Integrating the Individual and the Organisation*, New York.

Atkinson, J.W. and Feather, N.T. (1966) (Eds) : *A Theory of Achievement Motivation*, New York : Wiley.

Bailey, F.G. (1973) : "The Peasant View of Bad Life" in Shanin Teodar (Ed.), *Peasants and Peasant Societies*, Penguin Education Series, 299-321.

Baldwin, J.D. (1986) : *George Herbert Mead : A Unifying Theory for Sociology*, Newbury Park : Sage.

Bandura, A. (1977) : "Self-Efficacy : Toward a Unifying Theory of Behavioural Change," *Psychological Review*, 84:191-215

Behera, Chitta (1992): "Planting Trees Instead of Feeding Brahmins". *Down to Earth*, June 20, 41.

Bell, Denial (1976) : *The Cultural Contradictions of Capitalism*, New York : Basic Books.

Birney, R.C. *et al* (1969) : *Fear of Failure,* New York : Van Nostrand.

Blauner, Robert (1964) : *Alienation and Freedom,* Chicago : University Press.

Blumberg, P. (1968) : *Industrial Democracy : The Sociology of Participation,* London : Constable.

Borker, M.M (1987) : "Socio-economic and Psychological Correlates of Communication through Television in Nagpur District of Maharashtra", Ph. D Thesis, New Delhi : IARI.

Bowen, Maria, Maureen Miller, Carl R. Rogers and John K. Wood (1979) : "Learning in Groups : Their Implications for the Future" *Education,*100 (2), 108-116.

Braudel, Fernand (1988) : "History and the Social Sciences : The Longue Duree" In Aymard Maurice and Harbans Mukhia (Eds), *French Studies in History,* Vol I : 69-101 New Delhi : Orient Longmans.

Burowoy, Michael (1978): "Towards a Marxist Theory of the Labour Process : Braverman and Beyond", *Politics and Society* : 278-94.

—(1979) : *Manufacturing Consent,* Chicago : University of Chicago Press.

Chandra, Navin and Mehta, Prayag (1984) : *People's Self-Developement Action : The Case of Singari*, New Delhi : NLI.

Chaturvedi, Anil (1988) : *District Administration : The Dynamics of Discord*, New Delhi : Sage Pub.

Christie, R. and Geis, F.L. (1970) : *Studies in Machiavellianism*, New York : Academic Press.

Collins, B.E. and Guetzkow, H. (1964) : *A Social Psychological Group Processes for Decision Making*, New York : John Wiley.

Conger Jay A. and Rabindra N., Kanungo (1988) : "The Empowerment Process : Integrating Theory and Practice", *Academy of Mangement Review,* Vol. 13 (3), 471-482.

Dasgupta, Partha (1990) : "Well-being in Poor Countries," *Economic and Political Weekly,* August 4, 1713-1720.

Dasholi Gram Swaraj Mandal, *Hugging the Himalayas.* (1982) : *The Chipko Experience,* Chamoli, Garhwal.

de Charmas, R. (1968) : *Personal Causation*, New York: Academic Press.

Deci, E.L. (1975) : *Intrinsic Motivation*, New York : Plenum.

De, N.R. (1984) : *Alternative Designs of Human Organisation*, New Delhi : Sage.

De Silva, G.V.S et al (1979) : "Bhoomi Sena —A Struggle for People's Power", *Development Dialogue : 2.*

Dhingra, O.P. (1973) : "Participative Predisposition of Managers in the Indian Public Sector Industry", In Thakur, C.P. and Sethi, K.C. (Eds), *Industrial Democracy : Some Issues and Experiences,* New Delhi : Sriram Centre for Industrial Relations, 100-117.

Dreze, Jean and Sen, Amartya (1989) : *Hunger and Public Action*, Oxford : Clarendon Press.

Druckman, D. (1967) : "Dogmatism, Prenegotiation, Experience and

Stimulated Group Representation as Determination of Dyadic Behaviour in Bargaining Situation," *Journal of Personnel and Social Psychology*, Vol 6, 279-290.

Edward, Richard (1979) : *Contested Terrain : The Transformation of the Workplace in the 20th Century*, London : Heinemann.

Eisenberg, L. (1972) : "The Nature of Human Nature," *Science,* 176, 123-128.

Elias, N. and J.L. Scotson (1965) : *The Established and the Outsiders*, London : Frank Cass.

Emery, Fred and Thorsrud, Einar (1970) : *Democracy at Work*, Centre for Continuing Education, Australian National University.

European Economic Community (1975) : "Employee Participation and Company Structures", *EEC Bulletin Supp.* 8/75.

Fanon, Frantz (1968) : *The Wretched of the Earth,* Penguine.

Forward, J. (1969) : "Group Achievement Motivation and Individual Motives to Achieve Success and to Avoid Failutre,' *Journal of Personality,* 37, 297-309.

Finifter, A.D.A. (1972) : Dimensions of Political Alienation" In Ada W. Finifter (Ed) : *Alienation and Social System*, New York : John Wiley & Sons.

Fitzgerald, Thomas H.(1986) : "Why Motivation Theory does not Work" in *Harvard Business Review on Human Relation*, Vol. 4 : 29-41.

Fox, A. (1973) : Industrial Relations : A Social Critique of Pluralist Ideology" in J. Child (Ed), *Man and Organisation,* London : George Allen and Unwin.

Friedmann, John (1992) : *Empowerment : The Politics of Alaternative Development*, Cambridge (Mass.) : Blackwell.

Gecas, Viktor (1989) : "Rekindling the Sociological Imagination in Social Psychology," *Journal for the Theory of Social Behaviour,* 19(1), 99-115.

Gokulnathan, P.P. (1971) : "A Study of Achievement related Motivation and Achievement among Secondary School Pupils," *Doctoral Thesis*, Dibrugarh : University of Dibrugarh.

—and Mehta, Prayag (1972): "Achievement Motive in Tribal and Non-Tribal Assamese School Adolescents," *Indian Educational Review* 7, 67-90.

—(1976) : "Atkinson's Theory of Achievement Motivation Revisited," New Delhi : National Labour Institute, *Mimeo.*

Gottesfield, D.H., and Dozier, G. (1966) : "Changes in Feelings of Powerlessness in a Community Action Program," *Psychological Reports*, Vol 19, 987-995.

Gorupic, D. and Paj, I. (1971) : "Workers' Participation in Management in Yugoslavia," *IILS Bulletin,* 9, 129-72.

Gurin, P., Gurin G., Lao, R.C. and Beattie, M. (1969) : Internal External Control in the Motivational Dynamics of Negro Youth, *Journal of Social Issues,* 25 (3), 29-53.

Harman, W.W. (1977) : "The Coming Transfiguration," *The Futurist,* 11(2) Feb & April.

Herbst, P.G. (1962) : *Autonomous Group Functioning,* Tavistock : London.

Hill, Stephen (1981) : *Competition and Control at Work : The Industrial Sociology*, Cambridge, MA : MIT Press.

Hofstede, G. (1980) : *Culture's Consequences : International differences in Work related Values,* Beverly Hills : Sage.

Hyman, H.H. and Singer, E. (Eds.) (1968) : *Readings in Reference Group Theory and Research,* New York : Free Press.

Inkeles, A. (1969) : "Making Men Modern : On the Causes and Consequences of Individual Change in Six Developing Countries," *American Journal of Sociology*, 75, 208-225.

—(1978) : "National Differences in Individual Modernity," *Comparative Studies in Sociology*, 1, 4772.

—and D.H. Smith (1974) : *Becoming Modern*, Cambridge, MA : Harward University Press.

International Research Group (1981) : *Industrial Democracy in Europe*, Oxford : Clarendon.

Iyer, Radha (1991) : "Undrstanding Labour Management Relations Case of Siemens," *Economic and Political Weekly,* August 31, M101-110.

Jha, R.C. (1982) : Organisational Performance of Farm and Home Units of the AIR, Ph.D Thesis, New Delhi : IARI

Kanungo, Rabindra, N. (1992) : "Alienation and Empowerment : Some Ethical Imperatives in Business," *Journal of Business Ethics*, 11, 413-422.

Kanawaty, George, Einar Thorsurd, J.P. Semiono and J.P. Singh (1981): "Field Experience with New Forms of Work Organisation," *International Labour Review*, 120 (3), 263-277.

Khandwalla, P.N. (1984) : *The Fourth Eye : Excellence Through Creativity,* Allahabad : A.H. Wheeler.

—(1987) : "Organisation of the Future : A Strategic Organisation Perspecitve" in *Productivity Through People in the Age of Changing Technology*, New Delhi : NPC, 159-172.

Kluckhohn, F. and F. Strodtbeek (1961) : *Variations in Value Orientations*, Evanston : ILI Row and Peterson.

Kohn, M.L. (1969) : *Class and Conformity,* Homewood, IL : Dorsey Press.

—and Schooler, C. (1973) : "Occupational Experience and Psychological Functioning : An Assessment of Reciprocal Effects," *American Sociological Review*, (38) : 97-118.

—(1983) : *Work and Personality : An Enquiry into the Impact of Social Stratification*, Norwood, N.J. : Ablex.

Kubde, B.R. (1979) : "Study of Correlates of Work Involvement and Job Performance of the Personnel of Farm and Home Units of All India Radia," Ph.D. Thesis, New Delhi : IARI.

Kumaramanglam, S. Mohan (1971/1987) : "Public Sector ; Yesterday, Today and Tomorrow," *Socialist India, Annual*, May, 29; reproduced in *Mainstream*, May 30.

—(1973) *Coal Industry in India, Nationalisation and Task Ahead,* New Delhi : Oxford and IBH Publishing Co.

—(1973a) "Speech Delivered at the BCCL," *Coking Coal News*, Vol 1(12) and Vol II (1, 2, 3 and 4).

Likert, R. (1961) : *New Patterns of Management*, New York : McGraw Hill.

Maccoby, Michael (1975) : "Changing Work : The Bolivar Project," *Working Papers for a New Society*. Summer.

Marx, Karl (1844/1974) : *Economic and Philosophical Manuscripts of 1844,* Moscow : Progress Publishers.

Mahapatra, R.C. (1978) : "Workers' Participation in Management in Rourkela Steel Plant," *Indian Journal of Labour Economics*, 21 (1 and 2) 31-41.

Martimer, J.T., Lorence, J. (1979) : "Occupational Experience and the Self-Concept : A Longitudinal Study," *Soc. Psychol. Quarterly*, 42:307-23.

McClelland, *et al* (1953) : *Achievement Motive*, New York : Appleton (see specially pages 107-138, "Analysis of Imaginative Stories for Motivational Content.")

—(1958) : "A Scoring Manual for Achievement Motive," in J.W. Atkinson (Ed) *Motives in Fantasy, Action and Society : A Method of Assessment and Study,* Princeton, N.J. : Van Nostrand, pp. 179-204.

—(1975) : *Power : The Inner Experience*, New York : Irvington.

Mead, G.H. (1934/1964) : *G.H. Mead on Social Psychology : Selected Papers* (edited by Anlem Strauss) Chicago : University of Chicago Press.

Mehta, Manju (1988) : Achievement Motive in Backward and Non-Backward Class Higher Secondary School Rajasthani Boys,

Unpublished Report, Jaipur : University of Rajasthan.

Mehta, Prayag (1969) : *Achievement Motive in High School Boys and Training for it,* New Delhi: National Council of Educational Research and Training.

—(1970) : ''Need for Achievement in Socially Disadvantaged Secondary School Adolescents in *Modern Trends in Psychology*, Report of a Conference, Kanpur : Kanpur University.

—(1975) : Measuring Achievement Motivation, *Manas*, 22, 1-8.

—(1975a) *Election Campaign : Anatomy of Mass Influence*, New Delhi : National.

—(1975b) : ''Efficacy, Participation and Politics,'' New Delhi : PADC, Unpublished Manuscript.

—(1975c) : ''Developement of Efficacy in Working People,'' *National Labour Institute Bulletin*, 1,7-9.

—(1976) : *Managing Motivation in Educaiton*. Ahmedabad : Sahitya Mudranalaya.

—(1976a): ''From Economisim to Democratic Commitment: The Role of Wokers' Participation'', *Vikalpa*, 1 (4), 3946.

—(1976b) : ''Analysing Imagery for Social Efficacy,'' New Delhi: National Labour Institute, *Mimeo.*

—(1976c):''The Alienated Middle Managers,'' *NLI Bulletin,* 2, 94-96.

—(1977) : ''Employee Motivation and Work Satisfaction in a Public Enterprise,'' *Vikalpa*, 2 (3), 223-232.

—(1977a) : ''Efficacy, Participation and Politics Abstract'' in *ICSSR Abstracts Quarterly*, VI (3-4), 88-99.

—(1978) : ''Objective and Subjective Factors in Employees Satisfaction in Life and Work,'' *Indian Journal of Industrial Relations,* 2(13), 433-444.

—(1979) : ''Measuring Perceived Quality of Work Life,: New Delhi : National Labour Institute (Unpublished Manuscript).

—(1979a) : ''Participation of Rural Poor in Rural Development,'' *Occasional Paper No. 2/79,* New Delhi : NLI.

—(1981) : ''Political Processes and Behaviour,'' In *ICSSR Survey of Research in Psychology*, 1971-1976 (Part 2) New Delhi : Popular Prakashan.

—(1982) : *Manual for Personal Achievement, Social Achievement and Influence Motivation,* New Delhi : NLI

—(1983) : ''Political Efficacy and Participation in Socio-Economic Development,'' *Journal of Rural Development*, 2(6), 563-570.

—(1989) : *Bureaucracy, Organisational Behaviour and Development*, New Delhi : Sage.

—(1989a) : *Participation and Organisation Development*, Jaipur :

Rawat.

—(1990) : *Integrate Adult Education with Life : Feedback from Rajasthan*, New Delhi : PADC.

—(1992) : "Democratisation of Workplace" in Udai Pareek *et al* (ed), *Managing Transition : The HRD Response*, 111-130.

—(1994) : "Empowering People for Social Achievement : Motivation for Sustainable Development" in Rabindra N Kanungo and Manuel Mendonca (Eds.), *Work Motivation : Models for Developing Countries*, New Delhi : Sage : 161-83.

Mehta, Prayag and Nirmala Mohta (1974) : Achievement Motive research in India, *Indian Journal of Psychology,* 49, 320-336.

Memmi, Albert (1967) : *The Colonizer and the Colonised,* New York: Orient Press.

Milbrath, L.W. (1965) : *Political Participation,* Rand McNally, Chicago.

Mishra, S.P. (1979) : A Study of Farm Entrepreneurship in a Backward District of Bihar. Ph.D. Thesis, New Delhi : IARI.

Mitra, Amit (1992) : "Weaving a Common Destiny," *Down to Earth*, June 30, p.40.

Mills, C. Wright (1959) : *The Sociological Imagination*, New York : Grove Press.

Mohanan, N. (1981) : "A Profile of Beedi Workers in Cannanore District of Kerala" in G.K. Panikkar (Ed), *Kerala Dinesh Beedi*, Connanore : Workers Central Cooperative Society Ltd.

Murray, H.A. (1936) : "Techniques of a Systematic Investigation of Fantasy," *J. Psychol.*, 3, 115-143.

—(1938) : *Exploration in Personality*, New York : Oxford University Press.

Nandy, A.(1983) : *The Intimate Enemy : Loss and Recovery of Self Under Colonisation*, Delhi : Oxford University Press.

Nijhawan, H.K. and Chaudhary, Nirmala (1970) : "Anxiety, *n* Achievement and Vocational Aspirations," *Indian Journal of Psychology*, 16 (1), 17-30.

Oommen, T.K. (1990) : *State and Society in India : Studies in Nation Building,* New Delhi : Sage.

O'Toole, James (1973) : *Work in America : Report of a Special Task Force to the Secretary of Health, Education and Welfare,* Cambridge, Mass: The MIT Press.

Ouchi, G. William (1981) : *Theory Z : How American Business Can Meet the Japanese Challenge*, Reading, Mass : Addison-Wesley Publishing Co.

Pareek, Udai and Banerjee, D. (1976) : "Achievement Motive and

Competitive Behaviour, *Manas*, 23 (1), 9-15.

Passmore, William and Frank Friedlander (1982) : "An Action-Research Programme for Increasing Employee Involvement in Problem Solving," *Administrative Science Quarterly*, 27, 343-362.

Pateman Carole (1970) : *Participation and Democratic Theory*, Cambridge : Cambridge University Press.

Peters Thomas and Robert H. Waterman, Jr. (1982) : *In Search of Excellence : Lessons from America's Best Run Companies*, New York : Harper & Row Publications.

Pfeffer, J. (1981) : *Power in Organisation*, Marshfield, MA: Pitman.

Piaget, J.(1954) : *The Construction of Reality in the Child,* New York: Basic Books.

Ram, Bani (1981) : "A Critical Anaysis of Farm School on the AIR: An Instructional Programme of the All India Radio," Ph.D. Thesis, New Delhi : IARI.

Rahman, Anisur (1987) : "Participatory Rural Development and its Implications for Rural Employment Generation," *Programme on Participatory Organisations of Rural Poor*, Geneva: ILO, July.

Ramaswamy, E.A. (1985) : "Managerial Trade Unionism," *EPW*, 20 (21), M75-M88.

Rao, M.L. and Mehta, Prayag (1978) : "Measuring Implicit and Manifest Authoritarianism : Development and Standardisation of Tools", *Psychological Studies*, 23 (1),10-18.

—(1979) : "Communal Canker in Education : A Comparative Study of School and Family Environment", *Indian Educational Review*, 7587.

Ray, Krishnendu and Ravi Sundaram (1990) : "Socialism at the End of the Century-Reflections on an Epoch Passed," *EPW*, July 21, 1595-1606 and July 28, 1595-1605.

Reich, Charles (1970) : *The Greening of America*, New York : Random House.

Rice, A.k. (1958) : *Productivity and Social Organisation : The Ahmedabad Experiment,* London : Tavistock.

Rosenberg, M. (1979) : *Conceiving the Self,* New York : Basic Books.

Rosen, B. (1956) : "The Achievement Syndrome : A Psycho-Cultural Dimension of Sociological Stratification:, *American Psychological Review*, 21:203-211.

Rotter, J.B.(1966) : "Generalised Expectancies for Internal Versus External Control of Reinforcement ," *Psychological Monograph*, 80:1-28.

Roy, S.K. (1969) : A Re-examination of the Methodology of A.K.Rice's

Indian Textile Mill Work Reorganisation, *Indian Journal of Industrial Relations*, 5,2, 170-191.

Ryan, W. (1976) : *Blaming the Victim,* New York : Vintage Books.

SAIL (1988) : *Industrial Relations Scenario in SAIL*, New Delhi : Unpublished Report.

Schwalbe, M.L. (1986) : *The Psychological Consequences of Natural and Alienated Labour*, Albany, NY : State Uni. of New York Press.

Seeman, Melvin (1972) : "The Meaning of Alienation" in Ada W. Finifter (Ed), *Alienation and Social System*, New York : John Wiley & Sons.

Seligman, M.E.P. (1975) : *Helplessness : On Depression, Development and Death,* San Francisco : Freeman.

Setty, Bhaskar (1982) : "A Study of Entrepreneurial Characteristics of the Farmers in an Agriculturally Advanced District of Orissa." Ph.D. Thesis, New Delhi: IARI.

Sharma, Baldeo R. (1990) : "Managerial Unionism : Implications for Industrial Relations," *Indian Journal of Industrial Relations*, 25 (4), 335-353.

—(1991) : "The Determinants and Consequences of Relative Deprivation among Public Sector Managers", *Indian Journal of Industrial Relations*, 27 (2),1-25.

Shiv Kumar, A.K. (1991) : "UNDP Human Development Index: Computation for Indian States", *Economic and Political Weekly*, Oct. 12, 2343-2345.

Simonds, Rollin H. and John N.Orife (1975) : "Worker Behaviour Versus Enrichment Theory", *Administrative Science Quarterly*, 20, 606-612.

Sinha, J.B.P. (1968) : "The ***n*** Achievement, ***n*** Cooperation under Limited-Unlimited Resource Conditions." *Journal of Experimenatal Social Psychology*, 4(2), 233-246.

Sinha, B.P. and Mehta, Prayag (1972) : "Farmer's Need for Achievement and Change Proneness in Acquisition of Information from a Telecast", *Rural Sociology*, 37(3), 417-427.

—(1972a) : "Size of Land Holding and Farmers Achievement Motivation and Change Proneness," *Behavioural Science and Community Development*, 6(2), 244-251.

Smith, S.A.(1983) : "Taylorism Rules OK? Bolshavism, Taylorism and the Technical Intelligentsia in the Society Union 1917-41," *Radical Science Journal*, No. 13

Spencer, Kemeth, I. (1988) : "Technological Change, Skill Requirements and Education : The Case for Uncertainity" in

Richard M. Cyert and David C. Mowery (Eds.), *The Impact of Technological Change in Employment and Economic Growth*, Ballinger (USA) : National Academy of Science, 131-184.

Srinivas, B. (1989) : "Management plays truant-Workers initiate takeover plan," *Economic and Political Weekly,* vol. 24, No. 38,Sept. 23, 2113-2114.

Strodtbeck, F.L. (1958) : "Family Interaction, Values and Achievements" in D.C. McClleland *et al* (Eds.), *Talent and Society,* Princeton, NG, D. Van Nostrand.

Swanson, G.E. (1974) : "Family Structure and Reflective Intelligence in Children," *Sociometry*, 34 (4), 459-490.

Taylor, F.W. (1911) : *Scientific Management*, New York : Harper & Brothers.

Thursrud, E. (1972) : Democratisation of Work Organisation : Some Concrete ways of Restructuring the Workplace (Mimeo), Oslo: Work Research Institute, 15/72.

Toffler, Alvin (1980) : *The Third Wave*, New York : William Morrow and Campany, Inc.

Trist, Eric (1976) : *A Concept of Organisational Ecology*, Perth : The University of Western Australia.

Turner, R.H., and Killian, L.M. (1957) : *Collective Behaviour*, Englewood Cliffs, N.J. : Prentice-Hall.

Turner, R.H. (1976) : "The Real Self : From Institution to Impulse", *Am. J. Sociol.* 81:989-1016.

Turner, Jonathan H. (1988) : "A Behaviour Theory of Social Structure" *Journal of the Theory of Social Behaviour*, 18(4), 355-372.

Ulleman, J.S. (1972) : "The Need for Influence Development and Validation of a Measure and Comparison with the need for Power", *Genetic Psychology Monograph*, 85, 157-214.

United Nations (1954) : *International Definition and Measurment of Standards and Levels of Living*, New York : United Nations.

United Nations Development Programme (1990) : *Human Development Report* 1990, New York : Oxford University Press.

—(1992) *Human Development Report,* 1992, New York : Oxford University Press.

—(1993) *Human Development Report,* 1993, New Delhi : Oxford Uni. Press.

Veroff, J., Atkinson, J.W., Feld, S.C, and Gurin, G. (1960) : "The Use of Thematic Apperception to Assess Motivation in a Nation-wide Interview Study", *Psychological Monograph*, Vol 74, 12 (Whole Number 499).

Wignaraja, Ponna (1989) : "Towards a new Praxis for Sustainable

Development in Asia'' in Wignaraja, Ponna and Akmal Hussain (Eds), *The Challenge in South Asia: Development, Democracy and Regional Cooperation*, New Delhi : Sage Publication, 29-60.

Winter, David G. (1973) : *The Power Motive*, New York : Fress Press.

White, R.W. (1959) : ''Motivation Reconsidered : The Concept of Competence'', *Psychological Review*, 66, 297-333.

Zender, Alvin (1971) : *Motives and Goals in Groups*, New York: Academic Press.

Zimmerman, M. (1990) : ''Toward a Theory of Learned Hopefulness : A Structural Model Analysis of Participation and Empowerment,'' *Journal of Research in Personality,* 1, 77-86.

Index